Forming Dissenters

The Regulator Movement
in Piedmont North Carolina

Farming Dissenters

The Regulator Movement
in Piedmont North Carolina

Carole Watterson Troxler

Office of Archives and History
North Carolina Department of Cultural Resources
Raleigh
2011

Distributed by the University of North Carolina Press, Inc.
www.uncpress.unc.edu

Contents

Illustrations

Foreword

William S. Powell's booklet, *The War of the Regulation and the Battle of Alamance, May 16, 1771* (1949), went out of print in 2001 after six printings. Ten years later, Carole Watterson Troxler has updated and expanded the topic to include more information about the entire Regulator Movement, the climax of the battle at Alamance, and the aftermath leading up to the Revolutionary War.

Farming Dissenters: The Regulator Movement in Piedmont North Carolina tells the story of growing unrest among backcountry settlers in the 1760s and their efforts to make their grievances known to the governor and the assembly. Several key issues were up for debate, including the vestry tax to pay for Anglican ministers, corruption among local officials, and proving ownership of land. These three factors, in addition to continuing political and economic struggles between the backcountry and eastern residents, led to the events culminating in the Battle of Alamance on May 16, 1771.

Several editors on staff at the Historical Publications Section read the manuscript and made valuable edits to it. These included Dennis Isenbarger and Jan Poff of the Colonial Records Project, Special Projects Branch, and Kenrick Simpson, former head of the now defunct General Publications and Periodicals Branch. Staff members at the State Archives were helpful in locating maps, documents, and other images for use as illustrations. Two in particular were Doug Brown and Vann Evans.

Donna Kelly, administrator of the Historical Publications Section, shepherded the work through press, selected illustrations, and prepared the index. Susan Trimble designed and typeset the book, and Lisa Bailey proofread it. Bill Owens assisted in designing the book cover and was responsible for all marketing efforts.

Whether the Regulator Movement was a true precursor to the American Revolution remains controversial, even with the publication of this book. Recent archaeological research at the Alamance Battleground State Historic Site will hopefully shed light on the violence that occurred in Alamance County and add to a better understanding of the movement itself.

Introduction: The Regulators and Alamance*

PIEDMONT GRIEVANCES

During the two decades before the American Revolution, many North Carolinians were dissatisfied with the provincial government, feeling both alienated and cheated. Their quarrel was not with the form of government or the colony's laws but with abuses by colonial and local officials.

Grievances affecting the daily lives of colonists in the Piedmont included illegal fees, dishonest sheriffs and other local officers, and the inability of non-Anglican clergy to perform legal marriages. Scarcity of money also contributed to the state of unrest. Moreover, it was difficult to establish legal ownership of land in much of the colony's interior. A family could settle, build a house, and grow crops without buying land, but they had no assurance of keeping the land on which they had settled. Land was cheap but establishing title to it was frustratingly complicated. Typically, courthouse rings controlled local land offices and law enforcement in the new counties of the Piedmont frontier, and they could demand illegal payments for deeds and court papers. Courthouse rings retained power through political and business partnerships with members of the North Carolina legislature. The large Piedmont counties had few representatives in the assembly. Piedmont farmers distrusted the easterners who controlled the legislature—largely planters, lawyers, and merchants. Thus it was in the new Piedmont counties that the Regulator Movement began.

Displays of discontent were confined to petitions and minor clashes with local officials until the spring of 1768, when men calling themselves "Regulators" discussed issues in publicly announced meetings across the Piedmont and communicated by messenger between meetings. There was no membership in a "Regulator" organization. The meetings never had a single coordinating leader, though several men were prominent in the movement, including William Butler, Rednap Howell, James Hunter, Herman Husband, and Christopher Nation. Husband, a land agent well known among Quakers and Baptists between the Deep and Haw rivers, circulated political pamphlets that sought to effect peaceful reform. Along with a few other Regulators and Regulator sympathizers, he was elected to the legislature in 1769.

* Adapted and expanded from North Carolina Division of State Historic Sites Web page for Alamance Battleground http://www.nchistoricsites.org/alamance/alamanc.htm.

Some of the crucial Regulator stirrings originated within religious gatherings. In the British Isles, democratic church practices and convictions about equality and political participation had been forged in the 1600s; they accompanied certain immigrant sects to the colonies, particularly Presbyterian, Baptist, Congregationalist, and Quaker. Religious revivalism in the 1740s–1760s reconnected colonial communities with these traits, spread them in a nondenominational manner, and Americanized the practices by incorporating African features. The style and expressions of the emerging religious culture of the upland South, as well as its democratic tendencies and emphasis on individual value and responsibility, made North Carolina's Regulator Movement distinctive.

VIOLENT RESISTANCE

Like religious expression, violence was near the surface in the new and changing communities of the Piedmont. Some Regulators resorted to violence, particularly after efforts to secure their goals peacefully had failed. When government officials retaliated against them, Regulators refused to pay taxes and fees, attacked officials who administered the law, and disrupted court proceedings.

Royal governor William Tryon determined to bring the back-country revolt to a speedy conclusion. In March 1771, his council authorized him to call out the colony's militia and march against the rebel farmers. Volunteers for the militia were gathered, largely in eastern North Carolina. When the expedition got under way, Gen. Hugh Waddell with some Cape Fear and western militia was ordered to approach Hillsborough by way of Salisbury. Tryon and his militia proceeded directly toward Hillsborough from the eastern counties. Waddell's force was attacked by Regulators soon after leaving Salisbury, and Waddell turned back. On May 11, 1771, Governor Tryon and his forces left Hillsborough intending to rescue Waddell. When Tryon's group of approximately one thousand militiamen camped on Great Alamance Creek in the heart of Regulator country, they were aware that some two thousand Regulators were assembled four or five miles away.

THE BATTLE OF ALAMANCE

The battle began around noon on May 16, after the Regulators had rejected Tryon's demand that they disperse peacefully. Lacking leadership, organization, and adequate arms and ammunition, the Regulators were no match for the militia and its cannon. Many Regulators fled, leaving their bolder or better-armed comrades to fight on. The rebellion was crushed by the North Carolina militia. Nine militiamen were reported as killed and sixty-one wounded. The Regulator losses were much greater, though exact numbers are unknown. Tryon took fifteen prisoners; seven were later executed. Many Regulators moved on to other frontier areas to the west and south. Those who stayed were offered pardons by the governor in exchange for pledging an oath of allegiance to the government.

THE REGULATION AND THE REVOLUTION

The War of the Regulation illustrates the dissatisfactions of a large part of the population during the years before the American Revolution. The problems that gave rise to the Regulator Movement were not settled by the defeat at Alamance. The various issues that drove the Regulators were still alive after revolutionaries began putting together a state government following the Declaration of Independence. The foremost issue was land.

When the Revolution began, "the elephant in the room" in the Piedmont was the fact that most of the men who started the Revolution in North Carolina had sided with Tryon in putting down the Regulators. They had been part of the eastern-dominated legislature and the courthouse rings against whom the Regulators had raged. If the Piedmont—the Regulator country—were to support the cause of independence, some accommodation had to be made on the issues that had fueled the Regulator Movement.

Leaders of the American Revolution varied in their assessment of the Regulators, their actions, and their cause. During 1775–1776, North Carolina revolutionary spokesmen were annoyed and embarrassed to learn that Americans to the north, relying largely upon newspaper accounts of the Battle of Alamance, expressed sympathy with the erstwhile Regulators and tended to link the revolt of Piedmont farmers with the current struggle for independence. The Regulator Movement was linked with the Revolution more directly than by the perception of outsiders, and also more subtly. In areas of Regulator strength, issues connected with land and religion streamed through the Regulator years, gathering head, to be channeled skillfully by revolutionaries during the American Revolution. Regulator leadership had broadened the politicization of the North Carolina Piedmont.

1

Land Speculation and a
Geographic Imbalance of Power

"It Was Prety Currant . . . That the Lord Carteret's Land Was Dificult in the Titles"

Stresses from which the Regulator Movement emerged in the 1760s had reverberated throughout North Carolina's backcountry for years before the word "Regulator" came to be used there. The word "back-country" reflected the coast-oriented perspective of the colony's politics. The "back" country was the interior, land upstream from a river's head of navigation, unreachable by vessels that connected coastal settlements with each other and the world beyond the ocean. During the Regulator period, the Carolina backcountry was the Piedmont. Many of its earliest stresses dealt with land. Across most of the region in the mid-eighteenth century, it was hard, if not impossible, to know if a particular tract already belonged to someone, regardless of whether anyone appeared to be using it.

Part of the uncertainty concerning land ownership was embedded in the colony's original proprietary status and the resumption of royal control in 1729. In 1663, King Charles II had chartered a colony comprising present-day North Carolina and South Carolina, as well as lands to the west. He named it for himself, Carolina, and granted it to eight Lords Proprietors. The colony was their reward for assisting him in the restoration of the Crown and its Protestant state Church of England after eleven years as a republic in which the official church had embodied a populist form of Protestantism. The Proprietors' ownership of Carolina symbolized their continued cooperation with England's restored monarchy, with its Anglican state church, and with its largest landowners. By 1729, the original Lords Proprietors were long since dead, and political changes within the colony and the mother country had rendered proprietary control of Carolina obsolete. The Glorious Revolution of 1688–1689 and its aftermath had seen Parliament bestow kingship upon a new branch of the royal family, grant limited religious toleration for non-Anglican Protestants, and reserve top positions in the military, church, and administration for sons of the landed elite. Furthermore, neglect by the Proprietors had contributed to difficulties in Carolina. The colony was separated into North and South Carolina in 1712, and in 1729 the government bought the rights of seven of the Lords Proprietors from their descendants. The Carolinas were thereafter separate royal colonies. Quickly, the first royal governors of North Carolina granted large tracts of land to influential speculators. These grants were for thousands of acres each and included great swaths of the backcountry. Recipients of these grants—or their heirs and creditors—sporadically sent agents into the interior to sell tracts, but their surveys and legal documents were unsubstantial. Moreover, some absentee landlords preferred to rent out their investments rather than to sell them piecemeal. They continued to do so until revolutionaries confiscated the large tracts in the 1770s and 1780s.

Rather than buy land from the agents of absentee speculators, settlers who moved to the backcountry found it easier, cheaper, and more secure to obtain ungranted (or "Crown") land. For most of the area where the Regulator Movement developed, however, available land was not Crown land. It was Granville land, owned by the Carteret family, descendants of the sole proprietor who had not relinquished his land rights to the Crown in 1729. King George II in 1744 settled with John Carteret, Earl Granville, granting him title to one-eighth of the original Carolina colony. In effect, this "Granville Tract" or Granville District was the northern half of North Carolina, extending sixty to seventy miles south of the Virginia border. Gov. Gabriel Johnston and Earl Granville appointed surveyors to establish the Crown-Granville boundary. The surveyors started at Bath in 1743, and were well into the Piedmont by April 1746, when they stopped at the Haw River because crew members needed to return to their eastern farms for spring planting. They further observed that the land west of the Haw River did not have sufficient food for the men and horses in the spring, it being "very thinly Peopled." Surveying resumed in September and took the line to Cold Water Creek in present-day Cabarrus County;

King George II granted John Carteret, 2nd Earl Granville, title to one-eighth of the original Carolina colony. Portrait by Peter Pelham ca. 1710–1723. Image provided courtesy of the John Carter Brown Library, Brown University, Providence, Rhode Island.

a further extension was made in 1753. The line was not continued west until 1772, after the Regulator Movement. The location of the line east of Cold Water Creek was well enough known in 1753, 1762, and 1768 for the colonial legislature to cite it as a boundary when it created Rowan, Mecklenburg, and Tryon counties, but there could be uncertainty on the ground.[1]

A new map of Virginia in the early 1750s reflected increasing interest in the Granville District. The surveyors, Thomas Jefferson's father and a partner, extended their map sixty miles south of Virginia to include the district. Another surveyor recalled in 1753: "In the year 1746 I was up in the Country that is now Anson, Orange and Rowan Counties, there was not then above one hundred fighting men [but] there is now at least three thousand for the most part Irish Protestants and Germans and dayley increasing."[2] Indeed, Germans and Scotch-Irish (also known as Ulster Scots) were conspicuous among the newcomers, though many of them were second or even third generations of immigrant families who had settled in southern and western Pennsylvania in the early eighteenth century. At that time, the Pennsylvania interior had been known as "the best poor man's country" for its good cheap land and the colony's religious toleration. Land prices rose sharply with the birthrate, however, and the next generation moved into nearby Virginia or North Carolina for farmland. Furthermore, during the French and Indian War of 1756–1763, Indian scares in western regions of Pennsylvania and Virginia added to the push toward the new "best poor man's country" in the Carolina interior. Already, long-established trade corridors known as Indian trading paths provided access. Portions of these bridle paths were widened into wagon roads as heavier migration poured into what Regulator leader Herman Husband would call the second Pennsylvania.

In 1755 Husband remarked, "it was prety currant in Pensylvania, as I had often heard before I left there, that the Lord Carteret's land was dificult in the titles."[3] The difficulty about getting land in the Granville District was not its cost, as the price was low. Eight pounds four shillings Virginia currency, or about six pounds sterling, would buy 640 acres (one square mile) of "good" land in 1760, a cost of about five shillings per acre. The quitrent of two shillings per one hundred acres was the same rate as for Crown lands and was not enforced in any case. The biggest problem was the dishonest and abusive manner in which Granville lands commonly were administered. Earl Granville never had nor claimed to have any governing authority in the area. The Granville tract was simply a source of income that he had inherited.

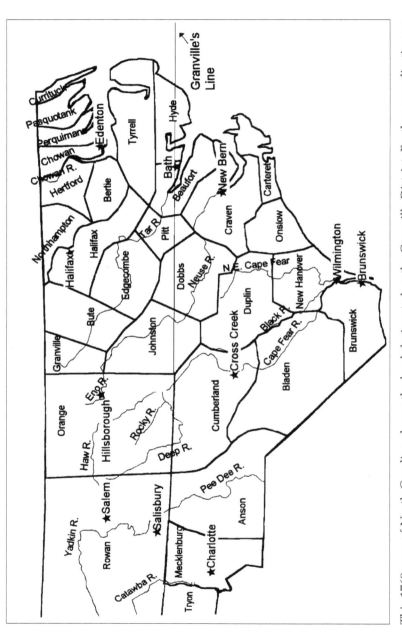

This 1769 map of North Carolina shows the land designated as the Granville District. Further complicating an already difficult system for gaining title to the land was the fact that several counties included Granville land and Crown land. From Wayne E. Lee, *Crowds and Soldiers in Revolutionary North Carolina: The Culture of Violence in Riot and War* (Gainesville: University Press of Florida, 2001), 23. Reproduced by permission of the author.

He delegated its management to men in business for themselves, who then turned the duties over to other men in business for *them*selves. Earl Granville's agent, Francis Corbin, and perhaps also land agent Thomas Childs, cheated both Granville and the land purchasers. The weight that Corbin, and later Childs, carried in Orange County is reflected in the names by which the new county seat was known after the original county courthouse near the Haw River was abandoned in 1754 in favor of its current site on the Eno River. Before the name "Hillsborough" was adopted (honoring the first secretary of state for the colonies), the new town on the Eno was known briefly as Corbinton and then Childsboro, following Corbin's removal from office in 1759.[4] Further west, a deputy agent in Rowan County, James Carter, was known for pocketing entry fees from men who had made improvements on land without registering them or any other claim to the land. Carter was free to demand payoffs and to reward favorites with land grants, as he was surveyor as well as land agent and register of deeds. As a trustee of the new town of Salisbury, he could also distribute its lots.[5]

Although the Granville land office was not a government agency, its loose structure and relative inattention to accounting followed the model of eighteenth-century bureaucratic laxness. In Britain and the colonies, lawmakers kept land taxes low or nonexistent by offering officials legitimate opportunities for making money from their offices instead of paying them salaries. Every administrative unit had a "fee table," which listed, for example, the amount of money a clerk should receive for registering a deed or that a sheriff would collect for serving a writ. Such fees were to be paid by the person for whom the public service was rendered. In London, the Privy Council, through the Board of Trade, set the fee table for each colony and included it among the general instructions issued to a governor at the time he took office. Fees were fairly uniform throughout the colonies, and they were consistently low. Exceptions might be made in areas of low population, where it would be expected that few fees could be collected. In the North Carolina Piedmont, the problem was not the fee table. Like the price of land, the officially sanctioned fees were low. The trouble came when the fee table was ignored, and officials collected what they could get away with. This became especially common in the large new counties of Anson, Orange, and Rowan, created by the North Carolina Assembly in the early 1750s. Each of these counties contained land that could be obtained from the Crown through county officials and the governor's office and some available from either the Granville land office or speculators.

North Carolinians sent petitions to Lord Granville complaining of abuses by his employees. In response, Granville strongly reprimanded Corbin and others, but the malpractices continued. In late 1758, approximately five hundred men appeared before the lower house of the legislature to complain that Corbin and his co-agent Joshua Bodley charged excessive and illegal fees. The House's minimal response required Corbin to publicly display the list of fees that Granville

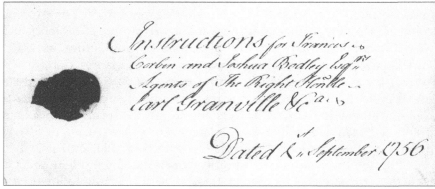

Instructions of Lord Granville to Joshua Bodley and Francis Corbin, September 1, 1756. Endorsement and last page shown. The overall tone of the document implies that Granville is not satisfied with the agents. From Colonial Court Records, Miscellaneous Papers, 1677–1775, CCR 192. Image provided courtesy of the North Carolina State Archives, Office of Archives and History, Raleigh, N.C.

officials were authorized to collect, and this confirmed the legitimacy of the complaints. A bizarre sequence of events followed. Corbin's clerk died unexpectedly, and his body was disinterred to make sure that he had not absconded to avoid prosecution. Soon thereafter, men in Edgecombe County stopped Bodley and forced him to remain at Enfield, which until recently had been the seat of Edgecombe County, and was still the location of the Granville land office. Seventy miles away at Edenton, approximately twenty-five men seized Corbin and took him to join Bodley. The agents had to post bond to appear in court to answer charges of extortion, and they were forced to sign a set of guidelines for granting Granville land. There are indications that grievances against corruption in the Granville agency were used by competing land speculators to produce this so-called "Enfield Riot" in Edgecombe County.[6]

"To Be Tied Neck and Heels and Be Carried over the Yadkin"

Competition among speculators was headed by Henry Eustace McCulloh. A self-acknowledged rake and thief, McCulloh was agent and attorney for his father, Henry McCulloh, a London merchant of Scottish background whose holdings of more than one million acres blanketed the western Piedmont. The elder McCulloh had helped Gabriel Johnston obtain the governorship of North Carolina in 1734 and had received his reward in land grants in the colony's interior. By 1750, McCulloh agents were said to be "Hawking [land] about in small quantities thro' all the back parts of the Province and quite thro' America even to Boston." During the next two decades, McCulloh's easiest money came from selling land with "improvements" (such as orchards, cleared fields, and buildings) to the very families whose labor had increased the value of the land. Contiguous McCulloh tracts of 100,000 acres dominated the present-day counties of Cabarrus, Davidson, Davie, Iredell, Mecklenburg, Montgomery, Rowan, and Stanly. Two other McCulloh tracts centered on present-day Alamance, Guilford, and Wake counties.[7] Surveying of the Crown-Granville boundary in 1746–1753 revealed that some of the Granville tract was on pre-existing McCulloh grants. This discovery further complicated land titles for settlers and created additional opportunities for higher fees, bribery, and favoritism, even after Granville and McCulloh agreed in 1755 that the latter's purchasers would not lose by the

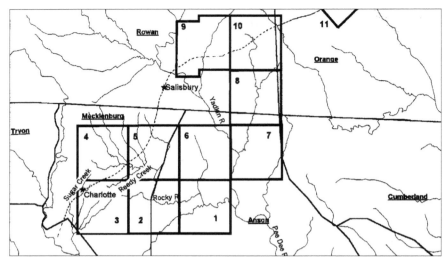

Henry McCulloh served as an agent for his father and for George Selwyn, who had inherited 100,000 acres in Mecklenburg County from a 1745 grant to his father. County boundaries are shown as of 1769. Tracts 2 and 5 belonged to Governor Dobbs, 1 and 3 to George Selwyn, and 4 and 7 to Henry McCulloh Sr. (Tract boundaries are approximate and are based on the 1738 survey plat printed in *North Carolina Genealogical Society Journal* 4 [1978]: 146, and on the map prepared by the late George Stevenson, former staff member of the North Carolina State Archives.) Reproduced by permission of the author.

Granville survey. The uncertain boundary with South Carolina compounded opportunities for confusion, chicanery, and frustration. Young McCulloh took up residence in North Carolina in 1761 as agent for his father and for George Augustus Selwyn, who claimed two tracts of 100,000 acres each in Duplin and Mecklenburg counties, inherited from a 1745 grant to Selwyn's father.

In the spring of 1765, a decade of grievances against McCulloh in the area between the Yadkin River and present-day Charlotte culminated in a series of confrontations between his agents and settlers on Sugar and Reedy creeks. Threats and negotiations centered on the price of land and settlers' rights to the improvements they had made as squatters. Like the Enfield Riot six years earlier, the Sugar Creek disturbances involved groups of settlers shaming and threatening agents of private land speculators, not surveyors for the Crown. Violence, though striking, was restrained. The targets of the "Sugar Creek War" were not only Henry Eustace McCulloh and his employees, but also local land speculators of the large and prominent Alexander family, who cooperated with McCulloh. The rioters used tactics they knew from generations of folk practices in the British Isles and from contemporary military and judicial punishments. For example, in response to McCulloh's refusal to accept their price for the land on which they lived, a crowd of approximately 150 men warned him that if he persisted in surveying, "the best usage he should expect to meet with, would be to be tied Neck and heels and be carried over the Yadkin." Military personnel, including the North Carolina militia, were accustomed to this humiliating punishment. On both sides of the Atlantic, group violence, or "riot," functioned as a tool to obtain wider community approval and legitimacy for the rioters' cause.[8]

McCulloh wrote his friend Edmund Fanning a description of the "Sugar Creek War" that reflects not only pique over his humiliation but also their shared understanding that governmental remedies could be made available to punish the rioters. He offhandedly referred to "the black act," a 1723 parliamentary law that empowered justices of the peace in Britain to take extraordinary measures against certain forms of group action. The black act was the English landed oligarchy's response to rural violence against their control. It was therefore a suitable model for addressing backcountry disturbances. McCulloh wrote:

> Mecklenburgh County 9th May, 1765
> Dear Ned
> Shall not the war of Sugar Creek be handed down to posterity? . . . Thy poor friend John Frohock—Abraham [Alexander] the father of the Faithful . . . have been in Troth—well Striped— Providentially detained by particular business I was not there—had I been present—I most assuredly & without any ceremony had been murdered; . . . Guns were brought for that particular purpose.—They declare solemnly— publicly, they will put me to Death:—they may be damned for a pack of ungrateful brutal Sons of Bitches:—I dont care:—I will tomorrow make my will: . . . Ned, thou shalt be one of my Executors & if the event should take place—one of their Executioners.—It made my heart quite full, when I first saw poor John [Frohock] . . . he got one damnable wipe across the Nose and Mouth,—and Abraham they say is striped from the nape of his neck to the Waistband of his Breeches, like a draftBoard; poor Jimmy Alexander had very near had daylight let into his skull:— a pack of Unmannerly Sons of Bitches as Abraham called them . . . . Cousin Billy [Alexander]—who will deliver you this can tell all about it:—he was one of the Thrashees,—John Frohock says I can hardly form an Idea equal to the horror of their Behaviour and Appearance.— Ned—. . . Shall not my soul see its Revenge?—By the Eternal God,—it shall not be for want of my utmost Exertions.—Didst thou ever hear of such a thing as . . . the Black act? But these things, at present Sub Rosa . . . . Surely my Cause is the Cause of Government.[9]

Since the men of Sugar Creek never tied McCulloh "Neck and heels," the Salisbury District Superior Court dropped the charges he brought against about fifty of them, and he forfeited several grants because challengers proved that he had not populated the land as required. As motivation behind the Regulator Movement, the outcome of eruptions like the Enfield and Sugar Creek disturbances was less significant than the underlying network of land speculators and county officials against whom the disturbances were directed. McCulloh's choice of Moses and Benjamin Alexander and their relatives as agents for his western tracts reflected a pattern of county-level power that had quickly emerged in the 1750s: multiple officeholding land speculators with ties to Virginia and eastern North Carolina, connected with other lawyers and merchants, staking out local access to land and fees. John Frohock was the Alexanders' counterpart in Rowan County, where he was responsible for the land of both the Crown and Granville. Frohock also enjoyed a family tie with the McCullohs; his brother was a son-in-law of Henry Eustace McCulloh's cousin. With several judicial offices and command of the county militia, Frohock's local power meshed with the eastern-dominated assembly in which he served.

The administration that regulated county officials was not the distant Board of Trade, but rather the local county court, the district court, and the colonial assembly. Of these, the lower house of the legislature and the justices of the peace in the county courts were the power pivots. The upper house of the assembly was the governor's council, appointed on an individual basis by the Board of Trade, generally on the advice of the governor and the other members of the council. The lower house, called the Commons House of Assembly, paralleled the elected House of Commons in London. In the third quarter of the eighteenth century, the lower house was the dominant branch of colonial government in North Carolina, exercising some of its powers by charter and others by tradition. It initiated most bills and, like the British House of Commons, had exclusive power to introduce or amend money bills.

The North Carolina lower house, more than any other unit of government, controlled and distributed power in the counties. Justices of the peace (JPs) were appointed by the governor, normally from names submitted by members of the lower house. JPs usually held office for two years and could succeed themselves. The legislature determined how many JPs each county would have, thereby creating the opportunity for new appointments. Typically, the representatives of a county would have first advisement in appointing new justices or renewing the commissions of current ones. As late as 1772, a North Carolina royal governor observed: "A great number of bad men . . . are . . . necessarily admitted into the Magistracy."[10] Like the justices, other county officers—coroners, registers of deeds, clerks, and sheriffs— held commissions from the governor but were selected on the basis of support from justices and county representatives in the lower house. Colonial sheriffs were very powerful, owing more to the medieval origins and statutory heritage of the office than to contemporary usage in England. The governor routinely appointed the sheriff from three nominees provided by the justices of a county. For example, in March 1754, the Orange County JPs nominated John Gray, Lawrence Thompson, and James Dickey. In this instance, they polled the grand jury and reported the votes of the jurors: ten for Gray, eight for Thompson, and six for Dickey.[11] Gov. Arthur Dobbs, who usually acted in accordance with the court poll, whether of grand jurors or JPs, appointed Gray.

After he became governor in 1765, William Tryon had to break a tie vote for his first appointment of an Orange County sheriff. From among Tyree Harris, Thomas Lloyd, and Thomas Hart, Tryon selected Harris. The new sheriff had previously provoked a complaint of having "acted partially in his office as a Majestrate." Harris and the Regulators antagonized one another while he was sheriff and afterwards. When the 1773 lower house sought to question him about his accounts as sheriff, Harris could not be found. The accounts concerned the county's back taxes for 1756–1761, which the legislature in 1764 had empowered him to collect. Scarcity of currency, particularly in the backcountry, had complicated the payment of taxes when due. The cumulative collection that Harris carried out was especially onerous. It was in "distraining," or seizing movable property such as cattle, cloth, or grain to sell for taxes, that Harris tripped the wire of farmers' anger and became a major target of Regulator resentment.[12]

Sheriffs and justices were assisted by constables, whom the JPs appointed. JPs also named the jurors for county courts and district superior courts. The district courts usually met twice a year at Edenton, New Bern, Wilmington, and Halifax. The Piedmont got a district court in 1762, when the legislature established the Salisbury District, and in 1767 a sixth district was added, to sit at Hillsborough.

In those counties where the Regulator Movement erupted, justices of the peace owned 40 percent of both land and enslaved laborers. Officers in the county militia and overseers of roads, many of whom were also JPs, were likewise among the wealthier residents. The governor appointed the top militia officers, who in turn appointed officers of the various companies in the county. Militia musters required attendance about two weeks a year. Work on county roads typically took an additional two weeks. The county justices appointed overseers of roads to supervise the work crews who cut and maintained roads. Legislation required free and enslaved men living in the vicinity of the road to serve on the crews, but there were so many exceptions that "the wealthy never worked as road hands, and the middling only infrequently did so."[13]

"When Fanning First to Orange Came"

In the large and increasingly populous Piedmont counties, courthouse rings quickly developed. Two features of the rings stand out: membership was small; and they were connected closely with the eastern leadership of the lower house of the assembly. The geographic imbalance in the assembly made the backcountry counties easy prey. In the 1750s, new county courthouses in Hillsborough, Salisbury, and Anson County became magnets for opportunists who were attracted by prospects of land speculation, collusive legal actions, and unsupervised collection of illegal fees. Granville land agents and surveyors found it easy to work with these speculators. While east-west political tension was not the sole cause of the turbulence generally referred to as the Regulator Movement, the geographical imbalance of power in the lower house of the legislature was crucial to the development and protection of the eastern-linked courthouse rings against which the Regulators raged.

Despite the rapidity with which the Piedmont was becoming populated, political power still lay with the east. Throughout the 1760s, the governor and his council, judges, and the Speakers of the lower house all lived in the older settled Tidewater area and acted from its plantation-based perspective. In effect, the only government officials from the backcountry were the two members of the lower house elected by each county. The Albemarle counties, by contrast, had five representatives apiece. Chowan, Currituck, Pasquotank, Perquimans, and Tyrrell together were no larger than Orange County and by 1766 had fewer free inhabitants; yet their twenty-five members overwhelmed the two from Orange County. Moreover, as the legislature created new Piedmont counties as settlers moved west, it simultaneously redivided the older eastern counties in order to maintain the numerical dominance of the east. This resulted in "perhaps the most glaring illustration of inequitable representation in all North Carolina history."[14]

The manner of electing members of the lower house also did little to contribute to its representativeness. Sheriffs conducted the elections. Before 1743 voters wrote the names of five candidates on a ballot and signed it, or had someone do so for them. The sheriff collected the ballots. After 1743 the voter recorded his choices in an open book under the sheriff's oversight. Beginning in 1760, votes were cast orally and recorded in election books under the sheriff's gaze. Candidates could observe the voting and inspect the books at any time. Polls remained open at the courthouse for one or two weeks to accommodate voters coming from distant parts of a county. Until 1743, the only voter qualifications were to be a male taxpayer over the age of twenty-one and to have lived at least one year in the county—a wide franchise. Beginning in 1743, the legislature stipulated a property requirement of fifty acres. The sheriff (and ultimately the justices and assemblymen who controlled the appointment of sheriffs) certified voters.[15]

The political difficulties with these arrangements in the eighteenth-century backcountry were neither their undemocratic nature nor their failure to match modern standards. In fact, little of this process would change after the American Revolution. The contextual problems, especially in the Granville District, were twofold. First, the role of sheriffs in the closed loop of local and legislative power meant that elections tended to keep that loop closed. The tighter the courthouse ring, the less difference an election normally made. Second, the difficulty of obtaining title to Granville land could disfranchise men who otherwise could have qualified to vote. Having the use of fifty acres or more was not generally a problem; obtaining legal validation of its ownership frequently was. Thus the framework was present for an elected lower house to be "representative only in the sense that it

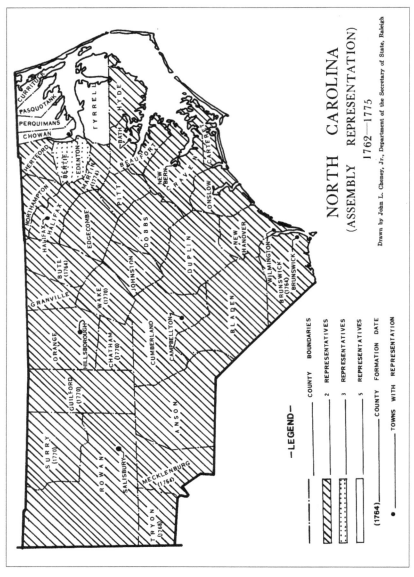

NORTH CAROLINA
(ASSEMBLY REPRESENTATION)
1762—1775

Drawn by John L. Cheney, Jr., Department of the Secretary of State, Raleigh

—LEGEND—

	COUNTY BOUNDARIES
	2 REPRESENTATIVES
	3 REPRESENTATIVES
	5 REPRESENTATIVES
(1764)	COUNTY FORMATION DATE
●	TOWNS WITH REPRESENTATION

Map from John L. Cheney Jr., ed., *North Carolina Government, 1585–1979: A Narrative and Statistical History* (Raleigh, N.C.: Department of the Secretary of State, 1981), 50. Reproduced by permission of the publisher.

was representative of the dominant class of local officials."[16] Even so, a county's courthouse ring and its "dominant class of local officials" were not necessarily identical, the latter being potentially larger and broader. Certainly, class tensions based on local inequities existed alongside anger toward abusive officials and resentment of eastern control. Indeed, the targets of all these resentments could be the same people. In the heat of the Regulator upheavals, insurgents indiscriminately took aim at all three targets: local class tensions, abusive local officials, and eastern control. The Regulators' perception of a linkage among their targets may have been as accurate as subsequent scholarly efforts to dissect them. This sense of a connection among the eastern oligarchy, county officials, and locals with legal ownership of several hundred acres set the political and social tone of the Regulator upheavals.

Edmund Fanning was the member of the Orange County courthouse ring who aroused the greatest resentment in that large county, which included all or part of twelve modern-day counties.[17] Fanning, a fourth-generation American from New York, was a lawyer and merchant. He continued to hold public office in New York as an absentee. His removal to Orange County seems to have resulted from kinship with Henry Tazewell, a lawyer in Williamsburg, Virginia. His eldest brother, the Reverend William Fanning, had been an Anglican minister in Carolina. Edmund Fanning was in Hillsborough by 1760, when the county court made him trustee of the newly incorporated town. His 1761 appointment as Crown prosecutor was followed by other local offices, including register of deeds, a particularly lucrative post. As a multiple officeholder, he truly could refer to Orange as "my darling my favourite County."[18] He went into business in Hillsborough with two recent arrivals from Virginia—Thomas Hart and Francis Nash. Hart was sheriff for multiple terms and a member of the assembly. Nash was a JP and clerk of court, as well as militia captain and a member of the assembly. The partnerships among Nash, Hart, Fanning, and other locals were political as well as commercial. After William Tryon became governor, Fanning and Tryon were close, and Tryon appointed Fanning as colonel of the Orange County militia regiment. To Henry Eustace McCulloh, Fanning was "Dear Ned."[19]

Public opinion condemned multiple officeholding, overcharging fees and fines, and economic manipulation by commercial legal actions. Lawyers in Orange County were said to charge five times the established standard for common legal services, such as drawing up

Edmund Fanning (1737–1818), a lawyer, land speculator, and colonial official, was an influential friend of Governor Tryon. His actions incurred the wrath of the Regulators, who wrote satirical songs and poems about him. Image provided courtesy of the Frick Art Reference Library, New York, N.Y.

deeds. Fanning was a special target and symbol, even before Tryon became governor. To observers, he appeared to get rich very quickly, and he was arrogant. Years later, a seventy-one-year-old Quaker who had sympathized with the Regulators recalled that he had been seventeen years old when his family moved to the Chatham section of Orange County in 1765. He first heard of Fanning at a wedding celebration where people were singing about him, using new words set to familiar tunes. The old man remembered the following lines. They may have been sung to the spinning tune, "Pop Goes the Weazel," then in common use:

> When Fanning first to Orange came
> He looked both pale and wearworn
> An old patched coat upon his back
> An old mare he rode on.
> Both man and horse won't worth five pounds
> As I've been often told
> But by his civil robberies
> He's laced his coat with gold.

The old Quaker further recalled that "Fanning . . . gained his seat [in the assembly] through the influence of Thomas Hart the sheriff to whom he promised a reward if he would get him elected and accordingly after he took his seat he brought in a bill and got it passed

Says Frohawk to Fanning, to tell the plain truth

When I came to this country I was but a youth.

My father sent me, I wasn't worth a crop.

And then my first study was to cheat for a horse.

I quickly got credit and straight ran away.

And Haven't paid for him to this very day.

Says Fanning to Frohawk tis a folly to lie

I rode an old mare that was blind in one eye

Five shillings in money I had in my purse

My coat it was patched but not much the worse

But now we've got rich and it's very well known

That we'll do evil enough if they let us alone.

This song ridiculed John Frohock and Edmund Fanning. The historian Archibald DeBow Murphey, who obtained three songs and other details of Regulator activity from interviews in the early 1800s, believed the songs were part of a much larger body of work by the teacher Rednap Howell or Howells. The songs were intended to arouse sympathy for Regulator activity and to celebrate it. Their structure was in the broadside tradition, with lines set to popular tunes to make them easy to sing and remember.

for giving to Thomas Hart one thousand pounds on account of loses [*sic*] as sheriff when he in fact had lost nothing. So said the Regulators. They complained that all the money went in this way." Also, he recalled Frohock's reputation for extortion of fees in Rowan County: "It was said that he charged 15 dollars for a Marriage License. Consequences was that some of the inhabitants at the headwaters of the Yadkin took a short cut. Took each other for better or worse and lived without any legal ceremony."[20]

2

Orderly Outbursts of
Backcountry Resentment

"A Poor Back Settler that Has Nothing but the Labour of His Hands"

The new colonial government building and governor's residence in New Bern known as "Tryon's Palace" became, like Edmund Fanning, symbolic of the grievances that came to a head in the Regulator Movement. The legislature's 1766 decision to provide a capitol in the Tidewater for the colony became a volatile symbol of the east-west differences, and the tax to pay for "Tryon's Palace" sharpened the frustration regarding local corruption and class tensions. One of the earliest histories of North Carolina observed that "this measure was thought, by many, to have laid the foundation of the series of disorders and commotions, which terminated in the battle of the Alamance. The grant of five thousand pounds was above the means of the province."[1]

"Tryon's Palace" was intended not only as a residence for the governor but also as headquarters for the administration of the colony. Until it was built, there was no central repository for records nor a set meeting place for either house of the assembly. In the tradition of many centuries, the government moved from place to place. Much of the English central government had followed this practice until the seventeenth century, having no fixed seat but traveling with the king and his court. Following that precedent, North Carolina's colonial

This engraving of Tryon Palace by William Tisdale appeared on the face of a counterfeit bill issued in 1775. Completed in 1770, the palace came to symbolize the grievances of the Regulator Movement. Image provided courtesy of the North Carolina State Archives.

government moved essential records in wagons from one session to the next. In the late 1750s, the legislature agreed on a place for a capital near present-day Kinston, but the Privy Council overruled the decision upon learning that the land belonged to Gov. Arthur Dobbs, and the legislature had to select another site. By 1765 there was sentiment expressed in the Piedmont to settle the government there, the fastest growing region of the colony. Hillsborough, then burgeoning beside the Trading Path, was the obvious choice. It had become, in historian Hugh Lefler's words, "something of the capital of the whole back country and this led representatives from the Albemarle and Pamlico Sound region and the Cape Fear to unite in favor of New Bern" as the seat of government to counter the backcountry's ambition.[2] The legislature decided in 1766 to build the governor's residence in New Bern and to pay for it with a uniform tax of eight pence on each taxable person, or "poll," in a household. The tax was to be collected, not in pounds sterling, which would have been uncollectible in the interior, but in "North Carolina proclamation money," the local tender of lower value, made temporarily legal by the legislature's "proclamation." The poll tax was resented in the backcountry because of the capital's apparent regional bias; men declared that they would never see "Tryon's Palace," for their trade took them only as far east as Cross Creek (present-day Fayetteville). Otherwise, their droving and other trading ventures led them to Hillsborough, then on to Halifax and Petersburg, Virginia, or to Salisbury or Salem, and thence to Charles Town, South Carolina. As a further irritant, the poll tax would be collected by the sheriff and therefore add to the tax gouging and fee abuse, which the Piedmont courthouse rings already embodied. Colony-wide, the poll tax was resented as an expression of the class bias of the tax-setting legislature. As one Mecklenburg County observer expressed it, "a man that is worth £10,000 pays no more than a poor back settler that has nothing but the labour of his hands to depend upon for his daily support." Driving his argument further, he claimed that the "back settler . . . must be still more grievously oppressed if he has a large family, which 'tis ten to one but he has, as the women in these parts are remarkable prolific."[3]

"Lawsuits Which Tends to the Great Disadvantage and Prejudice of Our Inhabitants"

Disorder pervaded the context of the Regulator Movement and was not limited to class tensions or riots, common occurrences in the eighteenth century. Disorder was part of the rapid influx of new settlers, the land grabbing, the insecurity of land possession, and the corruption that characterized local law enforcement. The closed local political arrangement was sanctioned by the next level of authority, the eastern-run House and council. Politically, therefore, the disorder in the backcountry was encapsulated.

Against that background, the origins of the Regulator Movement are conspicuous for stressing order, or at least orderliness. Spokesmen for emerging Regulator grievances pointedly acknowledged the authority of the county court as the local unit of the hallowed system of common law, their constitutional guarantee of the rights of Englishmen. The realization that local and eastern individuals were using the county governments as money machines did not prevent spokesmen from voicing their grievances in the county courts. When thwarted there, they continued to adapt court meetings and legal procedures as occasions for rituals of violence and humiliation.

A few years before the term "Regulator" is known to have been used in North Carolina, two Granville County men publicized the futility of utilizing county courts to address typical backcountry grievances. Reuben Searcy spoke for "Sundry of the Inhabitants of" Granville County when he wrote a petition "To the Worshipful Court" in March 1759, less than two months after the Enfield Riot in adjacent Edgecombe County. The petitioners' words to the presiding justices of the peace were blunt. Their target was Robert Jones Jr., a lawyer from eastern Virginia and a member of the lower house whose offices included attorney general of the colony and collector of rents for the Granville District. Searcy accused Jones of manipulating Gov. Arthur Dobbs by his "wiles and false insinuations" and of "impos[ing] on the inferior class of mankind" by collecting illegal and exorbitant fees, not only as Granville's agent but also as a lawyer and public officeholder. The petitioners asked the Granville County court to bar Jones from practicing law there because of his constant "chicanerie." Recently, Dobbs had removed the names of men in the northern part of the county from the list of appointees as justices of the peace. For this, the petitioners blamed Jones's "false and unjust Representations in

Arthur Dobbs (1689–1765) became royal governor of North Carolina in 1754 and served until his death in 1765. His administration was often at odds with the legislature. This engraving by James McArdell was based on a painting by William Hoare. Image provided courtesy of the North Carolina State Archives.

matters relating to our County of Granville." This reflected local rivalry for the office of JP and perhaps also Dobbs's concurrent wrangles with the lower house.[4]

Moreover, Searcy expressed the suspicion and fear with which many backcountry people regarded not only lawyers but also merchants and planters, who were the social and economic allies of lawyers in an economy that was chronically short of hard currency. Debt was unavoidable. Transactions that gave the appearance of barter in Piedmont mills, planters' stores, taverns, and merchant houses were recorded as "credits" for goods sold by individual customers and "debits" for goods bought by them. Buyers and sellers who frequented these businesses expected the settlement of accounts to accommodate their cycles of production and to be based on personal agreements and pragmatic principles of justice. Lawyers and their merchant/planter clients with connections in Petersburg, Charles Town, or eastern North Carolina sued in the county courts for debt (or trespass) to settle obligations on the basis of schedules and law book principles. Livestock, working tools, bedding, furniture, and crops might be lost to satisfy such cases and to pay court costs, as surely as such items could be distrained for taxes by the sheriff. Searcy's words suggest that flashy lawyers making unnecessary trouble was a new and unwelcome development in the 1750s in Granville County: "It has become a general practice and custom among chief of our Attornies . . . by the great volubility of speech . . . and [Jones] by his wiles insinuations and chicanerie . . . very frequently works on the passions of weak juries to blind their conception of Justice in order to gain his point so that *men flock daily to him to comence very trivial and frivolous lawsuits which tends to the great disadvantage and prejudice of our inhabitants.*"[5] It was not the legal profession itself but its practice for quick profit at the expense of "the inferior class of mankind" that drew Piedmont ire. In 1770, a Regulator spokesman would voice the distinction, approving of "such Men as have studied the Law from a Motive purely for the Good of their Country; but such as have studied and learnt the Law for Gain, *it is contrary to Nature and their Interest* to preserve our Liberties as they ought to be Preserved."[6]

As attorney general, Jones was a proper official to bring charges against the individuals who had detained the Granville agents at Enfield in January. Some of these men were arrested, but jail breakers released them. The records that survive do not provide an exact chronology of events, but when the lower house convened on May 15, Jones made a sworn statement that "he had heard it was intended by a great number of rioters to petition the court at Granville to silence him, the deponent, and that if no such order was made, to pull [Jones] by the nose and also to abuse the court." The Enfield rioters whose names are known were farmers of substantial means and not "a class-conscious mob of impoverished tenants"; even so, the image of the men of northern Granville County administering the common retaliatory insult of pulling the nose of the attorney general was provocative. The lower house, alarmed by backcountry threats of disorder, warmed to the protection of the Granville Proprietary's employees. However, Governor Dobbs did not heed their demand to prepare the militia to suppress riots wherever they might occur in the Granville District.[7]

George Sims and the Nutbush Address

Searcy and his extended family lived along Nutbush Creek in the northern section of what is now Vance County. In 1765, the Nutbush community produced a longer attack on illegal fee taking, titled "An Address to the People of Granville County by George Sims." The writer was a thirty-seven-year-old schoolmaster whose family had moved from Brunswick County, Virginia, some fifteen years earlier. Sims tried to avoid offending most of the Granville County justices of the peace, as Searcy seems to have done. The circumspect preface of his

"Nutbush Address" distinguished between "the common people," whom he claimed as his main audience, and "Gentlemen" readers, to whom Thomas Person facilitated access. Sims dedicated the address to Person.[8]

Person, like Sims, had moved from Virginia with his parents. For years a surveyor for Lord Granville, Person by 1765 had accumulated about twenty thousand acres. Appointed justice of the peace in 1756, he briefly served as sheriff in 1762 and two years later was elected to the lower house. As a representative, Person served alongside Granville's militia colonel and sheriff, Samuel Benton, a representative since 1760 and the target of Sims's attack. Both Person and Benton owned taverns, which facilitated their political activities. Taverns, also known as "public houses" or "ordinaries," served as centers of communication and commerce in the backcountry. Benton had been a JP since the creation of Granville County in 1746 and was longtime clerk of the county court. Months before Sims's Nutbush Address, Benton had influenced the legislature to create Bute County from the eastern portion of Granville and to designate a new county seat for Granville— on Benton's "Oxford" plantation.[9]

Sims's address continued the themes of Searcy's petition, adding details that would have been familiar to Piedmont listeners and readers. He detailed Benton's "abuses," but he could have been describing those of members of other county cliques as well. Herman Husband, the chief Regulator writer, would quote both Sims and Searcy, and the Nutbush Address stands as the classic statement of Piedmont grievances on the cusp of the Regulator Movement. Sims used his training in classical syntax to construct sentences based on rhetorical strategies. Read aloud, his words picked up political patterns and wove them together with hard-hitting rhythms of speech.

> It is not our
> *mode*, or *form* of *Gov*ernment,
> nor *yet* the *body* of our *laws*,
> that *we* are *quarrel*ling *with*,
> but with the
> *malpractices* of the *Officers* of our *County Court*,
> and the *abuses* which we *suffer* by those em*powe*red
> to *man*age our *public* af*fairs*.[10]

The constitutional ground of which the Granville County schoolmaster spoke was the 1689–1702 series of legislation by which Parliament had settled the issues raised first during the English Revolution of 1641–1649, then put on hold during the monarchy's restoration of 1660–1688, and finally brought back to the fore by the Revolution of 1688–1689. Seven decades later, this parliamentary reformulation of governmental authority and individual rights was common ground for English readers and listeners. Sims called it "the inexhaustible fountain, the source whence we draw our claims to these privileges that our situation as free subjects undoubtedly entitles us to." Other Piedmont petitioners of the Regulator period would appeal to this body of legislation as justification for their complaints.[11] The Nutbush Address was neither petition nor history lesson, but a call for cooperation to restore the traditional English legal system with its protections for individual persons, property, and reputations.

Sims attacked multiple officeholding and the illegal fees collected by colluding county officials and lawyers. As a local example, he cited Person's rival, Benton. When elected to the lower house, Benton was, according to Sims, "universally esteemed a person calculated for what is called a poor mans Burgess, . . . [but] all his transactions . . . have been for the benefit of that dear self of his . . . plundering his County to enrich [himself]." Sims detailed the sort of things that Searcy had decried as "chicanerie" six years earlier:

> The Clerks tell us their is no law to ascertain their fees, and therefore they are at liberty to tax our bills as they please, and the misfortune is[,] Gentlemen, that we are obliged to pay it, be it what it may; I think, Gentlemen, if there be no law to ascertain the Clerk's fees, there is no law to compel us to pay any fees at all. However, let us see what advantage Benton the poor mans Burgess makes of this deficiency in our law, if you give a judgment Bond for five pounds only, and this Bond goes into Court, the Clerk for only entering it on the Court docquet and issuing an Execution, charges you with forty one shillings and five pence [more than two pounds], I had it from Benton's own mouth, at which time he vapoured as high, and with the same confidence that a fighting gamester has, who is endowed with courage of a highwayman, with oaths and execrations that he had taken it and would take it.[12]

Sims offered an example of the consequences of this abuse of fees:

> Does not daily experience shew us the gaping jaws of ruin, open, and ready to devour us? Are not your lands executed your negroes, horses, cattle, hogs, corn, beds, and household furniture . . . taken and sold for one tenth of their value? Not to satisfy the just debts which you have contracted, but to satisfy the cursed exorbitant demands of the Clerks, Lawyers and Sheriffs. Here they take your lands which perhaps are worth four or five hundred pounds, and sell them at public vendue for about forty or fifty pounds. And who buys? Why the same villains

who have taken your . . . [movable] estate, and have the County's money in their hands. This has furnished them with money to buy off the rest of your livings. . . . [I]s it reasonable that they should rob the County to support themselves in such damned extravagancies, and laugh at us for being such simpletons as to suffer it?

Reaching further toward his audience, Sims re-created a familiar and fearsome scenario:

[L]et us make an estimate of the difference between getting our livings by honest industry and getting them by these cursed practices. We will suppose ourselves all to be men, who labour for our livings, and there is a poor man among us, who has dealt for about 4 or 5 pounds in such things as his family could not possibly do without, and in hopes of being spared from the lash of the law till he can sell some of his effects to raise the money; he gives a judgment bond to his Merchant, and before he can accomplish his design his bond is thrown into Court, and Benton the poor mans Burgess has it to enter on the Court docquet and issue an execution the work of one long minute. Well, Gentlemen, what has our poor neighbour to pay Mr. Benton for his trouble? Why, nothing but the trifling sum of forty one shillings and five pence. Well he is a poor man, and cannot raise the money. We will suppose Mr. Benton condescends to come to terms with him. Come (says he) and work. I have a large field and my corn wants weeding (or something like that). I will give you 1/6 [1 shilling and 6 pence] a day, which is the common wages of a labourer in these times till you pay it off because you are a poor man, and a neighbour I will not take away your living. Well how many days work has our honest neighbour to pay Mr. Benton for his trouble and expense in writing about a minute? Why, he must work something more than 27 days before he is clear of his clutches. Well the poor man reflects within himself. At this rate, says he when shall I maintain my own family. I have a wife and a parcel of small children suffering at home and I have none to labour but myself, and here I have lost a month's work and I do not know for what, my merchant not yet paid, I do not know what will be the end of these things; however, I will go home, and try what I can do towards getting a living. Stay neighbour [says Benton] you must not go home, you are not half done yet, there is a damned Lawyers mouth to stop before you go any further, you impowered him to confess that you owed £5, and you must pay him 30/ [shillings] for that, or, else go and work nineteen days for that pick-pocket at the same rate, and when that is done, you must work as many days for the Sheriff, for his trouble, and then go home and see your living wrecked and tore to pieces to satisfy your merchant.[13]

The abuse-fueled downward spiral of Sims's common man was relentless:

[I]f he has but one horse to plow with, one bed to lie on, or one cow to give a little milk for his children, they must all go to raise money which is not to be had. And lastly if his personal estate (sold at one tenth of its value) will not do, then his lands (which perhaps has cost him many years toil and labour) must go the same way to satisfy these cursed hungry caterpillars, that are eating and will eat out the bowels of our Commonwealth, if they be not pulled down from their nests in a very short time, and what need I say, Gentlemen, to urge the necessity there is for a reformation. If these things were absolutely according to law, it would be enough to make us turn rebels, and throw off all submission to such tyrannical laws. . . . But, *as these practices are diametrically opposite to the law, it is our absolute duty,* as well as our Interest, to put a stop to them, before they quite ruin our County.[14]

Sims's Three Measures and Three Rules

The Nutbush Address was a call to "the inhabitants of Granville County" for united action "to recover our native rights according to law, and to reduce the malpractices of the Officers of our Court down to the standard of law." Specifically, the schoolmaster proposed three measures and three rules. The measures: petition the governor; request the county court to halt all proceedings until the petitioners received the governor's response; and select a leader. Sims said he had already drafted statements to the governor and the court. He indicated a willingness to lead if selected and requested the "Gentlemen . . . the chief of you" to "name the man, I will be the first on his list to follow him through fire and water, life and death." He cautioned these rules: stay sober; keep the law; and "behave ourselves with circumspection to the Worshipful Court."[15]

If Sims counted on Person and certain other "Gentlemen" to shield him, he was apparently disappointed. Following the defeat of the Regulators in 1771, Husband quoted the Nutbush Address in his account of the Regulator Movement. He remarked that the writer of the address had been promptly indicted for libel and jailed, and that the case had remained unsettled in 1770. Husband indicated that Granville County men had responded to the Nutbush Address by petitioning the legislature "for redress of grievances, and against the male-practices of the Officers. The consequence . . . was, that the Officers sued the Petitioners . . . as Libellers; which action . . . was in suspence in the year 1770," and that "the Officers in the mean while, carri[ed] on their old Trade of oppressing and griping the poor Inhabitants."[16]

In 1748, an Act of Assembly was passed in the province of No. Carolina, for regulating the several Officers Fees within that province.

The 2d. sect. runs in these words. — Be it Enacted &c. That it shall be lawful for the several Officers within this province to take & receive in "proclam.n money or Bills of credit such Fees only as is appointed by this "Act for such service to wit,

Then follows the Enumeration of the particular Fees, of which the Fees of the public Register are set down thus.

For registring every Birth, Burial or Marriage	0 . 0 . 7
For registring a Conveyance, or any other writing, or giving a Copy thereof	0 . 2 . 8
For every certificate of Birth, Burial, or Marriage	0 . 0 . 7

This list of fees, based on a 1748 law, was presented during the 1769 trial of Edmund Fanning for extortion. From the Military Collection, War of the Regulation, (1768–1779), Box 1. Image provided courtesy of the North Carolina State Archives.

Husband's remarks indicate that Sims had followed through on the flourish with which he ended his call to action: "Here I am this day with my life in my hand, to see my fellow subjects animated with a spirit of liberty and freedom, and to see them lay a foundation for the recovery thereof, and the clearing our County from arbitrary tyranny. God save the King." For all his respect for the institution of the county court, Sims acknowledged that the multiple officeholders and fee gougers whom he attacked might block his polite plan of petitioning the governor against them. His third "rule" read, "Let us behave ourselves with circumspection to the Worshipful Court inasmuch as they represent his Majesty's person[.] We ought to reverence their authority both sacred, and inviolable, *except they interpose, and then Gentlemen, the toughest will hold out longest.*" [17]

In London, the ministry responded to petitions such as the one generated by the Nutbush Address with adamant condemnations of illegal fees and similar "shamefull and illegal . . . Demands and Exactions." The government ordered Gov. William Tryon to have the official fee table posted in every county and to require "all Public Officers whatever" to abide by it on pain of removal and prosecution. The new governor was ordered to make a full accounting of fees collected under his administration. These adjustments, while welcomed, came months after Sims and other petitioners had faced the wrath of local officials. [18]

3

A Century's Legacy:
Dissenter Religious Culture as
a Carrier of Political Expectations

Farming Dissenters: Land, Religion, and Regulator Inception

The deliberative, sober, and scrupulously legal approach that George Sims advocated in Granville County in 1765 was repeated in adjacent Orange County the following year by a quasi-organization known as the Sandy Creek Association. Its meetings, printed communiqués, and electioneering generally are cited as the beginning of the Regulator Movement. The association's originators maintained high profiles for the duration of the movement, but they never controlled it. With its Baptist-Quaker composition and its identification with Herman Husband, the Sandy Creek Association is a touchstone for understanding the substance and the dynamics of the Regulation.

The Sandy Creek Association of 1766 was a political network intent on electing Herman Husband and like-minded men to the lower house of the North Carolina legislature. Its concerns were the land abuses and cronyism that plagued the backcountry in the 1750s and 1760s, issues that had provoked a number of peaceful and violent outbursts, among them the Enfield Riot and Searcy's petition in 1758–1759, and Sims's Nutbush Address and the Sugar Creek War a few years later. The name chosen for the Husband-led political network, the Sandy Creek Association, reflected his agency in establishing a Separate Baptist settlement along Sandy Creek in the late 1750s. The word "association" had acquired a distinctly religious usage in mid-seventeenth-century England, where it came to be adopted by congregations united to advance a common cause.[1]

"More than Chiefly Inhabited by Dissenters"

Beginning in the seventeenth century, Protestants in British areas who were not communicants of the Church of England (also known as Anglicans and Episcopalians) were referred to as "dissenters" or "nonconformists." While the Church of England was governed by bishops, the Church of Scotland used presbyteries and other councils for governance. Presbyterians were not regarded as nonconformists in Scotland, where theirs was the state church. But elsewhere in the British Isles and in British North America, Presbyterians were considered dissenters, along with Congregationalists, Baptists, Quakers (Society of Friends), and other non-Anglican Protestants.

Dissenters in England, Scotland, Wales, Ireland, and their offshoot communities in America drew broadly from an intellectual base established in the sixteenth century by the church reformer John Calvin, who emphasized individual faith and practice. More distinctively, he formulated a new model of church governance to replace the traditional hierarchy of bishops, whose authority had originated with the papacy. Calvin and his colleagues reversed the flow of church authority, turning it upward from the local church through a series of representative councils, known as presbyteries and synods. While not antimonarchical, Calvin's writings denied any monarchical authority over individual churches or councils. In this regard, his was one of the more radical church polities produced by the Protestant Reformation. James I of England (James VI of Scotland) was not the first European monarch to fear the implications of Calvin's new framework when he chilled the hopes of Calvinist-minded petitioners in England in 1604: Calvinism, he thundered, "agreeth with a Monarchy, as God, and the Divell." Conspicuously, the government of the locale where Calvin's principles were showcased during his lifetime — Geneva, Switzerland — was a republic. Attempts to emulate the Geneva prototype were widespread in the sixteenth and seventeenth centuries, and some were successful. Thus, the British-based dissenting traditions shared Calvinistic roots with French Huguenots, German Reformed, Dutch Reformed, and other churches on the Continent. The importance of personal

John Calvin (1509–1564), a French theologian, expounded the doctrine of predestination. British-based dissenting traditions shared Calvinistic roots and made their way to the North Carolina Piedmont. This tradition was not dependent on an organized church. Reproduced from Google Images.

devotion among the British-based dissenting groups and their emerging Methodist brethren shared common ground with European-based religious traditions, especially German, Alsatian, and Swiss counterparts. These traditions entered the North Carolina Piedmont with Reformed, Lutheran, Moravian, and Dunkard (also known as German Baptist) settlers. These continental doctrines, as those of the British-based dissenters, held that the value of worship in the home and the community was not dependent on an organized church. Likewise, the responsibility for personal, home, and community worship did not come from outside.[2]

In North Carolina, the dissenter tradition was shaped politically by the Quaker experience during the eastern beginnings of the colony. By the end of the 1660s, the Lords Proprietors were encouraging Quakers and other dissenters to help settle their vast area. For roughly the next fifty years, Quakers flourished in northeastern North Carolina, their numbers dramatically increasing both by immigration from England and the older colonies and by conversion. The Society of Friends wielded significant political influence, particularly after John Arch-dale, an English Quaker, bought out one of the Proprietors and served as governor in the 1690s. In this welcoming atmosphere, many Quakers moved to eastern North Carolina whose descendants would settle in the Piedmont, along with Friends from Pennsylvania, Virginia, and other colonies.[3]

Then around 1700, both in England and in Carolina, proponents of the Church of England responded with fear and hostility to the growing numbers and political influence of the Quakers. As a result, Quakers in the Carolina colony lost political importance. To dismiss this Anglican reaction as a reflection of the intolerance of the age would be to miss its role fifty years later during the heavy population influx into the Piedmont, as well as its impact on the dissenter-infused culture that produced the Regulator Movement. More broadly, the anti-dissenter stance of colonial officials and the Church of England was produced during the 1600s, England's "Century of Revolution," when political revolt, civil war, class antagonisms, and religious ferment wracked England and reshaped Ireland and Scotland as well. As objects of official secular and ecclesiastical disfavor, dissenters resented the institutional privileges of the Church of England. Umbrage stiffened their solidarity and sanctioned their defiance, particularly in areas where dissenters' numbers or culture pre-dominated. These included sections of England, Scotland, Wales, and Ireland by 1700, and by the time of the Regulator stirrings, the North Carolina Piedmont.[4]

Dissenters in the Great Awakening: "The Duty of a Christianized People to Excite One Another"

The dissenter presence in the mid-eighteenth-century Piedmont was evidenced by the churches that appeared in the new settlements of the 1740s and 1750s. Moreover, the religious revivalism known as the Great Awakening and associated with the English preacher George Whitefield spread from New England and the middle colonies into Virginia and North Carolina in the 1750s and 1760s. Among Presbyterians in the middle colonies, many of whom would subsequently pour into the Carolina backcountry, religious ferment in the 1730s and 1740s drew on Scottish and Scotch-Irish communal worship practices of the previous century. Because it included some free and enslaved black people as worshipers and preachers, the Great Awakening incorporated African religious insights and practices. Public worship was dramatically energized, as it became more participatory. While dynamic preachers were the stars of the phenomenon, lay people were empowered by the practices and the sheer mass of the movement. The enthusiasm sparked the organization of new churches and began to characterize the general culture.

The widespread excitement was nonsectarian—Whitefield himself was an Anglican priest—but the most striking element called themselves Separate Baptists. On the eve of and during the Regulator Movement, their center of activity was along Sandy Creek in southwestern Orange County. Offshoot settlements and churches maintained ties with the mother church and its minister, Shubal Stearns. After the Regulator defeat at the Battle of Alamance, more than fifteen

Sandy Creek was the center of activity for Separate Baptists. Many Sandy Creek Baptists joined the Regulator Movement against Governor Tryon. This image of Sandy Creek Baptist Church, founded in 1755, is provided courtesy of the North Carolina State Archives.

hundred families of Separate Baptists reportedly left the area. Their migrations in groups to South Carolina, Georgia, western Virginia, Tennessee, and Kentucky thrust hundreds of congregations of Stearns's Separate Baptist tradition westward through the southern Piedmont and mountains, reinforcing and extending the dissenter tradition carried by others, largely Presbyterians.[5]

The most outspoken statements of the political tendencies of the dissenter tradition published in America were written by Presbyterian minister Alexander Craighead. Born in County Donegal, Ireland, Craighead moved to Pennsylvania as a child and spent his life shaping the emerging political and religious culture of the Virginia and North Carolina backcountry. Taking his inspiration from seventeenth-century Scottish theologians who rejected important aspects of Crown authority, Craighead precipitated a political disturbance in Pennsylvania in the 1740s. The Philadelphia printer Benjamin Franklin published Craighead's treatises against governmental authority in ecclesiastical matters. With the ramifications of his controversial positions and disruptions clinging to him, Craighead preached widely in the North Carolina Piedmont, both as a settled pastor and as an itinerant serving new settlements, for more than a decade before the Regulator Movement erupted. In 1758, he became pastor of Rocky River and Sugar Creek Presbyterian churches in present-day Cabarrus and Mecklenburg counties. He was active there when his parishioners confronted McCulloh's agents in 1765. Moreover, in Craighead's sermons and discourse, economic injustices suffered by Piedmont settlers were active religious issues. Drawing from a revivalist tradition of western Scotland that predated the Great Awakening by more than a century, the Scotch-Irish preacher and his followers were in the full thrust of the new movement. Whitefield regarded Craighead as "a worthy minister." Craighead published this statement in 1746 and continued thereafter to preach its theme: "If ever it was the Duty of a Christianized People to excite one another to enter into a Covenant with the Lord, it is certainly now."[6]

Thus an essential part of the history of the southern backcountry, and of the North Carolina Regulator Movement in particular, began in seventeenth-century Britain. The experiences and values of the dissenter tradition linked religious culture with yeoman pride and political participation a century before the Great Awakening of the 1750s and 1760s that framed and propelled the Regulator Movement. The Great Awakening re-energized the dissenter tradition of radical Protestantism in America, as similar processes would again forty years later.[7]

Resentment of official Anglican privilege was inherent in the dissenter tradition, grounded in seventeenth-century struggles in the British Isles. In England, the conflicts peaked in the late 1640s, when a victorious parliamentary army pushed through the trial and execution of King Charles I. They declared that England would have no royalty, and they wrote and enforced a constitution for the new republic. Many common people, who had not previously viewed themselves as political participants, were involved in the removal of the monarchy. Much of the new political activism had been fostered within local churches, many of which developed a religious culture quite different from that of the traditional Church of England out of which they had grown. Like the Anglican Church, the activist churches were both Protestant and anti-Catholic. Beyond this common ground and general doctrinal similarities, however, the activist congregations emphasized the individual, not just in private worship as did the Church of England, but especially in public worship; accordingly, public worship became more direct and simple and much less conceptual. Public worship and communal life in the new congregations were open to lay leadership, which connected the new religious atmosphere with political issues of the day and with the parliamentarians. As a result, when people from outside the traditional ruling classes participated in the events that eliminated the monarchy, they were also challenging the leadership of the groups who had helped the kings govern: large landowners, wealthy merchants, bishops, and the familial and commercial networks they maintained.

Widespread leadership experiences during the 1640s and 1650s, particularly in the parliamentary army and local religious groups, left a freed genie that could not be returned to its bottle. Kingship was brought back in 1660 in the person of Charles II, who soon chartered the Carolina colony and parceled it out to the Lords Proprietors. During the 1660s, the old political leadership regained its dominance, albeit with some modifications after 1688.

The movement that restored the monarchy in the 1660s also brought back the official Church of England. The religious groups that had grown out of and away from it were the religious heirs of the 1640s and 1650s activist congregations. The largest to survive the 1660s were the Quakers, Baptists, Congregationalists, and Presbyterians. For several years after 1660, worship among these dissenters was illegal outside an immediate family setting, and political and professional restrictions on dissenters continued for a century and a quarter after their churches attained legal sanction in 1689. The restored political leadership feared dissenters because of the connections linking dissenting religious culture with the common people and with republican political views. Monarchists suspected that at heart the dissenters wished to return conditions to the heady days of the 1650s when there had been no king and the only official churches had been the local congregations. From time to time after 1660, the government claimed to discover conspiracies directed toward this goal, and indeed the dissenting culture continued to speak and sing of the mid-seventeenth-century republican venture as "The Good Old Way."[8]

The lifetime of John Bunyan (1628–1688), an English Congregationalist and Baptist deacon and preacher, spanned the English revolutionary and counter-revolutionary years. Written while Bunyan was imprisoned for preaching outside the home, his book, *The Pilgrim's Progress*, was widely popular throughout English-speaking areas in the eighteenth century and conspicuous in the North Carolina Piedmont. When Robert Johnston and Richard Bennehan began selling books at Little River in Orange County in 1769, three of the thirteen titles were Bunyan's works. After hornbooks, spelling books, and Scripture, Johnston and Bennehan's best seller during 1769–1777 was *The Pilgrim's Progress*.[9]

The Covenanting Tradition and the Scotch-Irish

Impatience with restrictions on non-Anglican Protestants was at least as strong in areas of Scotland as it was in England in the late seventeenth century. There Presbyterian religious and ethnic identity enshrined two recent public covenants, the National Covenant of 1638 and the Solemn League and Covenant of 1643. The concept of covenant was grounded in the belief that an individual Christian had an all-encompassing compact with the deity. A covenant required mutual consultation and consent, and it was expected that agreements concerning religious practice and belief would be the subject of a covenant. Beginning in the 1560s, Protestant reformers in Scotland had adopted Calvin's "Presbyterian" model of church administration by representative presbyteries and synods. During the 1630s, the joint monarchy of Scotland and England attempted to return the Scottish church to the older Episcopalian model of administration by bishops that was still being used by the Church of England. The National Covenant was in response to this and other governmental alterations of religious practice. Five years later, the Solemn League and Covenant embodied a crucial political alliance. Scottish forces and English parliamentarians separately were fighting the army of King Charles I. In the Solemn League and Covenant, Parliament agreed to remove administration by bishops and replace it throughout the British Isles with Scotland's Presbyterian structure, in exchange for Scottish military assistance.

For a time after the monarchy was restored in 1660, Episcopacy was reinstalled in Scotland as well as England, thereby deepening the sense of grievance that bonded Scottish nationalism with Presbyterian identity. Scottish counterparts to the English dissenters during 1660–1688 were known as Covenanters, for their illegal adherence to the precepts embodied in the 1638 and 1643 covenants and the related Westminster Confession of Faith.[10] Following the Revolution of 1688–1689, the Presbyterian Church was restored as the national church of Scotland, but it lacked the democratic tendencies and clerical independence from the government that was associated with the covenants of fifty years earlier.

In the decades after 1689, various issues of discontent continued within Scotland—political, religious, local, and class-driven. They fueled a series of divisions, known as secessions, within the national church. Scotland's secessions were caustic, and they carried over into the north of Ireland with continued migration there. One effect of the divisions was to idealize seventeenth-century Scottish Covenanters, for each new movement identified with them. Moreover, all Presbyterians in Ireland were dissenters, for the Church of Ireland was Anglican, a circumstance that enhanced the Covenanters' veneration. Thus Covenanters had come to be remembered as folk heroes and heroines by Scotch-Irish people by the time their mass migrations extended to the southern Piedmont of North Carolina. With competing Presbyterian streams in Scotland, Ireland, and North America claiming Covenanters as godly and courageous forebears, their iconic attributes of personal responsibility and steadfastness in the face of persecution and Anglican privilege were remembered long after the secession issues and individual personalities lost their relevance in a new land.[11]

Moreover, Covenanter relevance was retained in America, notably in the Regulator area by Craighead. Taken in isolation, his insistence

Covenanters were the Scottish and Scotch-Irish parallels to English dissenters. Among North Carolina Scotch-Irish, Covenanters were icons of steadfastness in the face of persecution and the Anglican establishment. This scene depicts Covenanters worshiping in the Scottish Lowlands. Image from James Aitken Wylie, *The History of Protestantism with Five Hundred and Fifty Illustrations by the Best Artist* (London: Cassell, 1899), 595. Accessed through WorldCat at the HathiTrust Digital Library.

that all Presbyterians take the Solemn League and Covenant—the issue at the center of his controversy in Pennsylvania in the 1740s—might suggest that he was stuck on an issue that was both anachronistic and irrelevant in the colonies. In Craighead's vision, however, the Covenanting tradition was essential to a continuing reformation of individuals, congregations, and society. Further, when he preached that the covenants of 1638 and 1643 were necessary instruments of reformation for Christianity wherever believers lived, he was not an anomaly, either in his native Ireland or in Pennsylvania, Virginia, and North Carolina, where he accompanied other Scotch-Irish people. At the heart of his message, the popular preacher taught that the two Scottish covenants sprang from the vital compact by which a believer received divine grace. "Although we do not suppose them to be the same with the Covenant of Grace," he wrote, "yet we look upon them as another Obligation, binding us to all the duties of a Christian Life, as well as to the Duties which tend to *a publick Reformation of the Nation, of which the Covenant of Grace is the Spring and Foundation.*" By "publick

Reformation of the Nation," Craighead meant the removal of governmental restrictions on Presbyterian religious activities and, in particular, the dismantling of Anglican privilege.[12]

Anglican Privilege and Backcountry Grievances

Thus repercussions of political tension over religious issues were played out in the 1700s throughout the British Isles and in North America. In England, Ireland, and Wales, the primacy of the Anglican Church was a guarantor of the political establishment throughout the eighteenth century. As such, it was a touchstone of patriotism for people who were entitled to political participation and was resented by many who were not. Heavy baggage for any church to bear, these realities of eighteenth-century political life crossed the Atlantic with every person who emigrated to America from the British Isles.

By the time North Carolina's new Piedmont counties were organized, fresh efforts to ensure Anglican privilege throughout the colony contributed to backcountry grievances. A single outstanding example was attacked in one of Husband's publications, which he titled "A Sermon." It was a modification of a pamphlet, "Sermon to Asses," published in London in 1768. Husband was not the only American to reprint the pamphlet; it also appeared in Philadelphia and Boston in 1769–1770. The author was James Murray, a Scottish clergyman. Murray attacked the discriminations against dissenters and excise taxes as a burden on the poor. He also argued that an established church was inconsistent with a scriptural basis for a church. In plagiarizing and adapting Murray's "Sermon to Asses," Husband easily drew on issues in the North Carolina Piedmont, especially objection to a new vestry act authorizing taxation to provide salaries for Anglican ministers.[13]

Although the Anglican Church was the official church of the colony of North Carolina, it was largely a coastal church, with little presence in the interior except for the occasional itinerant ministers sent by the Society for the Propagation of the Gospel, the Church of England outreach for the colonies. Six vestry acts were passed by the colonial assembly, but five were struck down by the Privy Council before one was approved in 1765. These measures sought to organize parishes for the established church throughout the colony, with local boards, or vestries, to handle parish business, mainly poor relief. The Privy

Council rejected the otherwise unexceptional pre-1765 measures because they authorized the vestries to select the rector, a departure from church practice. The vestry laws were not a threat to freedom of worship, but they were a reminder that dissenting clergy were not authorized to conduct marriages without specific permission from the legislature, and they presented one more way in which the Tidewater-controlled legislature could levy taxes. Each vestry act was met by protest.

Significantly, while settlers were rushing into the Granville District from Pennsylvania, about eight hundred men in Anson, Orange, and Rowan counties signed petitions to George II and Earl Granville complaining that the legislature had passed a new vestry act in 1754. The petitioners described themselves as "loyal subjects . . . on the back frontiers of the Province of North Carolina in America." They explained that they were mainly Scotch-Irish Presbyterians, recently moved from Pennsylvania: "mostly originally from the North of Ireland, Trained & brought up under Presbyterian Church government and we & our forefathers have mostly resided sometime in the Northern provinces of Pennsylvania Jersey & New York &c." The petitioners implied that they had moved because they feared attacks during the French and Indian War. In the "Northern provinces" they said, "we were exempted from paying to or supporting any clergy save our own & came here in hopes of enjoying like freedom. But [we] find now our counties are constituted and laid out into so many parishes and . . . a late act of our assembly enjoyned all our vestrymen to swear to conform to the liturgy &c of the Church of England."

Further, the petitioners explained, "three counties are more than chiefly inhabited by dissenters where is ten large congregations seated in bodies, as birds of a feather are said to flock together, who amongst other grievances have not attained the Ordinances of the Gospel, our ministers being discouraged to settle here." They asked for exemption from any tax supporting Anglican ministers.[14] A comment made by Granville's surveyor in September 1758 may have referred to this petition or some activity connected with it. William Churton declared that "the 'mob,' about 700 strong, had formulated its demands into certain Articles. One Article demanded that the vestries should be abolished and that each denomination should pay its own ministers."[15] The petitioners cited "freedom" from taxes to support Anglican ministers in their former homes in the middle colonies. Pennsylvania in particular had been founded by and for English dissenters during their 1660–1689 troubles. During that period, the English government had occasionally encouraged dissenters to settle other areas of the middle colonies with little or no effort to establish the Anglican Church there.

Opposition to Anglican privilege was an issue for backcountry men and women of a British background, Scotch-Irish in particular. So was the broader issue of political and social humiliation of dissenters. There are indications that Germans in the southern backcountry guarded against being categorized as dissenters, knowing the disabilities the label could bring. The Crown and colonial legislatures had encouraged settlers to move directly from Germany to the frontier, and for this, an assurance of unencumbered religious practice was an important inducement. So was the funding by which the Society for the Propagation of the Gospel occasionally provided a German clergyman for a congregation of his countrymen in the southern backcountry. In Wachovia, the Moravians had a special, though tenuous, arrangement with the colonial legislature, which allowed the Brethren to administer their own parish. Officially, the Moravian lands were encompassed by Dobbs Parish and were under the ecclesiastical oversight of the Bishop of London; the Moravian leadership closely monitored this thin Anglican façade. Such an arrangement was a possibility for other non-British churches that had the status of a "state" church in any government enjoying amicable relations with Britain. Both Lutheran and Reformed churches in various German principalities met this unspoken but obvious qualification.[16]

4

Herman Husband, Crystallizer

"Harmon, that Hum Drum Old Fox"

As a term of church organization, "association" originated among Congregationalists and Baptists in England in the seventeenth century. It referred to scheduled meetings of representatives of autonomous member churches. Sandy Creek of the Regulator-era "Sandy Creek Association" is a tributary of Deep River in present-day Randolph County. Several families of New England Separate Baptists under the leadership of Shubal Stearns and Daniel Marshall moved to the Sandy Creek watershed in 1755. Herman Husband was the land agent for these Separate Baptists, who settled near him along Sandy Creek. Stearns and his followers had been shaped by the "New Light Stir" associated with George Whitefield's preaching in New England, and their infusion into the backcountry was basic to the Great Awakening in North Carolina and adjacent colonies in the late 1750s and 1760s. Nearly a decade prior to the 1766 Sandy Creek Association that sparked the Regulator Movement, Stearns in 1758 led the formation of a Sandy Creek Association as the centralizing polity for about one thousand Separate Baptists whom he and his colleagues served in churches in Anson, Granville, Orange, and Rowan counties. By 1760 the association included six North Carolina churches and one each in Pittsylvania and Lunenburg counties, Virginia. Thus, the name "Sandy Creek Association" had wide resonance throughout the backcountry when Husband and others began using it as a political label in 1766.[1]

Although Herman Husband was not present at the Battle of Alamance, it would be difficult today to conceive of a Regulator Movement without him. In part this is because he left more writings than other shapers of the movement, and his words inform any account of the Regulators and Alamance. Also, the words and concepts with which he articulated broadly held grievances were intimately familiar to the dissenter farmers for whom he spoke. Husband energized the 1766 Sandy Creek Association and the ensuing Regulator Movement with his idiosyncratic religious outlook and shaped both with his personal goals. At the height of the movement, a pro-Regulator song depicted a dialogue between Fanning and a crony, who expressed their astonishment at Regulator resiliency. It opened with these lines about Husband:

Who would have tho't Harmon, that hum drum old fox,
Who looks so bemeaning with his towsled locks,
Would have had resolution to stand to the tack;
Alas my dear Ned, our case is quite black.[2]

Husband was born in 1724 in Cecil County, Maryland. His parents reared their large family as Anglican, but when he was sixteen, Husband joined a New Side Presbyterian church after hearing Whitefield preach. Although an Anglican, Whitefield drew upon dissenter emphasis on the individual's spiritual birth through prayer and contemplation. Whitefield traveled widely in the colonies. He and many of his followers worshiped with and preached alongside enslaved and free black Christians, who, as mentioned earlier, contributed some African religious elements, in particular the intense spiritual breakthrough and its joyous celebration. Known as "pulling-through," the experience reinforced the value that the dissenter tradition placed on personal spirituality. The labels "New Side" and "New Light" for the Presbyterian congregation Husband joined in 1740 indicated its emphasis on this individual spiritual experience.[3]

Husband was a lifelong reader and writer, and he owned approximately eight hundred pamphlets and books when he died in 1795. About 1750, he wrote a memoir of his religious quest. Its long title was typical of seventeenth- and eighteenth-century books and pamphlets for which a descriptive title was a marketing tool: *Some Remarks on Religion, with the Author's Experience in Pursuit thereof, for the Consideration of all PEOPLE, Being the real TRUTH of what happened, Simply delivered, without the Help of School-Words, or Dress of Learning.* The memoir covered about fifteen years, beginning at age twelve. It is more analytical than the common run of the period's first-person religious accounts. While Husband included the usual dream and youthful angst, he gave most attention to the reading, conversations, and questioning by which he became a member of the Society of Friends. He depicted his New Side Presbyterian elders as patient, his relationship with them as cordial, and their differences as intellectual. He feared that they were "turning back to Old Presbyterianism, and a State of dead Forms." The memoir indicates that Husband went to the Quakers because he considered their worship and structure more open to leadership from "the Power of God."[4] He served on committees by which Friends counseled, or "laboured with," each other to maintain spiritual and behavioral discipline, and he was overseer of an informal local group, or "preparative meeting," in the late 1740s. Husband's

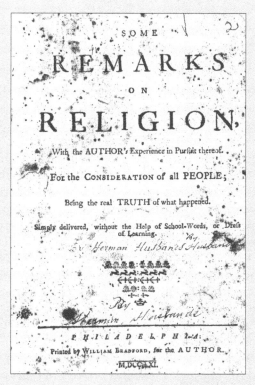

Title page of Herman Husband's memoir of his religious quest. Image provided courtesy of The Library Company of Philadelphia, Pa.

later writings would incorporate democratic and millenarian themes pursued by radical seventeenth-century English dissenting writers. He would draw on the Old Testament book of Ezekiel for a vision of a New Jerusalem in the backcountry, where landowning farmers and artisans might live in pristine democracy, employing a steady stream of free workers who would move there in pursuit of their own land. After the Regulator Movement ended, Husband would identify his vision with the land west of the Allegheny Mountains.

Although he did not mention her in his account, Husband's first wife died, leaving three children, about the time he wrote *Some Remarks on Religion.* He had received land in Cecil and Baltimore counties from his parents, who were prosperous planters, but by his late twenties, his career course was still undetermined. Trips to Barbados and to Bladen County, North Carolina, in 1750 and 1751 seem to have been trading ventures; at least his trading financed a preview of his prospects there.

Husband as Land Speculator
for the Dissenter Market

Husband turned to the North Carolina Piedmont in 1754, just as its great influx of settlers was getting under way, with the new counties of Anson, Orange, and Rowan established and the Granville line surveyed as far as present-day Cabarrus County. He traveled as an advance man for a land company consisting of himself and ten other substantial farmers and tradesmen in Maryland and Pennsylvania. They intended to establish a largely Quaker settlement in the North Carolina or Virginia backcountry. The excitement in the North Carolina Piedmont stimulated Husband. Quickly he saw his potential there as a land speculator, envisioning farms, mills, and related manufactories tended by industrious Christians—his New Jerusalem, as well as a new Pennsylvania. As quickly, Husband grasped the difficulties and injustices that small buyers faced in the new counties, particularly with employees of the Granville proprietary. He evaluated the situation and thought that he could fix what was wrong and make a good living while doing so.

Finding it essential that he go to Edenton to obtain Granville land for himself and his backers, Husband offered his services as an agent for settlers in the new counties whose efforts to obtain land from Granville officials had been frustrated. Armed with their stories of being cheated by surveyors and other employees, he found that Granville's chief agent, Francis Corbin, treated him with respect. After returning to Orange County, Husband in the autumn of 1755 wrote to Earl Granville, explaining the mistakes and dishonesty in the land office and suggesting how they could be addressed. He said that he enclosed a map he had made of rivers and mountains in the Granville tract. Neither the extent of Husband's ambition in writing Granville nor whether Granville replied is known. The value of the letter, as historian Roger Ekirch observed, is that it is "an idealization of aspirations shared throughout the backcountry."[5]

Husband envisioned a Carolina where land was easy to obtain; where labor and production would be untrammeled; where there was no privileged, or "Established," church; where the Indians still inhabiting it would remain on their land; where there would be no slavery; and, over it all, "a New Government of Liberty." The purpose of Husband's message to Granville was to explain what obstacles faced the settlers whose vision he summarized, which he characterized as "stuns" to settler expectations. These obstacles were graver than administrative abuses. The main "stun," he said, was slavery. Husband's parents possessed slaves, and he may have owned one in 1771. His attack on slaveholding was economic: "The first stun that I got was on a discovery of some of our northern men who had got a little money was corrupted already from that true Christian and Brittish disposition of encouraging our own poor, but are falling into that practice of buying Negro slaves." Better to spend money to hire free laborers, who then could buy their own land and provide the same opportunity for other poor people; Husband said this observation prevailed among the generality of newcomers.

Husband's second "stun" was the news that Gov. Arthur Dobbs had obtained from the assembly fresh authorization for taxes to support clergy and schools of the Church of England. This was the Vestry Act of 1754, against which eight hundred Piedmont settlers complained to Granville. Husband petitioned Dobbs and the legislature and sent Granville a copy, as the matter was not Granville's responsibility. "I have . . . travel[ed] some weeks past through the counties of Orange and Rowan looking for places for my self and friends to settle," Husband explained, having left Maryland to get "from under that yoke of bondage that our ancestors have brought us under, (to wit) the authority there given to the clergy." He acknowledged the Church of England to be the "most sound of any Christian sociaty in its foundation and pricipalls" but observed that involuntary financing of its clergy attracted "wiked designing men purely for the sake of such a maintenance," even dissenting clergy who were "turned out of their bread" for "misdemeanors among their own society . . . such a one if I mistake not is at present gapeing for a place on the Yadkin." He maintained that Anglicans as well as dissenters resented paying taxes to support the clergy.

Husband said that Corbin allowed him to examine land records on behalf of nearly one thousand men in Rowan and Orange counties who had told Husband that they had paid fees to deputy surveyor James Carter to file their entries for land they had settled and were farming. Husband said that Carter had followed through only for his "favourites," fewer than 10 percent of the fee payers. Husband judged Granville's system of granting land to be sound and fair. He observed that the extensive corruption among Granville's employees was keeping buyers off the market, even while newcomers thronged the area. Sensing speculative potential, Husband was convinced that once the corruption was curbed, the land market in the Granville District

North=Carolina,

Hermon Husband

ENTERS in the Office of the Right Honorable
JOHN EARL GRANVILLE,

Seven Hundred

Registered in

Lib.

Fol.

Acres of VACANT Land, lying in *Orange County on a branch of Sandy Creek the waters of Deep River adjoining his own Line including Ebenes Starns William Walker & John Fields improvem*

AND defires a Warrant to have the fame furveyed;
WHICH is granted, UPON CONDITION that fuch
Survey be returned into the faid Office, within Six
Months from the Date hereof, AND that the faid
Hermon Husband ————— do within Twelve
Months next enfuing the Day of making fuch Return,
take out a Grant of the faid Land; OTHERWISE
this Entry, and fuch Survey fo to be made thereon,
fhall be VOID and of no Effect. DATED the
Eleventh Day of *January 1761*

Witnefs

Jas Watson

Hermon Husband

Herman Husband obtained Granville grants for himself along Sandy Creek
and Deep River in Orange County. From Office of Secretary of State, Land
Office (Colonial), Granville Proprietary Land Office, Land Entries, Warrants,
and Plats of Survey, 1748–1763. Image provided courtesy of the North Carolina
State Archives.

would soar. His ten co-investors had instructed him to buy approximately one thousand acres for each of them. In addition, Husband determined to speculate on his own behalf: "The [Granville agents'] abuses had no other weight with me then as they turned to my advantage, as [while they existed] I could make a cheaper purchase of land. . . . I cleerly saw those abuses, how great and gauling soever to the inhabitants, was easily to be removed and on their removeall land [prices] would likely rise."[6]

Right away, Husband began the process of obtaining Granville grants for himself and his backers, and he also purchased land entries and surveys from people who had encountered bad luck with the granting process. Husband bought up entries from at least twenty men whose claims, largely along Abbotts and Richland creeks, turned out to be in McCulloh tracts. Most of these entries were for 640 acres each. In addition, he bought paperwork for Rowan and Orange land that had been claimed as a prior purchase by Granville's agent William Churton. In the Granville land office, Husband exchanged most of these surveys and entries for ungranted tracts concentrated along Sandy Creek and Deep River. He profited by facilitating settlers' exchange of insecure claims elsewhere for secure titles in the area where he would establish himself. Between December 1755 and March 1759, Husband *registered* deeds for seven thousand acres in Orange County, most of it as Granville grants in present-day Randolph and southern Guilford counties. He would register a similar amount in the area during 1764–1765. In addition, he bought from Granville and Granville's grantees about two thousand acres along the western tributaries of the Haw River, centered in present-day northern Guilford County, and 640 acres on Alamance Creek in today's western Alamance and eastern Guilford counties.[7]

Husband, Stearns, and the Origins of the Sandy Creek Settlement

Husband began buying land and claims at least six months before he wrote to Granville in the autumn of 1755. That spring, he returned to Pennsylvania and was shocked to learn that all ten of his partners had backed out of their plans because of North Carolina's new vestry act. "But poor I," he confided to Granville, "haveing purchased before the passing of this law, am not willing to quit my schemes that I there projected."[8] The extent of Husband's investment toward land purchases in the Granville tract at that point is not known, but that he was a speculator with land on his hands is indicated by transactions recorded in the Granville land office. The Quaker settlement he had intended for the "New Government of Liberty" had fallen through, but there were other dissenting congregations that could populate the society he envisioned, after buying land from him. As it happened, the 1754 Vestry Act would not be enforced, but Husband could not have foreseen that; in the meantime, its threat of future taxes to provide an annual income of £80 for every Anglican minister who might accept one of the new Piedmont parishes gave Husband another pressing reason to sell land to his fellow dissenters as soon as he could unload it.

Husband passed through the Shenandoah Valley at least twice in 1755 on journeys between Pennsylvania and his temporary location on Nutbush Creek in Granville County. Thirty miles from the north-south road through the lower valley, in present-day Hampshire County, West Virginia, lived a body of Separate Baptists. Most of them had moved recently from New England, with no fixed destination other than a southern colony, and they were dissatisfied with their location and the land. Their leader, Shubal Stearns, while in Connecticut had professed a call "far to the westward, to execute a great and extensive work." Stearns's careful biographer conjectures that Husband sought out the group as potential settlers, having heard of them from any of three larger Baptist congregations along his route. Indeed, Stearns wrote in June 1755 that some of their party had gone to North Carolina already. Stearns and the others visited Husband's place on Nutbush Creek that summer and from there settled in the Sandy Creek area with Husband. An indication of the relationship between Husband and Stearns was recorded in a 1756 land survey for which Stearns was a sworn chain carrier, his only appearance in the land records. Husband witnessed the grantee's signature to record the survey and grant. The survey was for Seymour York, who gave the land on which Sandy Creek Baptist Church was built. In effect, Husband witnessed the deed to the church.[9] Husband was a major source for farms in the heartland from which the Separate Baptist energy pulsed through the Piedmont during the decade and a half before the Battle of Alamance.

A visitor to the Sandy Creek area in 1772 was told that the original church had begun with sixteen adult members and had increased to more than nine hundred in three congregations by the autumn of 1758.[10] The earliest offshoot was at Abbotts Creek, where Husband

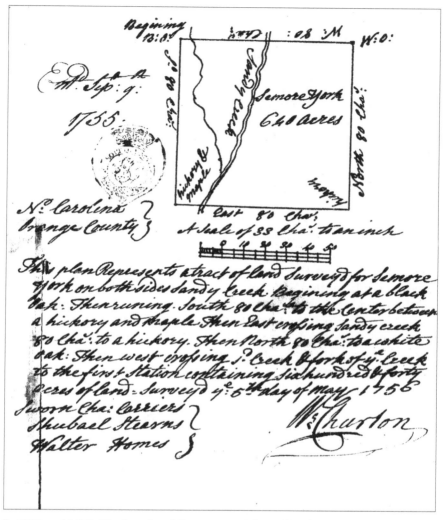

In 1756 and 1758, Husband and Stearns participated in the granting process for Seymour (Semore) York, who gave a portion of his land to build Sandy Creek Baptist Church. Stearns was buried there six months after the Battle of Alamance. Grant to Semore York, plat, September 9, 1755, Office of Secretary of State, Land Office (Colonial), Granville Proprietary Land Office, Grants of Deed, 1748–1763. Image provided courtesy of the North Carolina State Archives.

was obtaining unfulfilled entries and exchanging them for like acreages of Granville grants in the Sandy Creek area. During 1759–1769, deeds for Husband's sales to twenty-three individuals were recorded for land between or along Sandy Creek and Deep River totaling more than nine thousand acres. Except for one sale of 3,688 acres to a cousin, nearly all of Husband's sales were between 150 and 660 acres.[11] However, Husband's career as land speculator was soon curtailed. The Granville land office closed in 1763 because of Granville's death and uncertainties regarding his heir. After that, neither Husband nor anyone else could complete the land-granting process in the district. Husband's investment in land stood threatened from 1763 onward, in common with other settlers in the Granville District, but on a grander scale than most.

The 1772 visitor to Sandy Creek remarked that since the Regulator defeat in May 1771, some fifteen hundred Separate Baptist *families* had moved from the area, far more than left land records. Husband's transactions in the Granville office between 1754 and 1760, his sales of farm-sized parcels of land in the Sandy Creek-Deep River area, and the remaining unsold land for which he held entries and warrants all suggest that he had expected to continue to sell land in this way in the 1760s. People settled on land in the Sandy Creek area for which Husband had started the paperwork could have no expectation of land security following the Regulator defeat. On the contrary, their association with Husband would be a liability that adds credence to the 1772 estimate of an exodus exceeding fifteen hundred families after the Battle of Alamance.

The Charity Wright and Jehu Stuart Matter at Cane Creek

For the Sandy Creek settlement and the 1758 (Separate Baptist) Sandy Creek Association, Herman Husband was a business associate, land agent, and influential neighbor. He was not yet a political figure, although he was active in land matters in the county court. He emerged as a strident politician with the formation of the Sandy Creek Association of 1766, but on the eve of that development, Husband demonstrated his leadership within Cane Creek Monthly Meeting of Friends, which he had joined in December 1755. His behavior among Cane Creek Quakers is revealing. Its story is modestly labyrinthine, and the church records revealing it are coy, as records of conflict can be.

In December 1760, the minutes of the preparative session for the men's monthly meeting at Cane Creek recorded that a complaint was made "of Jehu Stuart for spreading scandalous reports on several young women." The men appointed two Friends to "labour with him and report to the next meeting," but in February 1761 it was noted that their counsels were ongoing. In April, the committee presented its "testimony against Jehu Stuart" to the men's monthly meeting, and they "approved and signed" it, language that usually denoted disownment of a member. Disowned members could attend meetings for worship but could not participate in discussions of business or mutual discipline, and their membership could not be certified if they sought to join a Friends meeting elsewhere. On the day of Jehu Stuart's disownment, April 4, the women's monthly meeting disowned Charity Wright "for having carnal knowledge of Jehu Stuart." The initial accusation against Charity Wright was not recorded, but it is clear that there had been a charge prior to April, and that the women's meeting had believed it. The women's cryptic minutes indicated only that committees had "extended . . . repeated labour" toward Charity Wright without getting the desired acknowledgment and repentance.[12]

The women's monthly meeting took unusual precautions in this case. Charity Wright's mother, Rachel Wright, along with fellow minister Abigail Pike, had taken the initiative for establishing a monthly meeting at Cane Creek and routinely traveled on business for the Society of Friends. Whether because of the leadership role of Rachel Wright, Stuart's notoriety regarding "several young women," or for some other reason, the women sent their action of disownment to the men's monthly meeting for approval. They had not sought approval for any of their previous sixteen disownments. The men's monthly meeting concurred.

It seems clear that Charity Wright denied any fault in the matter of Jehu Stuart and claimed that he had raped her: the men's monthly meeting for May 1761 recorded that "the friend appointed to publish the testimony . . . against Charity Wright report[s] he has not complied with the appointment by reasons she [Charity Wright] intends to appeal our judgment." The appeal was to the Western Quarterly Meeting in August, which blamed the fifteen-year-old girl for keeping "unseasonable" company with Stuart. The Quarterly Meeting acknowledged that she had been "Overcome and defiled by him" but blamed her for not resisting "to the Utmost of Her power his wicked and lustfull design." The Quarterly Meeting required a sincere apology, the routine path to reinstatement. Charity Wright refused, and so the girl who later would be a Friends minister remained disowned.[13] Subsequent developments in the Cane Creek Friends Meeting reveal that Rachel Wright continued to back her daughter's claim of innocence following the disownment, and that what became known as "Rachel

Wright's affair" opened a fissure in the Meeting that fed directly into the Regulator Movement.

In the years after 1761, a number of men in the Cane Creek Monthly Meeting would become Regulators, some of them leaders in the movement, and they would be disowned for taking up arms in violation of the Friends' avowed pacifism. After the demise of the Regulator Movement, several disowned Friends apologized for "getting out of the right line of truth and good order." They readily were readmitted. At least one of the former Regulator leaders from Cane Creek acknowledged a connection between the Rachel Wright controversy and Regulator activity. In April 1776, the Monthly Meeting recorded that "John Marshill [presented a statement] to this meeting condemning his getting out of the right line of truth and good order in Rachel Wright's affair, *which appears was the cause of his further disorders*, which this meeting receives as Satisfaction for the same."[14]

Husband and the Rachel Wright Controversy

Marshall did not analyze the links between the Rachel Wright controversy and Regulator activity at Cane Creek, but the chief connection was Herman Husband's leadership of the anti-Wright forces. The sparse records show him and other soon-to-be-Regulators to have been aligned against Rachel Wright for her defense of her daughter's innocence. The nature of her criticism of the monthly and quarterly meetings was not recorded but can readily be supposed. Charity Wright's biographer surmised that Rachel Wright's public objection to her daughter's disownment was strong enough to cause the women's monthly meeting "to feel the need of the support of the men's monthly meeting."[15]

Between early May and early December 1761, the Wright family moved outside the area served by the Cane Creek Monthly Meeting. Already a modest land speculator in Granville, Johnston, and Orange counties, Rachel's husband John Wright petitioned for and entered land on tributaries of the Wateree River, leaving records in both Anson County and South Carolina, as the boundary between the two Carolinas had not then been surveyed. In February 1762, the Cane Creek Monthly Meeting granted a certificate (or letter of transfer) to the Wateree Monthly Meeting on behalf of the Wrights' oldest son.[16]

THOMAS CHILD, *and* FRANCIS CORBIN, *Efqrs. Agents and Commiffion-ers of the Right Honourable the Earl* Granville, *&c.*

To *James Carter & Charles Robinson or either of them*

YOU are forthwith to admeafure and lay out, unto — — *John Wright* — — a Plantation, containing *Three hundred* Acres of Land, lying in *Anson* County, *on the place where he now lives including his Improvements* — — —

Obferving our Inftructions for running out Lands; Three Plats and Certificates whereof your are to return to us, within Six Months from the Date hereof: Or this Warrant to be void. Dated and Signed the *Eighteenth* Day of *July* 1755

Grant to John Wright, Anson County (1755), Office of Secretary of State, Land Office (Colonial), Granville Proprietary Land Office, Land Entries, Warrants, and Plats of Survey, 1748–1763. Image provided courtesy of the North Carolina State Archives.

Rachel Wright may have requested a certificate when her son did, but no record of such a request exists prior to November 1762, when she appealed to the Western Quarterly Meeting because Cane Creek had refused her application. The Quarterly Meeting noted that "Rachel Wright a member of Cane Creek Monthly Meeting being removed with her family out of the verge of that meeting [and having] requested a certificate to join in membership with another meeting, hath sent a complaint to this meeting against said monthly meeting of Cane Creek for unjustly detaining her certificate." A committee from the Quarterly Meeting investigated the complaint by visiting Cane Creek and learned from interviews what the minutes had not recorded about "Rachel Wright's affair." The committee reported in February 1763 that she "had been guilty of some disorders and had offered a paper to condemn the same which [Cane Creek Monthly Meeting] accepted for satisfaction only *some apprehended* there was a lack of sincerety in her which the committee reports *was the cause of her certificate being retained.*"[17]

One supposes that the "disorders" for which Rachel Wright had apologized consisted of supporting her daughter's claim of rape in the face of Cane Creek's disownment of her "for having carnal knowledge of Jehu Stuart." Essentially, the committee reported to the Western Quarterly Meeting that Cane Creek had denied a certificate to Rachel Wright because a persistent minority there was rankled by the acceptance of her apology some time earlier. Thus, the Quarterly Meeting in May 1763 judged that Rachel Wright's certificate had been denied because of "a division and separation" in the Cane Creek Monthly Meeting, not her behavior, and gave her a certificate. Cane Creek did not acknowledge the action until March 1767, for its "division and separation" ballooned with Herman Husband's encouragement of the anti-Wright minority during 1762.[18]

Husband spent most if not all of 1760 and 1761 in Maryland managing two copper mines and a smelter of which he was part owner, but he returned to his Sandy Creek home by the spring of 1762 and married Cane Creek member Mary Pugh in June. Presumably, he brought with him copies of *Some Remarks on Religion*, which he had published in Philadelphia in 1761. Readers and listeners influenced by the Great Awakening could then perceive Husband not simply as a land trader, miller, and man of affairs, but also as a spiritual pilgrim like themselves who related his own experience in direct, common language. Meeting minutes do not indicate whether Husband was present either when Rachel Wright "offered a paper to condemn" her "disorder" or later when the meeting received her request for a certificate. What is clear is that Husband was in the area prior to April 1762, after Rachel Wright's son had received a certificate. Husband publicly objected to Cane Creek's acceptance of her apology, even after the meeting had accepted it; and he defended the denial of a certificate following the acceptance of her apology on the grounds that the apology had been insincere.[19] A likely scenario is that he returned following the acceptance of her apology, complained against it after the fact, and then blocked the consensus that Quakers required for granting a certificate.

Husband as Shaper of the Cane Creek Disruption

Whatever the timetable of Husband's involvement in the Rachel Wright controversy, the original polarizing issue—Charity Wright's defiance—was not created by Husband. He stepped in and managed one side of the controversy successfully enough for the Western Quarterly Meeting to consider Cane Creek's condition "a division and separation" by May 1763. The disruption ensnared some of the Eno River and Deep River meetings as well, in support of Husband. Six months after the quarterly meeting acted in Wright's favor, the Cane Creek Monthly Meeting completed a course of action against Husband: "Hermon Husband being complained of for being guilty of Making remarks on the actions and transactions of this meeting [here] as well as Elsewhere as [is] his mind, and publickly advertising the Same, and after due labour with him in order to shew him the Evil of so doing, this meeting agrees to disown him, as also to publish the Testimony."[20]

If Husband had sought a platform, he had one now. He appealed to the Western Quarterly Meeting and the North Carolina Yearly Meeting with rhetorical prowess, accompanied by the signers of a "dissenting minute" from Cane Creek opposing his ouster. Cane Creek Monthly Meeting had disowned the signers as well. When the North Carolina Yearly Meeting ruled on Husband's appeal, they distinguished among claimants for reinstatement. First, they decided that the Western Quarterly Meeting "did not act Safe in . . . granting Rachel Wright a certificate," thereby reversing Wright's victory. Secondly, the yearly meeting conceded that the "dissenting minut Shewing a dislike to

Hermon Husband being disowned" was worthy of disownment in itself, but it asked Cane Creek to reinstate the signers for the sake of peace, that "we may Each of us labour for a meek and forgiving spirit so that what has happened may be done away." But the yearly meeting considered Husband a corrosive troublemaker, so he remained disowned. His parting salvo, however, moved them to rephrase his offensive actions as "Contrary to Right Seeing," rather than their original "Contrary to Truth."[21]

Thus, between 1760 and 1764, five successive issues unfolded at Cane Creek:

1. Charity Wright's sexual responsibility.
2. Rachel Wright's oral objections to the way the monthly meeting handled her daughter's case.
3. Herman Husband's objections to Cane Creek Monthly Meeting's acceptance of Rachel Wright's apology for her statements.
4. Husband's oral and written objections to the Western Quarterly Meeting's granting a certificate to Rachel Wright after Cane Creek had withheld it.
5. Mounting division between pro-Husband and anti-Husband factions following the departure of the Wright family.

The Cane Creek disruption strained the Western Quarterly Meeting, which encompassed meetings in the present-day counties of Alamance, Chatham, Durham, Guilford, Orange, and Randolph, the heart of what would be the Regulator area. The events of 1760–1764 illustrate the seriousness with which the relationship between church governance and individual spiritual awareness was questioned in at least one Quaker settlement in the Piedmont. Indeed, it is possible to interpret Husband's role in the Cane Creek disruption as articulating claims of individual conscience over the authority of the religious group.

Although Quakers were part of the dissenting tradition out of which the Great Awakening erupted, as institutions the Quaker meetings stood aloof from the emotion-filled, unusually large and long religious gatherings that marked the popular revivalism of the 1750s and 1760s. A century earlier, during the repression of English dissenters in the 1660s, Quakers had begun curbing their extreme individualists in the interest of the sect's security. The tightening of Friends' discipline in the eighteenth century further distanced them from another mid-seventeenth-century English group, the "Ranters," with whom Quakers had shared radicalism and ridicule.

When Husband had written *Some Remarks on Religion* a decade before the Cane Creek disruption, he had viewed the Friends' honoring of the Inner Light as supportive of spiritual birth fostered by the Great Awakening. In 1778, he would record a sharp distinction, chiding Quakers for a "false Conscience begat in you by . . . your Discipline, that false God, who sits in God's temple Mans Heart, by influence and Prejudice of Custom." Husband was perceived by some of his contemporaries at Cane Creek as a disruptive exponent of individualism in spiritual matters. A Delaware Quaker minister visiting Cane Creek early in 1765 noted that a "considerable number have unwarily got into a *ranting spirit*, . . . being led away by one Herman Husband."[22]

The Cane Creek issue that Husband took as his springboard suggests an additional concern, however. The earliest action in which Husband is seen to have been engaged was his attack on the sincerity of Rachel Wright's apology for the way she had supported her daughter's refusal to accept blame for having been raped. Attacking the sincerity of a personal apology to the meeting contradicted Husband's championing of individual conscience over the authority of the religious group. In terms of both Charity Wright's defiance and Rachel Wright's local leadership, Husband's attack served to protect the claims of patriarchal order and authority that prevailed in the general culture. Both Quakers and Stearns's Separate Baptists were conspicuous for women members preaching and praying in public.[23] Husband may have been uneasy with the relative access to leadership and personal travel available to Quaker women and exemplified at Cane Creek by Rachel Wright and Abigail Pike. (Pike had moved on to help establish the meeting that would become New Garden, in present-day western Guilford County.) Husband's second and third wives, both members of Cane Creek, left no evidence of leadership in the records. Discomfort with the relative gender equality of Friends would suggest that Husband's journey from Anglican to New Light Presbyterian to Quaker had left him with only a limited absorption of the social radicalism he encountered along the way.

Moreover, Jehu Stuart had boasted of several sexual conquests, but Charity Wright was the only girl to be charged in the overwhelmingly Quaker community. (In a similar action at Cane Creek, no female was accused when three young men were disowned "for Entering into an Engagement . . . to ensnare and debauch all the women they could, and [have] put the same in practice."[24]) Perhaps Husband seized Charity Wright's circumstance as an opening to displace some of the initial leadership of the settlement, in which the small-scale land speculator

John Wright and his minister wife were fixtures. Whatever conjectures arise, Husband's leadership style is perceptible at Cane Creek in the early 1760s: engaging, persistent, opportunistic, and articulate. He used existing issues to seize the moral high ground, to attract yeomen of substance and conviction to act with him, and to raise his own profile.

5

The Sandy Creek Network and Its Allies in the Regulator Movement

"Let It Be Judiciously Enquired"

Several of the men that Husband identified in his writings as fellow leaders of the Sandy Creek Association of 1766 were Friends in the Cane Creek, Eno River, and Deep River meetings who had sided with him in "Rachel's Wright affair" and had been disowned: Joseph Maddock, Isaac Vernon, Thomas Branson, John and William Marshall, and Jonathan Cell. After Husband was disowned, he married for the third time. His bride, Amy Allen, lost her membership in Cane Creek for marrying "out of meeting," as did members who attended the unsanctioned wedding. Her mother recently had married into the numerous Cox family, to which Husband's first wife had belonged. Several Coxes were disowned for attending the Allen-Husband wedding, along with other relatives of Husband's first wife. Coxes and Pughs (relatives of Husband's deceased second wife) were prominent among the Sandy Creek Associates.[1]

During the August 1766 session of Orange County court, the Sandy Creek network circulated a paper calling for popularly elected "delegates" to meet "at a suitable place where there is no Liquor" prior to the next quarterly court. In addition, the circular was read aloud in the courthouse. The paper proposed a time and place, as well as this agenda: "let it be judiciously enquired whether the free men of this Country labor under any abuses of power or not." Later this document was referred to as "Regulator Advertisement, Number One." Husband appears to have written it and to also have had a hand in writing the next two Regulator "Advertisements."[2]

In 1770 Husband compiled and published documents from the 1766–1769 events in which he had participated and linked them with his account of the events. He titled his pamphlet, *An Impartial Relation of the First Rise and Cause of the Recent Differences in Publick Affairs in the Province of North-Carolina and of the past Tumults and Riots that lately happened in that Province.*[3] He did not overtly distinguish between the 1766 Sandy Creek Association and the full-blown Regulator Movement; when he published *An Impartial Relation* in 1770, he championed the Regulator Movement and still hoped to control it. Nevertheless, the pamphlet's narrative gives the impression that by the end of 1767, Husband and other leaders of the Sandy Creek Association had lost whatever control over expressions of political rage in the backcountry

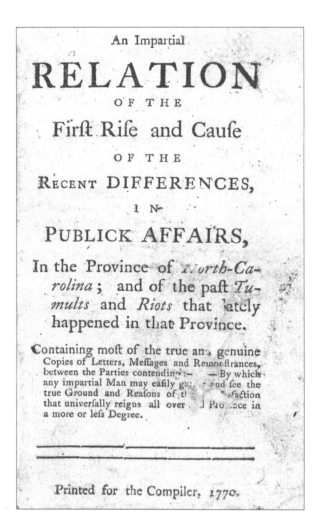

An Impartial

RELATION

OF THE

Firſt Riſe and Cauſe

OF THE

RECENT DIFFERENCES,

IN

PUBLICK AFFAIRS,

In the Province of *North-Ca-rolina*; and of the paſt *Tumults* and *Riots* that lately happened in that Province.

Containing moſt of the true and genuine Copies of Letters, Meſſages and Remonſtrances, between the Parties contending:— —By which any impartial Man may eaſily get, and ſee the true Ground and Reaſons of the faction that univerſally reigns all over the Province in a more or leſs Degree.

Printed for the Compiler, 1770.

Title page of Herman Husband's *Impartial Relation of the First Rise and Cause of the Recent Differences in Publick Affairs, in the Province of North Carolina. . . .* Image provided courtesy of the John Carter Brown Library, Brown University.

they may once have had. Husband himself saw anger over the poll tax, passed in 1766, as a turning point:

> The Rumour of giving the Governor *Fifteen Thousand Pounds,* to build him a House . . . conspired to give Rise to what was commonly called the Mob; which in a little Time altered to that of the Regulators. This new Association began in a different Neighbourhood, [i.e., not Sandy Creek] though they always mentioned and espoused the former [i.e., the Sandy Creek Association]; and People had entered into it by Hundreds, and it spread every Way like Fire till it reached *Sandy-Creek,* where the principal Men who were concerned in the Papers [a.k.a.

"Regulator Advertisements"] No. 1, 2, and 3, lived. There this new Scheme met with some Opposition, on Account that it was too hot and rash, and in some Things not legal. And though the *Sandy-Creek* People endeavoured to shew them the Danger of their Proceedings, yet [they] took Care at the same Time not to kill that Zeal for Justice and true Liberty.[4]

With the activity of the Sandy Creek Association of 1766, the critical mass necessary to support a political movement was achieved. By reading their paper in the August 1766 court, the network, in Husband's words, "had in View to carry Elections by the Majority, and . . . to confute a general prevailing Notion, that the Combination of Rogues . . . was so great, that it was in vain to try to out-vote them at Elections, which was the Method of Redress proposed. . . ."[5] The "new Scheme" that arose in the wake of the poll tax added nonpayment of taxes to the strategy of electoral challenges and implied physical resistance to tax collection. Henceforth, the original advocates of the Sandy Creek Association, largely Separate Baptists and Quakers, faced allies who did not share their values of nonviolence and pacifism. Indeed, the Great Awakening in general was not concerned with the nonresistance preached by its Anabaptist-Mennonite forebears and by John Calvin himself. The political support of nonpacifist allies, however, was deemed crucial to Husband's electoral ambitions and to the reform of county government that the Sandy Creek Association demanded. The emerging Regulator Movement lived with this dichotomy from its inception.

The procedure that the August 1766 announcement in court called for, a "judicious enquiry," was well within the common practice of a normally functioning county court in the traditional English and colonial usage. Grand juries made "presentments" of broad and narrow scope, with or without special instructions from the presiding justices. The justices then decided what action to take on the matters "presented" by the grand jurors. Unusual episodes of grand jury presentments could have effects ranging from mere venting of frustrations, to redress of the grievance by the county court, to attention to the issue by the legislature. The composition of the grand jury was decisive. The presiding justices and the sheriff named grand jurors from a pool restricted by a legislated minimum of land ownership. As late as 1769, Rowan County Regulators still were trying to use grand jury presentments against corrupt local officials. They related the cause of their failure: "about six or seven of us attended Salisbury general Court to indict our Officers; when, to our Astonishment, we found the Grand Jury to be composed of our inveterate Enemies, and of such as has been our greatest Oppressors—No less than five of them were old Sheriffs—In fine, there were but two or three but that were Limbs of the law."[6] The venerable and conservative practice of the grand jury presentment as a means to reform was not an option in Piedmont counties in the 1760s because of the closed loop of authority shared by the courthouse rings and their allies in the eastern-dominated legislature. It is significant that the first call for a public meeting in Orange County that could not be dominated by court personnel was issued while the county court was in session. Moreover, the circular was read aloud during the court. One of the Orange County representatives present, Thomas Lloyd, was said to sanction the call for the meeting.

During the following months, several such meetings were held, agreements made, records kept, and notices circulated. The common theme was agreement to pay no unlawful taxes or fees unless forced to do so, and then to "bear open testimony against" them, Quaker language. Generally, the participants agreed to attend meetings, contribute to defray the expenses of their efforts, and submit to majority decisions.[7]

"But We Were Disregarded"

Local officials declined to attend the public meetings called by the Sandy Creek network. With Fanning as their spokesman, the officers dismissed written summaries of the meetings, and, in the November 1766 court, Fanning said that he had sent the leaders a statement that would "silence them." Neighborhoods continued to elect representatives, who presented written requests to local officers to discuss issues with them. There was an expectation that such meetings would continue on a regular basis. Writing shortly after the Battle of Alamance, Husband recalled that it was backcountry officers, not Tryon, who in 1766–1767 had denounced such meetings as seditious and murderous in intent: "The G____r['s] fault, at this Period, seems to be chiefly Indolence; list'ning to Fanning, and giving himself no concern whether the People complained justly or unjustly."[8] Physical action was taken in April 1768 over the issue of distraint, the official seizure of movable property for payment of taxes. Approximately seventy men went together to Hillsborough and seized a horse that had been distrained as a fine for nonpayment of taxes. This was more than bearing "open testimony against" unlawful taxes. While the horse rescuers were in town, they fired shots into the roof of Fanning's house. As commander of the Orange County militia, Fanning ordered the captains to have their men ready to act if needed. In his description of the situation to Governor Tryon, there may be some exaggeration, but it does indicate widespread activity, as well as Fanning's arrogance:

> (O my favourite County and people how art thou fallen) [Orange County is] the very nest and bosom of rioting and rebellion—The People are now in every part and Corner of the County, meeting, conspiring, and confederating by solemn oath and open violence to refuse the payment of Taxes and to prevent the execution of Law, threatening death and immediate destruction to myself and others, requiring settlements of the Public, Parish and County Taxes, to be made before their leaders—Clerks, Sheriffs, Registers, Attornies and all Officers of every degree and station to be arraigned at the Bar of their Shallow Understanding and to be punished and regulated at their Will, and in a word, for them to become the sovereign arbiters of right and wrong.[9]

Tryon responded by notifying the militia in nearby counties to be ready to go to Orange, and he issued a proclamation ordering people who called themselves Regulators to disperse to their homes. To his superiors, however, the governor acknowledged sympathy with Regulator complaints. He reported to the Earl of Hillsborough, secretary of state for the colonies, that some sheriffs had embezzled more than half the money they were supposed to collect. Supervision of local officials belonged not to London, however, but to the colonial legislature. At Tryon's urging, the assembly passed a few laws regulating fees of county court clerks. The governor encouraged people in Orange County to petition the legislature for redress of their grievances, the standard English procedure.

Instead, they petitioned Tryon and his council directly, bypassing the lower house, a reflection of popular understanding of the political reality of that body's partnership with county officers. By the time the May 1768 petition, known as "Regulator Advertisement, Number Nine," reached the governor, hostility had ratchetted further. The new petition was signed by 474 people, at least 30 of them using German script. It complained that fees collected in Orange County were higher than the law allowed. The petitioners were quick to observe that "application has been made to our representatives [in the lower house, William Churton and Thomas Lloyd] to satisfy us But we were disregarded." As a result, they said, growing discontent threatened the "public peace." The petitioners rebuked the "heated unruly spirits" who had fired on Fanning's house. Even so, they insisted that the cause of their troubles was "the corrupt and arbitrary Practices of nefarious and designing men who being put into Posts of Profit and Credit among us . . . using every artifice, practicing every Fraud, and where these failed, threats and menaces were not spared . . . to squeeze and extort from the wretched poor."[10]

Rednap Howell and James Hunter presented the petition to the governor in June 1768. A teacher from New Jersey, Howell quickly engaged himself in the controversies that he found on his arrival in the Chatham area of Orange County and continued to promote Regulator issues when he settled in present-day Randolph County. Three surviving songs attributed to Howell satirized the Regulators' antagonists. He set his rhymes to familiar tunes, and they "were sung or rather roared by the regulators at their meetings," as Regulator sympathizer Joseph MacPherson recalled in 1810. He said that Howell had produced "perhaps 40" songs during the Regulator years. Howell's partner as Regulator emissary in 1768, James Hunter, likewise was articulate and would serve as messenger and spokesman for the movement several times during the next two years. Both Howell and Hunter, as well as Shubal Stearns, have been suggested as the author of one or more "Regulator Advertisements," as well as the pamphlet, *A Fan for Fanning, and a Touch-Stone to Tryon,* generally attributed to Husband. Hunter was in his early thirties, about a decade younger than Husband, and their land transactions in the 1750s had brought them together. Hunter had signed the 1756 petition to Earl Granville. He received a two-hundred-acre grant the following year, situated advantageously on the Trading Path and located near Husband on the western headwaters of Stinking Quarter Creek and Sandy Creek. MacPherson described Hunter as "next in point of wealth" to Husband, who was "the soul of the party."[11]

"From Hillsborough Town, the First Day of May"

Tryon's reception of the petition that Howell and Hunter presented was clouded by a fresh Regulator threat to Hillsborough. The renewed anger was in response to the arrest in May of Husband and William Butler on charges of inciting to rebellion. Thomas Lloyd had ordered their arrest on May Day, a day on which trouble might be expected. For centuries, British and European popular culture had sanctioned a break from the normal respect for authority on certain days, notably the half-year marks at May Day and Halloween and during Christmas. The county authorities went to the Sandy Creek area to take Husband and Butler. Regulators, protesting the arrest, described it as follows:

> Colo Fanning at the head of 27 armed men consisting chiefly of Sheriffs Bombs [sheriff's bums, i.e., undersheriffs or men temporarily deputized] Tavern Keepers, and officers after travelling all night were arrived by break of day on Sandy Creek, and had made prisoners Mr. Hermon Husbands & Mr. Wm Butler the former a Gentleman that had never joined the Regulators, had never been concerned in any tumults, and whose only crime, was his being active in trying to bring on the intended settlement. This extraordinary step of the Colonel's alarmed the whole County, Regulators or Anteregulators, all were unanimous in the recovery of the Prisoners; many who had till then opposed, the prevailing measures now went down with the foremost, as judging none were now safe.[12]

Swarms of men, variously remembered as between seven and fifteen hundred, responded to the arrest of Husband and Butler by surrounding the town in a manner that suggested hostile intent. Oral tradition held that Fanning and Isaac Edwards, the governor's private secretary, came out to negotiate. Fanning, holding a bottle of rum in one hand and a bottle of wine in the other, shouted across the Eno River to the men massed there. He asked them to send him a horse that he might cross with refreshments for a friendly drink and parley. Ninian Bell Hamilton, a seventy-year-old Scotsman living in the Sandy Creek area who later was remembered as having led the Regulators that day, reportedly responded: "Ye're nane too gude to wade, and wade ye shall, if ye come over!"[13] The image of Fanning crossing the Eno on foot, bearing libations, was encased in popular memory through a song, likely one of Howell's. Some verses had been forgotten before this remnant was written down from MacPherson's recital in 1810:

> From Hillsborough town the first day of May
> Marches those Mudering Traitors;
> They went to oppose the honest Men
> That were called the Regulators.
>
> Old Hamilton surrounded their town
> He guarded every quarter
> The Regulators still marching on,
> Full fifteen hundred after.
>
> [missing verses]
>
> At length their headmen they sent out,
> To save their town from fire
> To see Ned Fanning under Eno
> Brave Boys you'd admire.
>
> With hat in hand at our command
> To salute us every one sir
> And after that kept off his hat
> To salute old Hamilton sir.
>
> But old Hamilton like an angry man
> He still craved satisfaction
> For the taking of Husbands away to the town
> It was a most villainous action.
>
> [missing verses][14]

Edwards persuaded the crowds to disperse, assuring them that their grievances would be redressed. It was during the next few days that the petition known as "Regulator Advertisement, Number Nine" emerged, which Howell and Hunter took to the governor and council. This time, Tryon responded by admonishing all officials and lawyers to abide by the fee table and ordering that the tables be republished. He told Piedmont men to stop using the name "Regulator," to pay their taxes, and not to "molest" officials. Plainly, the vigilante prospect of the Regulator Movement alarmed Tryon.

6

The Gentlemen's Agreement
in Mecklenburg

Tryon's Alliance with Scotch-Irish Leaders

Tryon toured the Piedmont in the summer of 1768 in an effort to solidify his control over the area's militia. He expected more trouble at the September session of Hillsborough District Superior Court and also feared unrest at the Salisbury District Superior Court. The governor was keen to prepare for any one-two strike that Regulators might plan for the consecutive court sessions. Clearly, grievances that the Regulator Movement was articulating were shared by the rank and file of the militia throughout the interior counties. Moreover, some of the complaints were against local commanders of militia, who typically were also justices of the peace. Tryon could not afford to leave the reliability of militiamen to be decided when their support became urgent. His best success came in the crucial county of Mecklenburg.

Like Orange and Rowan counties and Anson County, out of which Mecklenburg was formed, Mecklenburg was in a sprawling western district. Mecklenburg officials exercised some authority in the present-day counties of Cleveland, Gaston, Lincoln, and Rutherford, as well as more direct administration in today's Cabarrus and Union counties. Tryon's success in stabilizing militia discipline in the greater Mecklenburg area owed much to the leadership and deference exhibited by the Scotch-Irish, who comprised the largest ethnic group in the county. Privileges of land engrossment and officeholding were enjoyed by a network of families who had more or less led a series of migrations from the western parts of the middle colonies. Alexanders, McNitts, and Polks headed the network. In land matters they worked closely with John Frohock in alliance with the interests of McCulloh and Fanning. The cultural tendency was for the leading men to communicate concerns to external authorities and negotiate on behalf of their people.

During the "Sugar Creek War" of the 1760s, this long-term deference of Scotch-Irish toward their more prosperous leaders had weakened in the area, as settlers who claimed squatter's rights (or more) challenged prominent local men who were working for land speculators. A 1777 satire on Mecklenburg politics reflected on two decades of an Alexander-Polk courthouse ring. "The Mecklenburg Censor" characterized the ring as complacently disdaining Mecklenburg farmers from a pedestal of wealth built from connivances in public office.[1] Presbyterian tradition recorded that in the 1760s the outspoken preacher Alexander Craighead denounced at least two of his church's elders for cooperating with land surveyors. At the same time, Craighead preached against oppression of the poor. Craighead died in 1766. With the influential and unpredictable Covenanter gadfly gone, Mecklenburg's Scotch-Irish leaders could comfortably rally their people without incurring his criticism. Joseph Alexander, ordained in 1768, was Craighead's successor.

The old issue of Anglican privilege in a land occupied by dissenters had resurfaced in 1765 with the assembly's passage of yet another act regarding vestries and local taxes for the support of Anglican ministers. County leaders readily could invoke Craighead's spirit for social solidarity against the new law, for his eloquence against the Anglican establishment was widely known; Tryon warily had taken note of Craighead as a Solemn League and Covenant preacher. Caution was needed, however. For the Mecklenburg leadership network—JPs, land agents, militia leaders, court officials—to protest the terms of the new law in general would have given credence to the complaints of Regulators. Yet the leadership risked overthrow if they did not protect their people, dissenters recently reinvigorated by the Great Awakening, from the enforcement of the Anglican establishment. About the time of Craighead's death, the Society for the Propagation of the Gospel sent an Anglican missionary to North Carolina, intending him to go to Mecklenburg County. When the Anglican arrived, Tryon and perhaps others in the east warned him that aroused dissenters predominated in Mecklenburg, mainly "Covenanters Seceders Anabaptists and New Lights," and that they hated the new act as much as they did the Stamp Act and were determined to prevent its enforcement. The missionary went instead to Northampton County.[2] The plethora of issues that had come together to fuel the Regulator wildfire were beyond the reach of Mecklenburg's leaders, but they seized the one issue they could champion with honor and without damage to themselves. Tryon's presence among them for two weeks in August 1768 gave them the opportunity to propose a deal: let us succeed in protecting our communities against the legislation of Anglican privilege, and our militia will serve under us against Regulator-led insurrection. Events at Hillsborough in September would confirm Tryon's trust in the Scotch-Irish gentlemen of Mecklenburg. In the months following, Mecklenburg's leaders would seek exclusion of Mecklenburg, Rowan, and Tryon counties from enforcement of the vestry act and related legislation, more than they could wrest from the lower house. Tryon himself did not obstruct them, and more than once he reminded his superiors in London, as well as Anglicans in North Carolina, that he "was greatly obligated by the support the Presbyterians have afforded government in my administration." The Mecklenburg petitioners pointedly observed that Presbyterian "freemen" there numbered more than one thousand, that they "hold to the established church of Scotland," and that they were "able to bear arms."[3]

Mecklenburg's champions were already in negotiation with Tryon and Fanning for the creation of a Presbyterian college in their midst. Fanning would emerge as its projected president. In March 1771, Tryon explained the unprecedented project to the secretary of state for the colonies: "Though the President is to be of the established Church and licenced by the Governor The Fellows, Trustees and Tutors I apprehend will be generally Presbyterians. The College being promoted by a respectable Settlement of that persuasion from which a considerable Body marched to Hillsborough in September 1768 in support of Government." At the same time, Tryon gave his assurances that new legislation authorizing Presbyterian ministers (but not other dissenting clergy) to perform marriages without compensating Anglican ministers for the fee was a well-earned "Indulgence" for Presbyterian "Attachment" in September 1768.[4]

Martin Phifer and the Mecklenburg Dynamic

The promised Queen's College (renamed Queen's Museum in deference to the Anglican establishment) was intended for Charlotte, the county seat of Mecklenburg authorized by the legislature in 1766 and again in 1768. The selection of Charlotte as the seat of government resulted from the local leadership's alliance with Tryon, McCulloh, Fanning, and the eastern-dominated legislature. The Alexander-Polk/ Frohock-McCulloh interest owned buildings in the new town. There was a precarious moment in the deliberations over the location of the county government. Martin Phifer, a justice of the peace and militia major in northeastern Mecklenburg County, for a time threatened to split his Scotch-Irish neighbors in the Rocky River settlement away from the Alexander-Polk ring that controlled the county.

> "An Act to ascertain Attorneys fees." As also
> "An Aadditional and explanatory Act to an Act intitled
> "an Act to regulate the several Officers fees within this
> "province, and to ascertain the method of paying the
> "same and to tax law suits".
>   Are two most salutary laws and I expect will prove
> in their operation very satisfactory and beneficial to the
> country.
>   "An Act to regulate the issuing of Marriage Licences."
>   Will better secure than formerly the fees due to the
> Governor and give him a summary way of calling the clerks
> regularly to account with him; a habit little known or prac-
> tised among some of them.
>   "An Act for authorizing Presbyterian ministers regularly
> "called to any congregation within this province, to sol-
> "emnize the rights of matrimony under the regulations
> "therein mentioned".
>   This Act I apprehended might be found by the Bishop
> of London, to whom I presume it will be referred, liable to great
> objections, therefore it was passed with a suspending clause
> till his Majestys pleasure should be known. If it is not
> thought too much to interfere with, and check the growth of

In this March 12, 1771, letter to the Earl of Hillsborough, Tryon transmitted the acts passed at the last session of the Assembly. He provided comments, some of which are very revealing. Note his comments about regulating fees for marriage licenses. From Tryon Letter Book, G.L.B. 1, 1764–1771, page 282. Image provided courtesy of the North Carolina State Archives.

A large landowner and merchant, Phifer was a Swiss native with influence among the numerous German-speaking settlers in his section of the county. He was a man of some prosperity and influence, having furnished provisions to friendly Indians and the fort on the south bank of the Catawba River during the French and Indian War. Phifer pushed for a Rocky River location for the county seat and thereby gained the votes of the Scotch-Irish in northern Mecklenburg. In 1764 and again in 1766, Phifer represented the new county in the lower house, along with a Scotch-Irish delegate, first Richard Berry and then Thomas Polk. A lasting combination of Germans and dissident Scotch-Irish threatened to unseat the Alexander-Polk clique. Regulator stirrings created electoral challenges to key figures in courthouse rings elsewhere: Frohock in Rowan, Fanning in Orange, Samuel Spencer in Anson, and Samuel Benton in Granville were conspicuous incumbents and Regulator targets. Why not the Polk-Alexander interest in Mecklenburg?

The latter pounced to thwart collusion between Phifer and any Scotch-Irish fringe formation. Militia colonel Moses Alexander attacked Phifer's limitations with the English language: "It was a dam'd scandal to send a man to the house of assembly that cant neither read nor write."[5] Furthermore, the Alexanders and Polks distorted Phifer's legislative record and thereby caught him in the backcountry quicksand of Anglican privilege.

In the lower house, Phifer did not have sufficient allies to block the Charlotte location, but in November 1768 he introduced a compromise empowering the Mecklenburg JPs, after seven years and with "the Consent of the Majority of the freeholders, . . . to sell and dispose of such Court House prison and stocks already built [at Charlotte], and to erect and build another Court House Prison and stocks *at any other place in the said County more Centrel.*"[6] Phifer's original bill passed its first reading in both houses. His fellow representative from Mecklenburg, Thomas Polk, countered with a bill to protect Charlotte. Phifer's bill then was "amended" to divide the county, creating a new county from its western extremities, not the northeastern section of Phifer's strength, and with no provision for ever moving the Mecklenburg seat. Significantly, the new county, to be named Tryon, would remain under the authority of the Mecklenburg sheriff. After the session ended, Polk and Moses Alexander spread word in Mecklenburg County that Phifer had introduced a bill to allocate the county's vestry tax to pay a German-speaking minister and teacher in the German settlements. There is no hint of such a measure in the House journal or session papers, which included Phifer's legislative activities.[7]

The rumor was political fodder for the directors of Mecklenburg's Scotch-Irish multitudes, for it doubly alarmed dissenters. Use of a vestry tax to benefit German speakers could be seen to validate the principle of broad taxation to benefit a religious minority. Ominously, it suggested a German-Anglican affinity, notwithstanding the Calvinism of the Piedmont's German Reformed and Dunkard groups. In a pro-Phifer effort, a German and two Scotch-Irishmen attested to Polk's and Alexander's misrepresentations of Phifer's bill and put their affidavits on record in the county deed book. In addition, about twenty members of the assembly defended Phifer, declaring the Alexander-Polk descriptions of his legislative conduct "false and scandalous . . . with an Intent to lessen . . . Fifer in the good opinion of the Freeholders [voters]." During the summer of 1769 electioneering, Thomas Polk claimed credit for having killed the phantom bill. Excitement magnified the amount of salary Phifer was said to have proposed for the German minister, from £30 to £136.[8] Phifer lost his seat to Abraham Alexander in the July 1769 polling, even as Regulators won assembly seats in backcountry counties east of Mecklenburg. Meanwhile, Tryon contributed personally to the salary of a young German-speaking schoolteacher and minister, Samuel Suther, in northeastern Mecklenburg. During the governor's two weeks in the county in August 1768, he divided his time between Phifer's home near present-day Concord and the lands of the Scotch-Irish leaders.[9]

Between two visits to Mecklenburg in August 1768, Tryon made certain his control of the Rowan County militia. Only one company refused to muster. Once his authority was secure, the governor raised the king's standard at Salisbury in an impressive military ritual lasting two days. During this time, he received a letter from four Presbyterian ministers in Orange County pledging their support to keep down rebellion: Hugh MacAden, James Creswell, Henry Pattillo, and David Caldwell. Their open letter to Presbyterians in North Carolina warned that Regulator oaths threatening nonpayment of taxes were unlawful. This and other communications were read publicly as Tryon massed nearly one thousand militiamen at Salisbury. The companies from Mecklenburg would add to that number, providing more than 20 percent of the force of nearly fifteen hundred militia from Granville, Mecklenburg, Orange, Rowan, and counties with whom Tryon would fortify the Hillsborough District court.[10]

7

Petitions, Court Proceedings, and Rioting in Hillsborough and Salisbury

In the Hillsborough District Superior Court, September 1768

The show of strength was effective. Unlike the largely eastern militia force that would defeat the Regulators at Alamance in 1771, the massed troops of September–October 1768 were Piedmont men. The court session proceeded as usual, though some of its cases were unusual. In addition to Husband and Butler awaiting trial, two other Regulators had been indicted for seizing a distrained horse. At the same time, Fanning had been charged with taking excessive fees for registering deeds. This session has been called "a perfect illustration of the centralization and power of the courthouse ring to which the Regulators had objected. Fanning, a defendant to be tried, and Maurice Moore, the presiding judge, were both colonels in the militia. Six other militia officers were members of the governor's council, and eighteen members of the Assembly also were among the militia officers."[1]

During the four months since the seizure of Butler and Husband, there had been many meetings of "Regulators," "associators," and "non-Regulators." Contemporary descriptions of their sessions used those terms to distinguish among, respectively: the more violent and radical voices; moderates generally eschewing violence; and sympathizers with the "Regulators and associators" who had not signed petitions or taken oaths—yet. Occasionally, prominent outsiders were invited to attend as mediators and messengers, for example the Hillsborough Anglican minister George Micklejohn and merchant Ralph McNair. The latter responded to Husband's request for legal documents and helped the more moderate element draft conciliatory petitions. The mediating efforts of Presbyterian minister David Caldwell rankled at least one Regulator among his two churches: it was said that James Hunter "withdrew [from Caldwell's congregation] because he thought the Doctor was not sufficiently enthusiastic in the cause of the Regulators."[2]

The headless nature of what is recalled today as "the Regulator Movement" was conspicuous during the four months that Husband considered his personal plight. Clearly, Fanning regarded him as his archenemy, and the governor was pleased to agree that Husband was the prime mover of insurrection in the Piedmont. It was widely expected that Fanning and his connections would convict and execute Husband and perhaps others at the September court. A cautious

Husband refused to attend some of the Regulator meetings, and he and others denied that he was a Regulator. Long-standing friends among his Quaker connections—John Wilcox, a merchant based at Cross Creek, and John Pyle, a doctor living on Cane Creek in Orange County—counseled against fleeing the colony and persuaded him to hire a costly eastern lawyer for his defense. An April 1770 sworn statement by an admirer of Husband recalled some of the tension and color of the summer of 1768:

> Some time before ye General Court was held at Hilsborough In September 1768, a Discoarce Commenly passed throughout ye Country yt Harmon Husbands would be then condemd and put to Death (through a suspision of being protector of ye Regulators). . . . When Court came on my Curiaucity led me to leave ye Regelaters who ware Incamped nigh ye town, and Endevour privately to Inspect into ye matter—When I went to ye town I was taken up by ye guard and took Before an officer who gave me Liberty to go where I saw fit through any part of ye town. As I walked a long I saw Collenel Edmen Fanning who was then viewing this part of ye Army they Being In an Exercising form ye drums Baiting and Coulers flying and as I drew nigh, ye Collenel Espied me and met me In a genteel manner, and said Well How Do you Do, Mr Mcferson, When I had answered He said, Well what temper is ye Regelaters in this morning—I said ye people seem temperate, But they take it Hard ye thee and other gentlemen Concernd therin should offer to touch Harmon Husbandses Life—touch His Life says He, He must be put to Death, Oh no, no Collenel Fanning Says I dont say so yts very Hard, He must says he must surely Die as sure as thee is Born of Woman. I considerd some part of ye Day whether I should tell Harmon or not what I had heard At length I told him, who said Well now I will go of[f]—I waited on him till he mounted his horse then rode by his side Discoarcing of ye matter, John Wilcox fell in with us as we Left ye Regelater Camp, and said to him, What Mr Husbands, are you a going of[f] he said yess I believe I had Best for if they get me into town I believe they will hang me—then Wilcox hastely rode before us and began to Lement in this manner Oh shocking, shocking my God I wish I had never been born, then he stopt his horse and was as I conceived much in anguish of spirit and says Mr Husbands But will you not stand tryal for If you Dont ye Country is Ruind is Ruined then Harmon said Doest think I had Better stand trial Yes it would be best Yes Sir it would And I will stand by you to ye very Last, During this Discoarce we had rode near three mile, when on a sudden Harmon Resolved to Return with Wilcox to town and advised me to ride home I being then on ye way which I did with a Sorrowful Heart.[3]

Husband estimated that 3,700 people gathered at Hillsborough for the court session. He described the atmosphere:

> Troops were raising in all Quarters, as was said, to guard the Court. The Effect of these Troops was, that every Man coming into Court was examined what Business he had. And every one who dared to own, that it was to complain of Officers, was ill used by the Guards and Soldiery, and scared away home; but some few who would not be scared away was ordered out of town by the Commanding Officers at a few Minutes Warning. None could stay but Prisoners, and them denied of Attornies, unless they would give Bonds for Fifty and to Three Hundred Pounds to each Attorney.[4]

The judges were Martin Howard, Maurice Moore, and Richard Henderson. The court took a mincing approach all around. Husband was acquitted. Butler was found guilty, however, and levied a fine of £50 and a jail sentence of six months. The two other Regulators were fined and sentenced at half of Butler's measure. Then all fines were suspended and the prisoners released. Fanning was found guilty of taking a fee of six shillings for registering a deed instead of the fee table stipulation of two shillings and eight pence. His fine was one penny for each of the five counts against him. A few weeks later, Tryon issued a blanket pardon for "all persons concerned in the late insurrection" except thirteen: James Hunter, Ninian Bell Hamilton, Ninian Hamilton, Peter Craven, Isaac Jackson, Herman Husband, Mathew Hamilton, William Payne, Malachy Syke, William Moffat, Christopher Nation, Solomon Goff, and John O'Neal.[5]

Richard Henderson (1735–1785), land speculator, judge, and politician, was appointed by Tryon as associate justice on the Hillsborough District Superior Court. During September 1770, he was caught up in the turbulence between colonial officials and the Regulators. This memorial silhouette in relief is provided courtesy of the North Carolina Museum of History.

In the Hillsborough District Superior Court, March 1769

The next session of the Hillsborough District Superior Court was in March 1769. Waightstill Avery, a newly qualified lawyer, kept a diary as part of his routine. In Mecklenburg County, Avery was a close associate of the Alexanders. In 1777, "The Mecklenburg Censor," satirizing that county's recent election, characterized Avery as "a lawyer mean in fame," who had offered to Hezekiah and John McNitt Alexander,

> my soul I'll sell,
> to serve you till 'tis sent to hell.[6]

Avery's entries for the March 1769 Hillsborough court days note what he thought significant and show the basic judicial issues still to be unsettled:

> March 16 & 17.—In company with the Judge [Richard Henderson], Col. Fanning, and Mr. Hooper, set out for Hillsborough.
> March 18, 19, & 20.—Where we arrived on Monday the 20th, having been waylaid by the Regulators who had formed an Ambuscade to kill col. Fanning. . . .
> March 22.—Sup'r Court was opened.
> March 23.—The Evening was spent in a great crowd of Lawers and others—narrowly escaped being intoxicated.
> March 24 & 25.—Business of Court went on.
> March 26.—Heard the Rev'd John Micklejohn preach a well connected, cunning, Arminian[7] discourse, which was highly applauded by all the Bar and Bench.
> March 27.—Harman Husbands was tried for Insurgency, and acquitted.
> March 28.—Col. Fanning was tried for Extortion in the Register's Office. A flood of indictments being thrown in against him by the Violence of Faction.[8]

The governor, writing to his immediate superior, the secretary of state for the colonies, described the March 1769 term of Hillsborough District Superior Court in his coverage of events in the Piedmont:

> By letters I have lately received from the back country the Sheriff of Orange County [John Lea] as he was going to serve a *Capias* on two or three of the late insurgents was seized tied up to a tree and received

from them a severe flogging. I have however the satisfaction to be informed by other letters that this act of outrage is not countenanced but disapproved by the body of the people who called themselves regulators. These matters I have laid before the Council who have desired to postpone the consideration of them till further intelligence is received from the back country. The Attorney General writes me that James Hunter was brought to tryal at Hillsborough last month [March 1769] but that the jury bringing in an insufficient verdict the Chief Justice awarded a new tryal at the next court, and that everything appeared quiet. Hermon Husbands who was and is still believed to have been at the bottom of the late disturbances took his tryal at the same court and was acquited for the want of proof.[9]

Herman Husband described the events of the March 1769 court in considerably more detail than either Avery's private diary, the governor's report, or the court minutes. The only case he described seems to have been Hunter's, for it fits Tryon's summary of the case. Husband said that the jury "mixed among Men before they gave" the verdict, and "by hearing others Sentiments, they disagreed to it when given in; And this was repeated so often . . . that the Jury was discharged at the Bar, after a Verdict agreed to, and then disagreed." Husband acknowledged a freer atmosphere during this term:

> No Troops being raised against us, . . . People flocked in to make Informations. But besides the Difficulty of attending Courts from thirty to sixty miles, and the Officers threatening to sue for malicious Prosecutions, and take all other Advantages of the Law. — Besides all this, the Attorney-General did not attend the two or three first days of Court; so that most of the People had gone Home.
>
> Some Informations, however, was made after he came, and a few of them tried, in which the Officers was all convicted, except in one Instance, and immediately that one prosecutor was sued.

There was some hope among the Regulators that the acting attorney general, William Hooper, might be of some assistance in bringing charges against corrupt officials. The Boston native was a Wilmington lawyer. In the absence of the king's attorney, he had been appointed deputy attorney by his friend Tryon. During the recent district court at Salisbury, Hooper had, at the request of the Regulators, drawn up a bill of indictment against John Frohock. The Regulators expected that Hooper would be similarly useful in Hillsborough. Husband was rueful in his disappointment in the future signer of the Declaration of Independence:

We observed the Deputy Attorney [Hooper] and both Associate Judges lodged with him whom we looked on as our chief Enemy [Fanning], and Cause of our oppressions.—So that Men of common Modesty was deterred from applying to [Hooper]. . . .

Some, who had more boldness than others, apply'd to Deputy _____ [Hooper], and made Information against the Clerk of the Inferior Court for taking . . . [excessive] Fee on a Common Attachment.—He told them he must have the Informations in Writing.—They found a Clerk, and carries it in writing.—Then it wanted a Date, or name, and then something else, till at length they got one almost right; but had gone from Office to Office so often, that one of the clerks D——d them for a pack of Sons of B——s, and denied serving them.

Deputy Attorney came also out of his fortification into the Street, and complain'd he had been so much harassed, that he was almost sick. . . .

Next day Deputy told W——B——r [William Butler] he would hear no more of us; and as [Butler] made Complaint of this to the court, Deputy said, it was a Lie.[10]

Such charges against officers as Husband described were not only difficult to make but also hard to make stick, and they left little trace in the historical record. An exceptional example has survived. In March 1769 Henry and Sarah Bray conveyed two hundred acres of land to Adam Moser. Fanning was due no fee for registering the deed, but he demanded and received six shillings in North Carolina proclamation money. A charge was brought against him in the March 1769 court. The record of indictment was retained in London but not in Hillsborough.[11]

The 1769 "Instructions"

Husband and other Regulators were successful in the July 1769 election. Backcountry farmers and planters voted their resentments against merchants and lawyers and reduced the overall representational power of the networks they regarded as blocs of their creditors. Regulators and their sympathizers were elected to the assembly to represent Anson, Granville, Halifax, Orange, and Rowan counties. Fanning and Frohock, both prime targets, lost their seats in Orange and Rowan counties, respectively. So did Samuel Benton in Granville County, whom George Sims had singled out in the Nutbush

Address four years earlier. Thomas Person, Benton's rival, retained his seat. Husband and John Pryor would represent Orange County for the first time, having polled 642 and 455 votes, respectively, to Edmund Fanning's 314. Pryor had been one of the original JPs of Orange County and was a Regulator.[12]

The momentum was at hand for the Regulators to address the backcountry's grievances through legislative means directly, rather than handing signed petitions to elected representatives who were unsympathetic to their issues. Husband and Pryor took to the legislature from some of their constituents a document titled, "Instructions from the Subscribers Inhabitants of Orange County to their Representatives in Assembly." The petition may be regarded as representative of issues aired during postelection public meetings in several counties and may have originated in campaign documents. The Orange County "Instructions" contained sixteen clauses, each addressing a specific

"Instructions from the Subscribers Inhabitants of Orange County to their Representatives in Assembly." This October 27, 1769, petition expressed concerns about different issues. Three of sixteen clauses are shown here. From General Assembly Session Records, October-November 1769, Lower House Papers, Petitions rejected or not acted on. Image provided courtesy of the North Carolina State Archives.

issue. The total number of signatories is unknown, but forty-seven signatures are on the document that survives in the House records. The names link the petition with present-day areas of northwestern Chatham, northeastern Randolph, and southern Alamance counties.

The concerns expressed in the petition involved elections, taxes, court procedures, land, and religious privilege. The petitioners wanted votes to be cast "by ticketts," or written ballots, and urged the House to exercise its parliamentary authority to scrutinize elections in which improprieties were alleged. Electoral "scrutiny" was a procedure by which the House obtained a sheriff's polling documentation and ruled on the validity of the election. The petition also called for graduated taxation and for taxes to be paid in produce so long as there was inadequate currency in circulation. Anticipating the creation of more colonial currency, the petitioners wanted money to be put into circulation quickly; they requested local loan offices that would accept land as security for currency. They repeated earlier requests to limit fees to their legal maximums but also asked that some officials be paid salaries and receive no portion of the fees.

Of all the issues addressed, land received the most attention. The petitioners actually asked that distraint be used when back payment of quitrents was charged, as that method was the legal, familiar, and "easy" way. What they opposed was the working alternative to distraint: suit for the land itself. Quitrents were so low that a lifetime of nonpayment would result in a sum so small that the traditional recourse of collection by distraint of movable property would not threaten a landholder's security. Neither would it bring any significant income to Granville or the Crown. What was happening, according to complainants, was that county officials were bringing suit for nonpayment of quitrents, then, using the scarcity of currency as an excuse, the courts were ordering the land to be auctioned. At such forced sales, the land went cheaply to those with ready cash or a network of credit, so that merchants and lawyers were buying up the land for speculation.

The petitioners believed that such legal maneuvers were in breach of common law usage, and they appealed to the assembly to inform the king of this great evil. In the same vein, they wanted London to know that Tryon and the council were granting land inconsistently with his instructions as governor, ignoring the headright limit and the terms of the grant. The Granville land office remained closed, six years after the earl's death. (He had willed the tract to his mistress, and the resulting challenges in English courts continued into the nineteenth century.) Meanwhile, people continued to move onto the tract, clearing land, building houses, and making similar improvements with the hope of buying the land that they occupied. The petitioners wanted an inventory of improvements on ungranted Granville land to be made, and they sought acknowledgment of some privilege of seniority. The request was consistent with the practice regarding Crown land.[13]

Portions of the petition emphasized localism, combined with a disregard for the personnel of the county court and the district superior court. Petitioners wanted some of the debt cases that currently came before the county court to be tried before justices of the peace, with local juries. They desired these cases to be heard "without lawyers" and with no appeal. Finally, the petitioners wanted all religious groups to be placed on an equal footing with regard to the performance of marriage ceremonies within each sect. This petition repeated some of the issues addressed in a far more obsequious petition from Orange and Rowan counties a year earlier.

A petition similar to the Orange "Instructions" was presented from Anson County. Bearing 261 signatures, it included a preamble reiterating complaints about illegal fees and corrupt lawyers and officials. The preamble climaxed with the statement: "That the Violation of the King's Instructions to his delegates, their artfulness in consealing the same from him; and the great Injury the people thereby sustains: is a manifest Oppression." The final request in the Anson petition reflected the last item in its preamble: "That Doctr Benjamin Franklin or some other known patriot be appointed Agent, to represent the unhappy state of this Province to his Majesty, and to solicit the several Boards in England." Colonial legislatures routinely hired agents to transact their business with London officials. Franklin was one of several men, both American and British, whose effectiveness in this capacity was well known. For decades, Regulator oral tradition would link Franklin with Husband as collaborator and correspondent, originating perhaps from Husband having his pamphlets printed in Philadelphia. (Franklin was not in America during the Regulator years.) The Regulators knew that they would receive no satisfaction from North Carolina's current London agent, Henry Eustace McCulloh.[14]

Husband introduced the Orange County version of the petition on October 27, the fourth day of the session, the first three having been spent in routine opening exercises, such as swearing in new members, hearing the governor's speech, and appointing committees. He presented

"The Petition of the Inhabitants of Anson County being part of the Remonstrance of the Province of North Carolina." This October 9, 1769, petition laid out seventeen points, in addition to a seven-point preamble, complaining about taxes, exorbitant fees, and corrupt officials. The opening portion of the petition and items 16 and 17 are shown here. A few signatures appear at the end as well. From General Assembly Session Records, October-November 1769, Lower House Papers, Committee of Propositions and Grievances. Image provided courtesy of the North Carolina State Archives.

it as a petition from constituents, a first step in drafting a bill for the consideration of the House. The usual procedure, continued from English usage, was for a member to present such a petition to the Speaker of the House in a general session. The Speaker would either refer it to the appropriate committee, or, if he saw no consensus to fulfill its requests, let it "lie on the table for consideration of the members," as the formula read. On the other hand, a call for vote and resulting majority approval would require the Speaker to refer the petition to a committee. In the tradition of parliamentary autonomy, the Speaker was elected by the House. The current Speaker was John Harvey of Perquimans County. Husband and Pryor seem to have prepared petitions, or drafts for bills, concerning the various subjects that the Orange petition treated; legislative minutes recorded that "Mr Husband moved for leave to read sundry petitions from the Inhabitants of Orange County." This was the main item of business for the day. There was no vote taken, and Harvey ordered that "the Petitions and other papers lie on the table for the consideration of the Members." Once tabled, the petition never resurfaced. The political lines were taut in the new lower house, but the weight of the east remained decisive.[15]

The assembly did look into the most recent Orange County election—the one by which Pryor and Husband had been elected. On the same day that Husband presented the petition, the committee on privileges and elections ordered a scrutiny of the election in an effort to exclude Pryor and Husband from the House. A challenge to the election had been lodged as the last item the day before Husband presented the Orange petition. The chairman of the committee on privileges and elections who ordered the scrutiny was Richard Caswell, a foe of Regulators, who would become the first governor of the State of North Carolina. The scrutiny cited electoral supervision by sheriff's assistants Laurance Van Hook and John Pyle. Van Hook lived on Dry Creek west of the Haw River in present-day Burlington, and Pyle lived in the Cane Creek settlement. Husband had come armed with an affidavit with which to respond to the challenge, and he presented it in the House immediately before introducing the Orange County petition.[16]

Husband served on a nine-member committee that undertook "to state and settle public accounts." Undoubtedly, it was the committee assignment that he wanted. The colony's sinking fund had been discussed in Piedmont meetings during 1768 and 1769. An Orange-Rowan petition to the legislature in October–November 1768 had addressed the fund, and Regulator legislators were keen to investigate it and arrange for its supervision. The committee made some headway, and the governor claimed to be astonished by its report. Upon receiving it, Tryon dissolved the legislature after a session of eighteen calendar days.[17] During the Stamp Act crisis a few years earlier, there had been some Piedmont praise for anti-Stamp Act expressions in the east; in particular, the Sandy Creek Association's first "Advertisement" had mentioned the Sons of Liberty in appreciative terms. Now that Parliament had repealed the Stamp Act only to follow it with the Townsend Acts, anti-government murmurs were arising from among North Carolina's eastern establishment, reason enough for Tryon to terminate the legislative session. Regulators and their supporters may have elected some of their own to the lower house, but they could not set its course.

The Calm before the Hillsborough Riots

In the modern imagery of the Regulator Movement, the Hillsborough court riots of September 1770 are surpassed only by the Battle of Alamance. The rioting that occurred during the Hillsborough District Superior Court session was contradictory to the movement's order-centered, and orderly, beginnings. The court riot suggests a change in direction, spiraling downward toward tragedy and defeat. Even so, the sensational violence that racked and wrecked the town for two days was no indication that the Regulator Movement had totally veered off its course into a sputtering trajectory of outrage. The old insistence on order and orderliness endured and was demonstrated by the conduct of the Regulator spokesmen at the Hillsborough court. It was evident again in Regulator preparations for the next superior court scheduled for the backcountry following the Hillsborough disaster.

The September 1770 riots were a reaction to the placid triumph gained by Fanning and his allies in the March 1770 session of Hillsborough District Superior Court. Their unaltered mastery may have been especially galling as a sequel to the brief autumn 1769 assembly in which Piedmont representatives had made no headway toward legislative redress of grievances. Nothing had changed.

There was no intimidating militia outside the court to chill Hillsborough's March atmosphere. It was the unrelenting business as usual that chilled it. There were legal challenges to men who were both militia officers and JPs, brought by known Regulators. In turn, there were countersuits against Regulators and suits against them for slander and for damages by debt. There are not enough surviving records to make judgments about the justice of individual cases. The extant records do indicate that the JPs won most of their suits, and the Regulators lost theirs. Fanning lost no case, either as plaintiff or defendant. The Regulator leader James Hunter lost his suit against Fanning but apparently prevailed against JP Michael Holt II. Abner Nash, Husband's expensive lawyer, won a £350 debt case against him. This and other charges were, according to James Hunter, a concerted effort by several officials to intimidate Husband from any further challenges to illegal fees and extortion. Hunter wrote to Maurice Moore the following November: "Every body believes there was a joint confederacy of extortionate officers to cow him [Husband] from bringing their extortions to light; and I believe, had such evidence been allowed, it would have appeared so to the jury. . . . Husband had [received] several messages before the court [met] that 300£ was the sum agreed on for him to pay. . . . [T]hat sum would pacify them, for it was no matter to whom it was paid, so it went among the fraternity." A number of Regulators were charged with nonpayment of fees. They were either summoned to the next district court or taken into custody.[18]

"The Consequence . . . is Wooden Shoes and Uncombed Hair": Taking the Hillsborough Court

The next court opened quietly on Saturday, September 22, 1770. Adam and Henry Whitsell (Weitzel) took the oaths naturalizing them as British subjects, a routine procedure.[19] The court reconvened on Monday morning, proceeded with two other routine matters, and then was interrupted. The superior court clerk disdained to chronicle in the minutes what happened, but an Orange County record book noted the following:

> Several persons stiling themselves Regulators assembled together in the Court Yard under the conduct of Harmon Husbands, James Hunter, Rednap Howell, William Butler, Samuel Devinney, & many others insulted some of the Gentlemen of the Bar, & in a violent manner went into the Court house, and forcibly carried out some of the attorneys, and in a cruel manner beat them. They then insisted that the

Judge should proceed to the Tryal of their Leaders, who had been indicted at a former Court, and that the Jury should be taken out of their party.

Therefore the Judge finding it impossible to proceed with honor to himself and Justice to his Country, adjourned the Court till tomorrow morning 10 o'clock, and took the advantage of the night & made his escape, and the Court adjourned to Court in Course.[20]

The judge was Associate Justice Richard Henderson. Following his nighttime departure, he went to Granville County and five days later wrote Tryon an account of the abbreviated session. The skeletal basis for all subsequent accounts, Henderson's letter is the only eyewitness description of events in the courthouse, other than the brief entry in the Orange County record book. Like the entry, Henderson's letter noted that the violence in court was directed toward lawyers, and that the Regulators' only demand was that their indicted leaders be tried—but with new juries, not the jurors whom the JPs in the county courts had assigned to the district court.

Courthouse rings relied upon control of jury selection to maintain their power. Juries were an issue, particularly in cases in which improper collection of fees was alleged. Such an allegation was part of most of the Regulator cases, whether the individual Regulators were plaintiffs or defendants. Officers who might be convicted of fiscal irregularity were not the only people endangered by these charges; so too were the sureties who had given bond for them when they took office. If a sheriff, for example, were convicted of malfeasance, his sureties stood to lose hundreds of pounds. Routinely, some of the justices of the peace served as sureties for sheriffs and other county officials. In this way, a JP had a vested interest in the personnel of trial juries when officials for whom the JP had stood as surety were involved in litigation. Regulators had fingered this problem early in the conflict. A petition headed by James Hunter was presented to Judge Henderson on the Saturday that he opened the September 1770 court. He promised to respond to it on Monday. The emphasis that Hunter and other Regulators placed on jury selection when they interrupted the court on Monday suggests that their petition concerned juries. An Orange County petition to the superior court justices that was presented three weeks after the September 1770 court linked jury selection with the other Regulator grievances; signed by 174 people, it may be the petition that Hunter gave Henderson on the opening day of court. The document, a long and rambling statement, always returned to the theme of jury selection, and included this observation:

> As for the Objection . . . that it is hard to find Jury Men but what is prejudiced to one Side or 'tother, this Objection has not the least Foundation . . . no more than if a Gang of Horse Thieves had been numerous and formidable enough to have engaged the same Attention and Concern of the Publick. . . . [T]hey and all who espouse their Cause knowingly are as to Numbers inconsiderably small only that they have the handling the Law chiefly in their own hands. . . . To sum up . . . our Petition in a few Words it is namely these *that We may obtain unprejudiced Jurys.* . . .[21]

Henderson said that the courthouse was crammed on Monday morning, "as close as one Man could stand by another." Some carried clubs, whips, or switches. Then Jeremiah Field, who lived in present-day eastern Guilford County,

> came forward and told Me he had something to say before I proceeded. . . . Upon my informing Fields that He might speak on, He proceeded to let Me know that He spoke for the whole Body of the People called Regulators, That they understood I would not try their Causes, and that their Determination was to have them tryed . . . and if I would proceed to try these Causes, it might prevent much Mischief; They also charged the Court with Injustice at the preceeding Term and objected to the Jurors appointed by the Inferior Court and said they would have them altered and others appointed in their room.

Henderson said that this went on for approximately thirty minutes, until someone "Cried Out 'Retire, Retire, and let the Court go on,' upon which most of the Regulators went out and seemed to be in Consultation in a party by themselves." Henderson then conducted court in peace for a short while. The next interruption occurred when Regulators attacked a lawyer as he was about to enter the courthouse. The lawyer escaped to a nearby building. That broke the ice for an attack on Fanning. Regulators came into the courthouse, dragged Fanning "off the Bench where He had retired for protection and Assistance," hauled him by the heels out to the street, beating him all the way. Fanning also fled to the safety of another building. Henderson feared that he himself might be attacked, but he related: "it was not long before James Hunter and some other of their Chieftons came and told Me not to be uneasy for that no Man should hurt Me *on proviso, I would set and hold Court to the end of the Term.* I took Advantage of this proposal and made no scruple at promising what was not in my

Intention to perform: for the Terms they would admit Me to hold Court on were that *no Lawyer, The Kings Attorney excepted*, should be admitted into Court, and that they would stay and see Justice impartially done." That was the extent of the Regulators' interference with the court. Henderson continued to hold court for "four or five Hours." Meanwhile, the rioting out of doors was carried out by individuals who were more interested in whipping justices of the peace than in seeing "Justice impartially done" in court. Henderson said they "severely whiped . . . Thomas Hart, Alexander Martin, Michael Holt, John Sitterell (clerk of the Crown) and many others," and that "Colo. [James] Gray, Major [Thomas] Lloyd, Mr. Francis Nash, John Cooke, Tyree Harris and sundry other persons Timously made their Escape."

Henderson's account of the following day's riots was based on what he had heard, for he slipped out of Hillsborough that night, "by a back Way, and left poor Colo. Fanning and the little Borough in a wretched Situation."[22] Henderson was told that Fanning had been chased out of town on foot and his house and wine cellar plundered and all but destroyed. Other merchants also apparently left town.

Meanwhile, back at the courthouse, a document that usually has been referred to as the "Regulator Docket" was produced. The manuscript has been interpreted as an indication that the Regulators conducted mock trials after Henderson departed. But the document does not record any such trials. The so-called Regulator Docket is either the original docket of the district court over which Henderson presided on Monday or a careful transcription, for its legal terms and abbreviations are consistently accurate. The only exceptional feature is the final column of the docket, in which comments are written. The remarks are simple commentaries on the outcome of cases. Whoever recorded these comments approved of some decisions and disliked others, suggesting that the cases were tried in the usual manner during the "four or five Hours" that Henderson was on the bench. The following quotations are typical of the comments in the remarks column of the docket:

> "The Man was sick. It tis damned roguery"
> "Has gone Hellward" [i.e. the litigant had died prior to court]
> "Right enough"
> "Executed by a damned Rogue & Bill not sufficient"
> "All Harris's are Rogues"[23]

Such entries match the mood of the petition to the superior court justices: "the consequence of not bringing these Men Subject to the Law

Frank:

*Who would have tho't Harmon, that hum drum
  old fox.
Who looks so bemeaning with his towsled locks,*

*Would have had resolution to stand to the tack;
Alas my dear Ned, our case is quite black.*

Ned:

*And who would have tho't Hunter, so seemingly
  mild,
Would have been so gigantic, mischievous and
  wild,
I tho't him a fool, and I took him for one;
Alas my dear Frank, our cause is undone.*

*Like Turkish Bashaws they bear absolute sway;
Alas my dear Frank we must all run away.*

Eli W. Caruthers thought Rednap Howell wrote this satirical "conversation"
between Francis Nash and Edmund Fanning—two enemies of the Regulators.
In 1842 he published it in a biography of David Caldwell. The song's rhythm
fits an eighteenth-century broadside tune that became enshrined in American
folk memory in the nineteenth century as "Sweet Betsey from Pike."

is wooden Shoes and uncombed Hair . . . [i.e., poverty, and] though there is a few Men who have the Gift or Art of reasoning yet every Man has a feeling and knows when He has Justice done Him as well as the most learned."[24]

Scorn for "the Convention Ratified at Salisbury"

Whatever the Regulators' intentions at the Hillsborough court, their leaders did not wish to repeat the experience. Their preparations for the March 1771 superior court for Salisbury District reflect on the events of the September riot in Hillsborough. A few hundred Rowan County men camped in the woods near Salisbury before the court was scheduled to convene. A delegation, apparently led by James Hunter, approached two of their Rowan County opponents, John Frohock and Alexander Martin, with a proposal for settling disputes over excessive fees. Frohock and Martin later told the governor that when they visited the Regulator camp on the Yadkin River, they found the Regulators "peacably disposed beyond expectation." The Regulators acknowledged that Frohock and Martin were among the causes of their

Alexander Martin (1740–1807), merchant, lawyer, governor, and senator, also served as a justice of the peace at the Hillsborough Court. In September 1770, a mob of Regulators took over the court and assaulted several lawyers, including Martin. Image provided courtesy of the North Carolina State Archives.

complaints and seemed eager to explain their intentions. They told Martin and Frohock that they:

> came with no Intention to disturb the Court or to injure the Person or property of any one, only to petition the Court for a redress of Grievances against Officers taking exorbitant Fees, and that their Arms were not for Offence, but to defend themselves if assaulted. These were the general Answers of their Chiefs, though there were several Threats and Menaces of whipping flung out by the lower Characters among them against some particular persons but not by the general voice. We told them there was not any Court, that from this late Behavior the Judges did not think it prudent to hold one at Salisbury under the direction of Whips and Clubs.[25]

The two parties proceeded to work out an agreement concerning fees and to name members of a joint arbitration board. Then the Regulators celebrated by riding through Salisbury shouting "Hurrah" and left. Frohock and Martin, pleased with themselves, wrote to Tryon of their breakthrough. Apparently Martin and Frohock were sincere. Tryon thought they were, as his icy response to their treaty with the Regulators indicated. He replied that if they were extortionists, that was their own problem, but they had no right to compromise authority. Furthermore, he already had called out the eastern militia to march against the Regulators: "This measure is not intended to impede nor has it the least reference to the agreement between you gentlemen and the Regulators, though it is expected in the execution of it more stability will be added to our government than by the issue of the convention ratified at Salisbury."[26]

Tryon's sarcasm reflected his conviction that the Piedmont was given over to rebellion and required the strongest measures a governor could legally take. With the exception of Henderson's letter, every account he had received of the September 1770 Hillsborough events had been given by people whom the Regulators had accused of corruption. The governor immediately showed these accounts to Thomas McGuire, the attorney general, and pointedly asked: is there evidence in the accounts to support a charge of treason, and can persons charged for such actions be tried in a court in eastern North Carolina? The attorney general replied that "riot" was the most serious charge for which warrants would be legal, and that "the Insurgents . . . if apprehended, must *under the present Court Law* be tried in the District where the offense was committed." Further, he wrote, "As to pointing out to your Excellency . . . the most Effectual ways to bring the offenders to condign punishment, . . . there is no process that can issue

... that would bring about that great End." He suggested that Tryon call out militia "in particular Counties" to be ready to march westward, advice that suited Tryon's identity as a professional soldier. (Prior to his governorship, Tryon had obtained the rank of lieutenant colonel in the First Regiment of Foot Guards.) The attorney general also advised the governor to convene the assembly promptly and let it change the law.[27] Both Tryon and McGuire understood that before this new law could be reviewed and disallowed in London, they could use it to intimidate the Piedmont, decimate the Regulators, and put them to flight. That is exactly what happened at the Battle of Alamance.

A Law "Altogether Unfit for Any Part of the British Empire"

The resulting session of the assembly was the first to meet in Tryon's Palace. Fanning again was a member of the lower house, the first representative of the town of Hillsborough. There were threats from Regulators to prevent his taking a seat, even if it meant burning New Bern. To protect the town, a trench was dug between the Neuse and Trent rivers, and militia from nearby counties were embodied. To dilute the strength of Regulators in massive Orange County, the legislature created new counties at its edges: Chatham, Guilford, and Wake. Similarly, Surry was carved from northern Rowan. This meant new county courts and additional militia regiments, but the representational dominance of the east was not threatened by additional backcountry members of the House.

The new law that embodied the attorney general's advice was the "Johnston Riot Act," passed in January 1771. Samuel Johnston, an Onslow County planter who would be governor and United States senator after the Revolution, introduced the measure. The law authorized prosecution for riot in any county of the colony, regardless of where the offense occurred. The felony of "riot" was defined to include failure of any group of ten or more people to disperse within an hour after being ordered to do so by a JP or any officer assisting him. The new law specifically authorized the governor to use the militia to put down the Regulators, and it declared any person resisting or fleeing arrest to be an outlaw. The statute was to be in effect for one year, beginning March 1, 1771, but its terms were retroactive to March 1, 1770, so as to include the September 1770 Hillsborough court riot. Portions of the act were in clear breach of statutory and common law, and the Privy Council later rejected them as "full of danger in its operation, and irreconcilable to the principles of the Constitution, . . . altogether unfit for any part of the British Empire."[28] The six men who would be hanged near Hillsborough following the Battle of Alamance would be tried and convicted under this law.

While the Johnston Riot Act was under consideration, the lower house expelled Herman Husband. The resolution against him cited a reputation for "libel" and said he was "unworthy of a seat in this Assembly." The House vote expressed a consensus that he was a Regulator, and that he had promoted disorder in Orange County. That evening, Tryon consulted his council for "the expediency of preventing him from returning into the back settlements to inflame anew the insurgents," and accordingly Attorney General McGuire had Husband arrested for libel and jailed in New Bern. He remained under guard for weeks until a grand jury refused to indict him. Word of Husband's expulsion and arrest, fortified by details of the Johnston Riot Act, brought out an estimated 2,200 men to Cross Creek. Their plan to march on New Bern was dropped only after Husband was released in February, after which he returned to Sandy Creek.[29]

The publication at the center of Husband's expulsion and libel charge was a letter that James Hunter wrote and Husband submitted to the *North Carolina Gazette.* It was an open letter that Hunter wrote to Maurice Moore, one of the judges of the Hillsborough District Superior Court. Hunter accused Moore of having obstructed justice in 1768 when several charges were made against Fanning for assessing illegal fees.

Thomas Sitgreaves was paid five pounds on April 22, 1771, for assisting with Herman Husband's incarceration after being expelled from the assembly. From Military Collection, War of the Regulation, (1768–1779), Box 1. Image provided courtesy of the North Carolina State Archives.

Moore was no friend to Fanning, and he showed some toleration for Regulator activities throughout 1766–1771. At the height of the 1768 tension, Moore had written tersely to Fanning, decrying the "Calumn[y]" of Moore's having been "ascribed . . . as . . . [the] Author and Encourager of the Insurrection in your County." Husband printed this note in his 1769 electoral pamphlet, *An Impartial Relation*. By this, Husband implied that Judge Moore had lost his nerve to oppose Fanning. Moore responded with an open letter in the *North Carolina Gazette* defending himself. A new turn came when Hunter, safe in Orange County, answered Moore with his own open letter in November 1770, which Husband provided to the *North Carolina Gazette*. Hunter boldly delineated events in the September 1768 Hillsborough District Superior Court from a Regulator perspective, impaling Moore and the entire court system for obstructing justice in order to protect a network of corrupt officials. Reflecting two years of frustration since Fanning's fine of one penny for extortion, Hunter fingered the North Carolina oligarchy's court puppetry:

> You say, if any person has been unjustly dealt by, let him apply to the law, and he shall be redressed. Alas! Sir, some of us have attended court, court after court, this two years and upwards, with our complaints, to your knowledge, and have almost brought ourselves to the brink of ruin by attending court, and paying the cost of malicious prosecutions; and are no nearer redress than we were at first.[30]

8

Tryon's Militia,
Regulator Confrontation,
and the Battle of Alamance

From Tryon's Palace to Alamance Creek

With authorization under the Johnston Riot Act, Tryon's campaign to extirpate the Regulator Movement was a matter of moving eastern militia westward and accepting whatever additional recruits Piedmont militia commanders could raise. In February Tryon was appointed governor of New York, a post he ardently desired. Although his good news did not reach him for several weeks, it must have lightened his spirit and also that of Fanning, who would accompany him to New York. Tryon's last acts in North Carolina were to deal dramatically with the Regulator business. He authorized a court of oyer and terminer in New Bern, and its grand jury indicted thirty-nine men on sixty-two charges. The governor planned to have them tried at a special term of superior court for Hillsborough District during the upcoming military campaign, but the justices protested in fear. One of them suggested that Tryon wished to ensure more violence against the court now that the Johnston Riot Act had been passed, and that the governor was willing "to sacrifice his judges to increase the guilt of his enemies."[1] Following the Battle of Alamance, Tryon summoned justices for a court of oyer and terminer in Hillsborough to try the indicted men and others.

On March 18, the four members of Tryon's council who were present unanimously approved his intentions for the militia force he was raising:

> [To take] a Sufficient Body of forces from several Regiments of Militia, and to March with them into the settlements of the Insurgents, and reduce them by force to an Obedience to the laws of their Country. That while the forces are in their Settlements, to support the Sheriff in the levying the Taxes due from those people; to protect the Election of a new member for Orange County in the Room of Herman Husband Expelled; and to aid the commissioners in Running the dividing line Between Orange and Guilford County's, none of which Acts of Government, can be carried into execution unless Strengthened with a Military force.[2]

Before requesting his council's concurrence in the expedition, Tryon showed them an intercepted letter that Rednap Howell had written to James Hunter a month earlier. Howell had started for New Bern during the excitement arising from Husband's arrest and imprisonment there. Stopping at Halifax, Howell wrote to Hunter.

Tryon used the inflammatory content to influence his council; today the letter between two Regulator leaders three months before the Battle of Alamance gives some insight into their intentions and expectations, as well as current rumors.

On my setting out for Hallifax my Horse fell sick which detained me some time so that on my arrival here I had certain information that Herman was at Liberty so that I found it needless to raise the Country but I am satisfied it would be easily done if Occasion required however I have animated the people here to join the Regulation on saturday come 2 weeks they are to have a meeting for that purpose if it once takes a Start here it will run into the neighbouring County's of Edgcomb, Bute and Northampton and this will undoubtedly facilitate Justice to poor Carolina, I will now inform you of such things as I have learn't since I left home. At NewBern the Gov. called a Gen. Muster of 1100 Men after treating them at yours & my Expence he tried to prevail on them to March against the Rebels but on one Mans absolute refusal he ordered him to turn out of the Ranks for a Traitor which [he] very readily did and all the Regiment followed or were following him, the Governor perceiving his mistake says Gentlemen you mistook me I only meant should they come down and destroy all your livings would you not fight them, they answer'd Yes on which he dismissed them, they then gathered in Company's of 6, 8, 10 and 12 Growling & swearing would the Mob come down they would join them. In Dobbs a Gen. Muster was called for the same purpose but only 7 Men Attended I am informed the Clerks places in the New County's [offices of clerk of court for Chatham, Guilford, Surry, and Wake] are parcell'd out among the Quality One Cooper is designed for your County [Guilford], but if you suffer any Rascal to come there may eternal Oppression be you[r] lot . . . pray you will reserve that morsel for yours to serve, for as the whole Province is in your favor, you may do as you list in that respect I understand Butler and you are to be Outlawed, despisse it, laugh at it, We hear that the Governor has sent a Proclamation to you importing as the French and Spaniards are now at War with us, it's a pity to breed a Civil war among ourselves, that the Chief Cause of the Trouble Was the counterfiet Money which the Great Men were to Blame [for], artful V——n if he could have raised the Province on us he would soon have told another Tale, however if this be true the day is ours in spite of Lucifer; I give out [announce] here, that the Regulators are determined to whip every one who goes to Law [files a suit], or will not pay his Just Debts, or will not agree to leave his cause to men where disputed [arbitration], that they [Regulators] will choose Representatives, but not send them to be put in Jail; in short to stand in defiance; and as to theives to drive them out of the Country. I leave the Plan to your consideration.

Howell's reference to prospective officers for the new county of Guilford attests to the possibility that certain individual Regulators, rather than opposing courthouse rings *per se*, wanted to replace the current rings. The prominent Husband-Fanning animosity in particular is subject to this interpretation.[3]

Despite the mustering difficulties in eastern North Carolina that Howell reported, 73 percent of the militiamen who served under Tryon in the campaign against the Regulators were from the eastern counties. They were encouraged to enlist by a bounty of forty shillings (£2) in addition to their pay of two shillings per day. The bounty was roughly equivalent to two weeks labor or 270 pounds of flour. Tryon expected families of militiamen to use the money to hire help for spring planting in the absence of their menfolk. Further, when the assembly revised the militia act in 1768 in expectation of further Regulator disturbances, it mandated a fine of £10 for refusal to serve against "invasion or insurrection." The law authorized militia officers to impose the fine "by action of Debt, in any Court of Record in this province."[4]

Even so, in the Piedmont, militia commanders found that calling out their men was a very hard sale. From "the North side of Orange County," a group who called themselves "True Friends to Government" petitioned Tryon in protest of the militia muster, saying that it was directed against the wrong people. They complained of the expense of the 1768 campaign, but declared that they would be glad for "every man to take his horse out of the Plow tho at a busy time of the year" to assist the governor if he was "realy determin'd to suppress all the disturbers of the public peace and to punish according to their deserts the Original offen[ders] in government." The petitioners attacked "the legislature of this Province" for abandoning "the Constitution of Great Britain" in defiance of North Carolina's colonial charter. Apparently referring to the Johnston Riot Act, they said the legislature "paid very little regard to that Bullwark of life the habeas Corpus." It was not a submissive petition.[5]

Tryon began the expedition with a force of approximately eight hundred militiamen from the Neuse, Tar, and Cape Fear divisions. About 270 men joined them as they moved westward. On May 9, the force of less than eleven hundred militia was camped on the Eno River near Hillsborough. They were from Beaufort, Carteret, Craven, Dobbs, Johnston, New Hanover, Onslow, Orange, and Wake counties, and about 14 percent of them were officers.[6] Meanwhile, the governor directed Gen. Hugh Waddell with some of the Cape Fear division to Salisbury, where he was to collect militia from the western counties

To his Excellency the Governor of North
Caroline — an humble address from the Inhabitants
of the North side of Orange County —

Wee his Majestys most loyal subjects
have heard of the formidable commotions in our County which is
like to be attended with great cost to the Pro
vince — And we humbly think that it is Quite
needless to disburse such large sums of money
for so mean purposes as to reward men for
destroying the tranquility of government —
after mature deliberation, it was the general
resolve of our people that if your Excellency
came up at the head of your army for every man
to take his horse out of the Plow tho at a busy
time of the year and wait on your
Excellency to know for certain whither you
are realy determind to suppress all the distur
bers of the public peace and to punish
according to their deserts the Original offenders
in government. If so we are willing and ready
to assist you all in our power to suppress
or remove any nusance that may be an obst
ion to good government — But if your

[page break]

they paid very little regard to that Bulwark
of life the habeus Corpus when they enacted
for a law. the Court of Oyer to be held at
Newborne for the tryal of riots. where the
accused Persons must attend tho living in the
most remote part of the Province — Notwithstanding the
Judges are also appointed to attend the Circuit
at the expence of government — we wait your
Excellencys answere and subscribe ourselves
                    True Friends to government

and bring them to join the main body. When Tryon wrote to Waddell on May 1, their estimated date of rendezvous was May 13 or 14. Waddell mustered 280 officers and men, largely from Anson, Mecklenburg, Rowan, and Tryon counties. At Salisbury, Waddell expected to find gunpowder from Charles Town. Its transport was supervised by Col. Moses Alexander of Mecklenburg, Tryon's commissary. But when the artillery wagons crossed the old militia training ground on Martin Phifer's land, nine young Regulator sympathizers among the Rocky River Scotch-Irish destroyed the powder. Then Regulators near the Yadkin River blocked Waddell's effort to move eastward to his rendezvous. Weakened already by desertion, Waddell's force of about four hundred men was compelled to retreat and would not reach Tryon until nearly a month after the Battle of Alamance.[7]

When Tryon learned of Waddell's setback, he moved his forces from the Eno in the direction of Salisbury. An early account of Tryon's movements, using sources no longer extant, indicated that Tryon was afraid that the Regulators would reach the Haw River before he did and compel the militia to fight its way across the river:

> Accounts were . . . received that the regulators were advancing, with the avowed intention of opposing the governor's march, and fears were entertained, they would reach Haw river soon enough to obstruct his pasage, the ford of that stream being so easily defended, that, on that contingency, the crossing of it must have cost a great deal of blood. The inhabitants of the neighborhood being generally disaffected to the government, no intelligence, that could be relied upon, was to be obtained, except that the regulators were in considerable numbers and determined to give battle.[8]

The Orange County men were placed at the front of the line of march and to the right of the larger Carteret County unit. Each flank had a small fieldpiece, and a third at the center of the rear faced outward. The militia crossed the Haw, apparently without incident, but Tryon's orders for May 13 include this entry: "His Excellency having been Informed that the Army had committed outrages on the property of the Inhabitants settled on the Road contrary to his express commands . . . He does once more strictly forbid every Person belonging to the Army from taking or disturbing the property of any Person whatever as they will on complaint receive the severest Punishment . . . besides making restitution."[9] Providers of food to the force, either in their settlements or by bringing it to camp, were reimbursed.

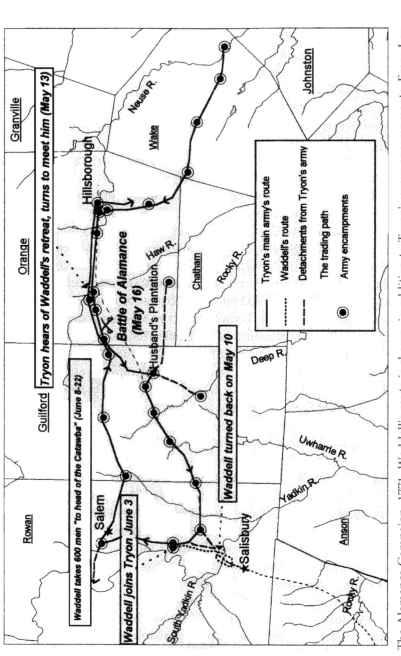

The Alamance Campaign, 1771. Waddell's route is shown, in addition to Tryon's army encampments. From Lee, *Crowds and Soldiers in Revolutionary North Carolina*, 80. Reproduced by permission of the author.

After crossing the Haw River and Great Alamance Creek, the militia made a "strong post" south of a long-used Trading Path ford of that creek near the terminus of present-day Rocky Cliff Trail.[10] Tryon knew that a large body of Regulators was gathering four to five miles to the southwest on the Trading Path, the main road to Salisbury. Orders for the days prior to the May 16 encounter include:

Monday May 13: "No Officer or Soldier to pull off his Cloaths or stir out of Camp without Orders, the Officers to . . . not suffer the Soldiers to make the least noise in case of alarm but to remain perfectly Silent after they are formed. the Signal upon an alarm to be 'Stand to your Arms' instead of Drum beating. . . . Large Fires to be lighted as soon as the Army arrives at Camp, in the front Rear and Flanks, at two hundred Yards distance from the Lines."

Tuesday May 14: "One third of the Army to remain under Arms all Night to be relieved every two hours by the like Number. . . . an Officer and fourteen Men [of the quarter guard] to take charge of all Prisoners, who are to be kept in the rear of the Line."

Wednesday May 15: "The light Horse to keep their Horses Saddled and bridled all Night, Ten of them to form a grand Guard about half a Mile from the Camp a little off the Road to Salisbury, and to have three Videtts out, one in the Center, and one on each Flank to be visited by the grand Guard and relieved every two hours. In case of alarm Notice to be immediately sent to inform the Commander in Chief, and to maintain their Ground or retire slowly to the Camp as the case may require. . . .

After Orders—The Army Marches tomorrow at seven O'Clock without Beat of Drum. One Waggon with Provision, another with Ammunition, and a third with the Surgeons Medecine Chest, to accompany the Army. . . . Note, when [on] the March the discharge of three Pieces of Cannon will be the signal to form the line of Battle, and five the signal for Action."

Thursday May 16: "The Governor Orders that all the wounded of the Army be brought to his own Tent and the greatest care taken of them, the wounded of the Rebells brought to Camp to be taken care of."

Standard security practices of the period included the commander's selection of two different passwords each day, a "parole" and a "countersign." Tryon's word choices indicate his frame of mind during those days.

May 13: Waddell/Charlotte
May 14: America/Steady
May 15: New York/Albany
May 16: Great Alamance/Victory[11]

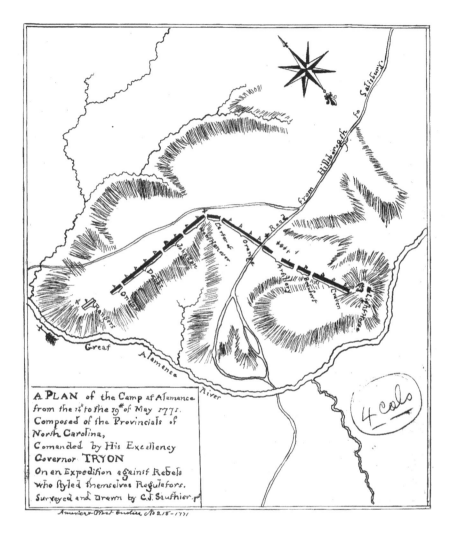

"A Plan of the Camp at Alamance from the 14th to the 19th of May 1771." This tracing was adapted from a map prepared by Claude Joseph Sauthier (1736–1802). It shows, topographically, the location and position of troops at the camp of the North Carolina militia under the command of Governor Tryon. Image provided courtesy of the North Carolina State Archives.

"The Lives of His Majesty's Subjects are Not Toys"

The battle between a body of Regulators and the North Carolina colonial militia that transpired on May 16, 1771, became a symbol in the Piedmont of popular resistance against oppression. In the late 1840s, when it was clear that there would be a new county carved out of western Orange, the name "Alamance" was suggested, reflecting strong memory of the unequal encounter. In the years immediately following the battle, its main legacy was outrage that it had occurred at all. This is the unmistakable impression held by old Regulators who were interviewed by historians Archibald DeBow Murphey and Eli Caruthers in the nineteenth century. Murphey (1777?–1832) was born during the American Revolution and expended much of his considerable energy and intellect recording interviews and collecting manuscripts to document the revolutionary era in North Carolina. A lawyer and judge, he lived at present-day Swepsonville near the place where Tryon's force crossed the Haw River. Caruthers (1793–1865) was a Presbyterian minister who for forty years served churches in Guilford County, some of whose members had been active Regulators. Caruthers's extensive interviews with survivors informed his three volumes treating the 1760s–1780s in Piedmont North Carolina.[12]

Tryon knew that he would be exposed to censure for the battle. He fortified his reports of the campaign with copies of his prebattle exchanges with the massed Regulators. Within weeks of the encounter, a member of Tryon's council attacked his actions in the press.

But if local people were outraged that a battle occurred at Alamance, what was the purpose of the Regulators' gathering and encamping under arms along the main road? They knew that the governor was on the way at the head of a large body of militia. Did the Regulators not expect a fight? There is no reason to suppose that all "Regulators" came to Alamance with the same intent. During the mounting crisis, Regulator activists and sympathizers exhibited varying patterns of behavior. Presumably, these differences reflected variant intentions and expectations and, perhaps, different moral, ethical, and civil norms within the Regulator ranks. Inasmuch as Husband was acknowledged as a formative leader of the movement, it must be significant that people "who knew him well" in 1771 told Caruthers decades later "that his Quaker principles would not let him fight." Caruthers continued: "It is believed by many that his aim was to carry his point by making such a display of numbers and by manifesting such a determined spirit that the governor would be obliged to yield." Caruthers's parishioners who had been Regulators or had known Regulators maintained an oral tradition of there having been about two thousand Regulators and sympathizers at Alamance, but no more than half of them were armed. People went in response to a call for support: "As the Regulators knew that they could not fight the governor with any hope of success without cannon, runners were sent out in every direction, on the news of [Tryon's] approach, to collect as many as possible, with a view of presenting to the governor such an array of numbers as would make him feel the necessity of a compromise."

Caruthers's informants convinced him that most people who styled themselves Regulators and gathered near the militia camp "certainly did not expect that there would be any blood shed; and therefore many who started with their guns left them by the way, either hid in hollow trees or deposited with their friends . . . because some wiseacre had said, 'if you take your guns, the governor will not treat with you.'" Others kept their guns, "although they went not expecting to fight," simply because "they were in the habit" of carrying guns "wherever they went."[13] Regulator sympathizer Joseph MacPherson told Murphey that the Regulators did not know until the day before the battle that the militia from eastern North Carolina were with Tryon. Orange County had the largest contingent of militia of any county, and gathering Regulators and spectators may have believed they would face only Piedmont units.[14]

There are several eyewitness accounts of the battle and of the hours preceding it. Those accounts agree with Tryon's on many points. All show Tryon importuning the Regulators in what appears to be a genuine effort to avoid bloodshed. Negotiation was not an option for the governor, however, at least on his essential demands. He ordered the assembled men to surrender their leaders and disperse, declaring them to be in a state of insurrection until they did so.

The last exchanges between the governor and the insurgents demonstrate their final points of view. At six o'clock in the evening of May 15, the following "Petition of us the Inhabitants of Orange County" was delivered to Tryon at his camp. It was signed "in behalf of the Country" by John Williams, Samuel Low, James Wilson, Joseph Scott, and Samuel Clark. It was not an optimistic document, the petitioners expecting that the governor would again refuse to do what the Regulators had repeatedly asked him to do.

_The Interest of a whole Province, and the Lives of his Majestys Subjects, are not Toys, or matters to be trifled with. Many of our common

People are mightily infatuated with the horrid alarms We have heard; but we still hope they have been wrong represented. The Chief Purport of this small Petition, being to know whether your Excellency will hear our Petition or no: We hope for a speedy and candid answer. In the mean time, your humble Petitioners shall remain in full hopes and Confidence of having a kind answer.

Delivered to his Excellency at Alamance Camp the 15.th Day of May 1771. — Six O'Clock in the Evening.

The last written communication the Regulators are known to have sent Tryon on the evening before the battle contained the signatures of five men signed in the name of Orange County inhabitants. It reminded Tryon that "the Lives of his Majesty's Subjects, are not Toys, or Matters to be trifled with." This excerpted copy of the original was recorded in CO 5/314 pt. 2, pages 181 and 182. Image reproduced by permission of The National Archives of the UK.

We have often been informed of late that your Excellency is determined not to lend a kind Ear to the just Complaints of the People in Regard to having roguish Officers discarded . . . and Sherifs and other Officers . . . brought to a clear . . . Account. . . . We would heartily implore your Excellency, that . . . you would . . . let us know, (by a kind answer to this Petition) whether your Excellency will lend an impartial Ear to our Petitions or no; which, if we can be assured of, We will with Joy . . . [give] a full Detail of all our Grievances, and remain in full hopes . . . of being redressed by your Excellency, in each and every [one] of them, as far as lies in your Power; which happy Change would yield such Alacrity . . . that the sad presaged Tragedy of the warlike Troops marching with Ardour to meet each other, may by the happy Conduct of our Leaders on each side be prevented. The Interest of a whole Province, and the Lives of his Majesty's Subjects, are not Toys, or Matters to be trifled with. . . . The Chief Purport of this small Petition, being to know whether your Excellency will hear our Petition or no.[15]

Reading the Riot Act

On the following morning, Tryon sent a reply "to the people now Assembled in Arms who Style themselves Regulators." He did not accept their lecturing him or their claim to have level ground for "Leaders on each side." Addressing "you who are Assembled as Regulators," he told them: "to lay down your Arms, Surrender up the outlawed Ringleaders, and Submit yourselves to the Laws of your Country, and then, rest on the lenity and Mercy of Government. By accepting these Terms in one Hour from the delivery of this Dispatch you will prevent an effusion of Blood, as you are at this time in a state of War and Rebellion against your King, your Country, and your Laws."[16] Tryon's formula was a familiar one, both in its wording and in its time limit. Used frequently in the eighteenth-century Anglo-American world, the order followed the provisions of the Riot Act of 1715, a measure that had strengthened the coercive power of JPs and other magistrates in the wake of the Jacobite rebellion of that year. In the face of insurrection, which was the usual meaning of the word "riot," local magistrates were empowered to mobilize the militia to attack the rioters. The law stipulated that one hour before such a militia action, the magistrate must read the law to the rioters as a warning to disperse, a practice formalized as "reading the Riot Act." Tryon, in his warning on the morning of May 16, was reading the riot act to the Regulators. Further, he was acting under the provisions of the Johnston Riot Act, which a member of Tryon's council, Samuel Cornell, described as "calculated exactly for these Villains."[17]

The Regulators attempted to delay the militia attack. First there was an effort toward a prisoner exchange, for the Regulators held two militiamen (John Baptista Ashe and John Walker), and the militia had seven Regulators. Second, Robert Thompson and Robert Matear were said to have gone to Tryon to assay a compromise. Tryon refused to negotiate and considered them prisoners. When Thompson proceeded to leave, he was shot. Regulators in their old age concurred that Tryon himself shot Thompson. Even council member and judge Maurice Moore, who heard of the incident secondhand, did not question that Tryon had killed Thompson. About six weeks after the battle, he addressed Tryon in an open letter to the *Virginia Gazette*: "I can freely forgive you, Sir, for killing Robert Thompson at the beginning of the battle: he was your prisoner, and was making his escape to fight against you."[18] Whether the battle was already under way when Thompson was killed is not known. On May 30 and June 6, the *Virginia Gazette* published accounts of the battle received from letters and visitors to the Williamsburg office. At least one of the newspaper's informants asserted that Tryon's shooting of Thompson started the fighting: "his Excellency was much insulted by them, particularly one Fellow, whom he shot dead on the spot, as he was approaching him; that this happened but a very short Time before the Expiration of the two Hours allowed them by the Governor, upon which the Engagement began."[19]

A third effort to avert a fight was made by the Presbyterian minister David Caldwell, who had mediated between the governor and the Regulators on previous occasions, and who rode back and forth between the two camps several times on May 15 and 16. During the morning of the sixteenth, Tryon promised Caldwell that "he would not fire on the Regulators until he had fairly tried what could be done by negotiation." Tryon apparently meant that he would not fire on the Regulators without giving them one more chance to surrender their leaders and disperse. Caruthers, in his biography of Caldwell, thought the clergyman represented the Regulators on the morning of the battle in one last attempt "to effect a compromise." Caldwell's final report to them was that Tryon would not yield. He advised those against whom there were no charges pending to "quietly return home." He told those who had laid themselves liable to "submit without further resistance,

David Caldwell (1725–1824), Presbyterian minister, educator, physician, and statesman, tried unsuccessfully to thwart any bloodshed by serving as a mediator between Governor Tryon and the Regulators. Image provided courtesy of the North Carolina State Archives.

promising that he and others would obtain for them the best terms they could. . . . [He] had got scarcely out of sight when the firing commenced."[20] Herman Husband rode away at the same time.

"This Began the Engagement, a Little before 12 O'Clock"

Eyewitness accounts differ about how the fighting started. Caruthers assumed that Francois-Xavier Martin, who wrote the pioneering account of the battle in the 1820s, got his information from people who had been in Tryon's camp. Martin said that before the attack, and following Tryon's reading of the riot act, the governor sent an adjutant to receive the two prisoners the Regulators were holding. The adjutant returned with the message that the Regulators would surrender the prisoners "within half an hour." Thereupon Tryon again sent the adjutant, who told the Regulators that the time was up and they must lay down their arms or the militia would open fire. To that demand, the renowned Regulator response of "fire and be damned" was returned. It may have been at this point that Robert Thompson decided to leave Tryon's presence, and the governor killed him.

Along with the Regulator "fire and be damned," another well-worn image of the opening of the battle is Tryon rising in his stirrups at the head of the militia, ordering " 'fire, fire on them or on me.' " Plainly, some privates were reluctant to start shooting. Martin's sources and Cornell's account, which Martin may have used, stressed the bravado of Regulators in the front line before the fighting started, baring their breasts and taunting the militia. Cornell said that some of the Regulators ran to the militia front line and "wounded some of our men wt Cutlasses" while they waited out the hour. There was also prebattle alcohol accompanied by fistfighting.[21]

The basic cause of differences between what Caruthers's informants remembered and early accounts based on militia officers' telling of events was the placement of the eyewitness. Caruthers's former Regulators and spectators missed the opening exchanges, and to them the start of the battle came out of the blue. They concurred that the militia started it. Each "company" of Regulators had its own captain and acted on its own, another factor in the varying experiences of eyewitnesses.

The question of placement heightens interest in Joseph MacPherson's recollection of the battle. MacPherson said he was close enough to Tryon's adjutant to hear him read, yet the twenty-three-year-old Quaker was present as a spectator. If indeed MacPherson did hear the aide, it may have been his delivery of Tryon's refusal to allow the Regulators thirty more minutes to release their two prisoners. MacPherson's description does not refer to Tryon's proclamation with its hour-long truce. According to Murphey's notes, MacPherson recalled:

> The governor's aid first came forward first to the party of the regulators and read a proclamation. Macpherson stood near him. The Regulators [said they] required an hour to return an answer. The messenger wheeled his horse and returned to his own friends and the firing immediately commenced on the part of Tryon with cannon. He had 4 field pieces and two 6 pounders. At the first fire the balls struck the ground at some distance in front of the Regulators and Macpherson heard one of Tryon's men say, "I told the gunmen he aimed too low."[22]

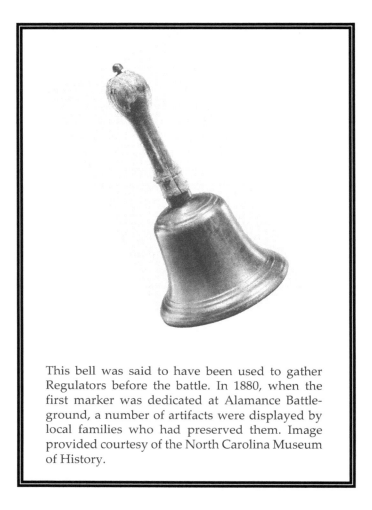

This bell was said to have been used to gather Regulators before the battle. In 1880, when the first marker was dedicated at Alamance Battleground, a number of artifacts were displayed by local families who had preserved them. Image provided courtesy of the North Carolina Museum of History.

Tryon sent at least one flag of truce. Caruthers's impression was that there were two, the first coming just prior to the start of the fighting, immediately after the shooting of Thompson. All agreed that the Regulators shot at the flag bearer(s) and that the flag(s) fell. MacPherson, describing what Caruthers considered the second flag, observed that "The meaning of this no body knew except an old Scotchman who had served in the army, and who called out, 'it's a flag, don't fire.' Three or four rifles were however fired." One early account stated that Tryon did not initially employ his cannons: "Such was the disorder of the action, that the artillery was idle for the first hour during which time the conflict was equal and well sustained. When the artillery, however, was brought to bear the contest ceased on both sides as if by magic; and the Regulators (who were without even a swivel), as they recovered from their panic, fled in dismay and confusion; and were pursued in a similar state of disorder." Caruthers was told that the battle opened with the militia discharging five cannons; this is consistent with the order of May 15 indicating that number of cannon shots as the signal for action. Hugh Williamson, writing in 1812 and generally dismissive of the Regulators, added this detail: "Colonel Fanning, who commanded the left wing, unused to action and deficient in courage, fell back with the whole of his regiment, except captain Nash with his company," while "the cannon did great execution."[23] Cornell did not flinch from saying that a cannonade opened the battle:

> His Excellency gave Orders to Colo. [James] Moore, who had the Command of the Artillery, to fire, who instantaneously obeyed the Order by firing one of the Cannon. This began the Engagement, a little before 12 o'Clock, when immediately ensued a very heavy and dreadful firing on both sides, which continued about 2½ hours. When the Rabble were so galled by the Artillery & so hard pressed by our men, they were oblijed to give way; we pursued them about a mile thro' the Wood, took a great Quantity of their provisions Baggage &c also sixty three horses, & about 30 prisoners which were brought to our Camp; the killed & wounded on our side are about 70, but of the rabble there were upwards of 300.[24]

Both Cornell and Tryon anticipated criticism for bringing heavy artillery in the first place. Tryon explained that the militia had expected to be attacked while crossing the Haw and Deep rivers, which were "wider then the reach of Musket shot." In March he had requested "two Light field pieces" and took "Six Swivel Guns half Pounders from Fort Johnston." He could not take cannon from the fort, because they were "mounted in Carriages not fit for Field Service." At the same time, he ordered six drums and four flags: "two Union, and two with Red Fields, the Union in the Upper Canton." Nothing indicates the presence at Alamance of any British soldier or army officer other than Tryon, but there had been an "Artillery Company of Sailors Raised at Wilmington" for the expedition.[25]

When the fighting began, the Regulators were massed near the road by which the militia had approached the field. Tryon described their early success and his response: "The Action was Two Hours but after about half an Hour the Enemy took to tree Fighting and much annoyed the Men who stood at the Guns which obliged Me to cease the Artillery for a short Time and advance the first Line to force the Rebels from their Covering. This succeeded and we pursued them a Mile beyond their Camp." Gideon Wright, one of Tryon's officers from Surry County, told his Moravian neighbors that Tryon's method of flushing the Regulators "from their Covering" was to burn the woods. "Many had taken refuge in the woods," Wright related. "The governor ordered the woods to be set on fire, and thus the poor helpless fellows were roasted alive. Their charred corpses were found later." This was understood to refer to wounded men. Other visitors to the Moravian settlements,

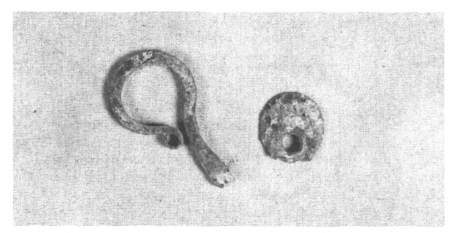

In December 2010, the Alamance Battleground Research Project, a collaborative effort between the Division of State Historic Sites and the Office of State Archaeology, recovered 120 battle-related artifacts at the site. Shown here is a screwdriver-like tool (*left*) used to remove and replace exhausted flint and the "top jaw" of a flintlock musket hammer (*right*). Since part of the hammer and the tool to change flint were found in close proximity, their placement suggests that the owner of the musket may not have been able to replace the flint and dropped both items. He may have been shot or fled from the battle with his inoperable weapon. Image provided courtesy of the two agencies mentioned above.

from both sides of the conflict, said that many Regulators fled after expending their ammunition in the first flush of fire.[26] Newspapers published descriptions of the encounter, piecing together whatever direct observations came to hand, with considerable reprinting, pruning, additions, and flourishes. One wrote:

> There was such confusion as cannot well be described. Some who had no guns attempted to rally those that had; and some gave up their guns to such as were willing to face the enemy. . . . [After] the second fire from the cannon[,] they all soon fled and left the field except James Pugh from Orange county, and three other men who had taken a stand near the cannon. They were defended by a large tree and ledge of rocks. Although half the cannon were directed against them, they could not be driven from their position, until they had killed fifteen or sixteen men who managed the cannon. Pugh fired every gun, and the other three men loaded for him; but at length they were surrounded. Pugh was taken prisoner: the others made their escape.

Caruthers printed this extract, adding: "It has been the uniform testimony of the Regulators in this section [eastern Guilford County], that they did not fly until their ammunition failed." These informants had with them only the ammunition they generally carried for hunting.[27]

Estimates of the duration of the fighting ranged from about one hour to two and one-half hours. Tryon declared a truce immediately afterwards for burial of the dead. It is conventionally repeated that nine men were killed on each side and that sixty-one militiamen were wounded, along with an unknown number of Regulators. Early sources originating on either side estimated the other's deaths in the twenties. Cornell calculated the total "killed & wounded" at about seventy militia and more than three hundred Regulators. Tryon hanged one prisoner, James Few, on the spot. Few was a threat to Fanning, and MacPherson told Murphey that Few's execution was "at the instigation of Fanning." Fanning was reported to have either raped or seduced Few's fiancée. Eighteenth-century language with respect to such matters leaves the issue unclear. If it was rape, or even perceived as such, the incident symbolized Fanning's being beyond the law. Tryon explained to his superiors that his summary execution of Few, authorized by the Johnston Riot Act, was to appease the militia who thirsted for Regulator blood.[28]

North Carolina

Return of the Army whilst Encamp'd at Herman Husbands on Sandy Creek 22 May 1771.

Detachment	Colonel	Lieut Col	Major	Captain	Lieutenant	Ensigns	adjutand	Qu Mas	Clerks	Serjeant	musicks	Drummers	Rank & file	Chaplain	Surgeon	Mates	Servants	Waggoners	Women	Horses	Waggons	Carts
Craven	1	0	0	3	3	3	1	1	3	6	0	3	144				3	0	0	10	0	3
Carteret	1	0	0	3	3	1	1	1	1	2	0	1	53				3	1	0	7	1	0
New Hanover	1	0	0	2	2	1	1	1	1	4	0	2	81				3	1	0	8	1	0
Onslow	1	0	0	2	2	2	1	0	2	2	0	1	42				2	0	0	6	0	0
Johnston	1	0	0	2	2	1	0	0	2	4	1	1	54	1	2	2	2	1	0	6	1	0
Orange	1	0	1	4	4	4	1	2	4	8	0	3	162				3	2	0	13	2	0
Beaufort	1	0	0	1	1	1	0	0	0	8	0	1	35				2	2	0	2	0	0
Dobbs	1	0	1	2	3	0	1	2	2	6	0	2	160				2	1	0	18	0	0
Artillery	1	0	0	1	0	0	0	0	0	2	0	0	110				6	6	2	28	4	1
Light-Horse	0	0	0	1	0	0	0	2	0				22				0	0	0	23	0	0
Rangers	0	0	0	1	1	1	0	0	0	2	0	0	54				0	0	0	5	0	1
	8	2	2	22	22	20	10	2	20	24	2	17	917	1	2	2	26	11	2	126	10	7
Commissary															2	2	2	12	0	48	12	1
Hospital																	2	2	0	8	2	
Wake	1	0	0	1	1	1	0	0	0	2	0	2	46				1	1	0	3	0	1
Light Infantry	0	0	0	1	1	1	1	0	0	2	1	0	54				0	4	0	12	1	0
Ammunition																	4		0	16	4	0
	9	2	2	24	24	22	11	2	22	28	3	18	1017	1	2	2	31	12	2	213	39	9

NB The Wake Detachment and the light infantry did not join the army before the 20 may.
Wm. Tryon

Tryon kept his militia in the Regulator area for several weeks after the battle to punish and intimidate the inhabitants. His offer of pardon to Regulators who would surrender their arms and take the oath of allegiance had wide exemptions, but he claimed that approximately three thousand men "submitted." Many of those who came in claimed not to have been at the battle or to have been there without arms. Tryon believed neither claim. Similarly, when the governor sent Waddell to the counties west and south of Orange, his order was "to force the Inhabitants to a submission to Government."

Tryon targeted the farms and mills along Deep River, Rocky River, Richland Creek, Cane Creek, and Sandy Creek, destroying crops, burning homes and barns, driving off livestock, and "requisitioning" flour from the mills. He boasted that his men were well supplied with flour and beef, with no necessity for buying any supplies during the campaign. There seems to have been a preference for Baptist beef and Quaker flour. Tryon regarded Quakers as sympathetic with the Regulators when not overtly active with them, and he entertained no distinction between pacifist and nonpacifist Separate Baptists. After this whirl of destruction, the governor returned to Hillsborough to conduct hangings. He had hoped to include Herman Husband, James Hunter, Rednap Howell, and William Butler in the executions, offering a reward of one hundred pounds and one thousand acres of land for the capture, dead or alive, of any of them, but to no avail. Waddell was thwarted as well in his efforts to identify and capture the men who had destroyed his ammunition dump.[29]

Tryon's harshness in the Regulator area was attacked by an anonymous contributor to the *Virginia Gazette*, who lashed out in an open letter to the governor:

> [T]here was no necessity, Sir, when the people were reduced to obedience, to ravage the country or to insult individuals.
>
> Had your Excellency nothing else in view than to enforce a submission to the laws of the Country, you might safely have disbanded the army within ten days after your victory; in that time the Chiefs of the Regulators were run away, and their deluded followers had returned to their homes. . . . But, Sir, you had farther employment for the army; you were, by an extraordinary bustle in administering oaths, and disarming the Country, to give a serious appearance of rebellion to the outrage of a Mob; you were to aggravate the importance of your own services by changing a general dislike of your administration into disaffection to his Majesty's person and government, and the

riotous conduct that dislike had occasioned into premeditated rebellion. . . .

From the 16th of May to the 16th of June, you were busied in securing the allegiance of rioters, and levying contributions of beef and flour. You occasionally amused yourself with burning a few houses, treading down corn, insulting the suspected, and holding courts-martial. These Courts took cognizance of civil as well as military offences, and even extended their jurisdiction to ill breeding and want of good manners.[30]

9

Regulators as Victims:
Repercussions of the Militia Attack

"Those Unhappy, Ill-fated Victims"

On June 15, a special court at Hillsborough tried fourteen prisoners who had been seized under the provisions of the five-month-old Johnston Riot Act, convicted twelve, and sentenced them to death. At the scheduled execution four days later, Tryon "postponed" the execution of half of them "until the king's pleasure" could be known, the protocol for requesting pardons. In London, there was no hesitation in granting them. The fortunate men were James Stewart, James Emmerson, William Brown, Forester Mercer, James Copeland, and Hermon Cox. The other six men, including James Pugh, Robert Messer, Benjamin Merrill, and Robert Matear, were hanged near Hillsborough on June 19, 1771. Tryon staged the executions with such attention to detail that a newspaper writer observed that the governor brought to mind "an undertaker at a funeral." (Six years later, a New York observer would remark that Tryon "never let slip any opportunity of appearing consequential.")[1] The hangings were Tryon's final

Six Regulators were hanged near Hillsborough on June 19, 1771. This memorial plaque, located at Alamance Battleground, depicts the hanging of James Pugh of Randolph County. Image provided courtesy of the Alamance Battleground State Historic Site.

acts of drama in North Carolina. His Regulator campaign enabled the forty-two-year-old governor to leave the colony in a column of smoke, taking Fanning with him. They sailed for New York eleven days after the Hillsborough executions. The new North Carolina governor, Josiah Martin, delayed his own departure from New York in order to confer with Tryon, who granted the thirty-four-year-old first-time governor only a cursory interview. Martin quickly perceived that Tryon's departure from the deeply divided colony had included an element of face saving, both for Tryon and his superiors in London. Martin would seize his opportunity to calm the politics of his new domain.[2]

Meanwhile, some sense of how news of the encounter spread was recorded by a Moravian diarist at Bethabara, who summarized what was said by Regulators who stopped there after the battle. The town first learned of the battle the day after, when two men arrived from Salisbury with "the unpleasant news that there had been a hot skirmish between the Governor's troops and the Regulators." Then, on May 18:

> Late last evening two Regulators came to our Tavern, and today others came at intervals. Some had been in the skirmish, others had been near by, and had been told of it. The most important point seemed to be that the terrible cannonading of the Governor's troops had badly frightened the Regulators, who had thrown down their arms and run, even leaving the hats and coats which they had taken off before the engagement.

On May 19 someone from Tryon's camp arrived and also "reported that the Regulators had fled after the first fire from the cannon." Two days later, a Regulator and "friend" told a Bethabara resident that "they had stood the first two rounds" from the militia, "during which many of their people had fled, and then they also had retired some distance; at a spring they had seen many hats and guns lying, but only three men, who were nearly dead. One, the lower part of whose body was shot away, begged him for God's sake to give him a drink, and he had brought him water in his hat. Another had part of his skull shot away." The diarist's comments indicated that after the dead and wounded were cleared away, the curious continued to visit the battle site. Being on the Trading Path, it was easily accessible. The Regulators, as defenders of the spot where they had spent the night, had purposely tried to keep the militia on or beside the road, where they were clear targets. The Regulator dead were buried at the site, and their grave mounds were still visible in 1849, when historian Benson Lossing sketched the battleground. Local lore also recorded that hunters salvaged "an incredible number of balls" that had lodged in trees during the fight, "which the hunters have since picked out, and

This view is from the north side of the Salisbury Road. On the right is the cavalry, with Tryon mounted on a white horse. On the left are the trees, rocks, fences, and hedges from behind which the Regulators fired at the militia. In the center of the field are a few Regulators who had fallen in battle. Image from William Edward Fitch, *Some Neglected History of North Carolina; Being an Account of the Revolution of the Regulators and of the Battle of Alamance, the First Battle of the American Revolution* (New York and Washington: Neale Publishing Co., 1905), facing page 218.

therewith have killed more deer and turkies than they killed of their antagonists."

An "unknown man," whom the Moravians implied was Husband, came to Bethabara on May 19. He wanted the local doctor to go to the home of James Hunter, a few miles from the battle site, where there were about twenty wounded Regulators who needed attention, and "the surgeon who was with them did not have the necessary instruments."[3] In addition, Tryon's surgeons treated wounded Regulators and militia in the governor's camp and at the home of Michael Holt II, the militia captain and justice of the peace who lived nearby.

Holt had been a subject of Regulator ire in his capacity of JP and land agent for McCulloh. Regulators had whipped him in Hillsborough, and as a captain in the militia at the time of the battle, he was ranged against them. Yet his condemnation of the governor's actions

North Carolina militiamen who died during or shortly after the Battle of Alamance were buried with military honors at the site of Tryon's camp shown here. Present-day image provided courtesy of the author.

was unmistakable when he was interviewed by a visitor during the interval between the Regulator upheaval and the outbreak of the American Revolution. The visitor published his travel account a few years after the Revolutionary War, when British readers were eager for information about America. The interview is remarkable for Holt's candid attitude concerning the Regulators. Evidently, Holt traced the Regulator Movement from its causes through its tragic climax. Regrettably, the visitor, John Ferdinand Dalziel Smyth, did not record exactly what Holt said. Nevertheless, Smyth's account plainly indicates that Holt thought the Regulators had been badly mishandled. Moreover, Holt convinced his visitor that the Regulators in general had acted responsibly and well within their political and legal rights. Holt blamed others for the insurrection. Smyth prudently refrained from naming the person or persons whom Holt had fingered as responsible for the Regulator troubles and the Alamance tragedy. At a minimum, Holt must have blamed Tryon and Fanning. Some of Tryon's contemporaries who were more forthright than Smyth agreed that the governor's chief characteristic, vanity, made him easy to manipulate.[4] Smyth spent an entire day and two nights with Holt, but the only topic of conversation that he recorded was the earful Holt gave him about Regulator issues. Even with its tantalizing omissions, Smyth's account demonstrates the importance of Regulator concerns in the area during the early 1770s.

Smyth was an Englishman who had moved to Maryland several years earlier and established a plantation. His stop at Holt's occurred on a trip from Salem to Hillsborough. Smyth wrote of his visit:

> After a long, but pleasant, ride down the eastern side of the Allamance Creek, I arrived at night at the house of a Mr. Michael Holt, a Dutchman, whose plantation was adjoining the creek, near the place where it enters the Haw River. . . . Mr. Holt, although a High Dutchman, or rather the son of Dutch or German parents, for he himself was born in America, is a very loyal subject, and entertained me with great hospitality. He is a magistrate, possesses a considerable property, and has a large share of good sense and sound judgment, but without the least improvement from education, or the embellishment of any kind of polish, even in his exterior.
>
> In the course of a long interesting conversation, with which he entertained me, and really afforded me a great deal of satisfaction and information by his sensible, blunt, and shrewd remarks on every subject occasionally, he explained the whole grounds, proceedings, and termination of that most unfortunate and much to be lamented affair of the Regulators, which made so great a noise in North Carolina, their scene of action, as well as in all America besides.
>
> But to avoid throwing reflections and censure, however just or otherwise, *on characters of persons still in existence, out of whose power it is now ever to atone for their former, perhaps ill-timed, unfortunate, and mistaken conduct*, I shall suffer it to rest in oblivion, only observing that those unhappy, ill-fated victims, the Regulators of North Carolina, were, and still are among the worthiest, steadiest, and most respectable friends to British government and real constitutional freedom. . . .[5]

The Road beyond Alamance

John Dalziel Smyth and Michael Holt II met again a few years later, in far less pleasant circumstances than the time Smyth spent on the Alamance. At the start of the Revolution, both men were Loyalists, and they were imprisoned together for a while in Philadelphia. They talked again, with Smyth remarking, "I . . . had the melancholy, mortifying satisfaction of seeing and conversing with my old friendly, hospitable

Dutchman once more." Their being together again in this way illustrates a peculiar conundrum in the Regulator areas at the outbreak of the Revolution: the relationship between Regulator activity during 1765–1771 and the choice of allegiance, either to the Crown or to the emerging state government, in the years following 1775.

Holt was imprisoned along with other Loyalists (also known as Tories) whom revolutionaries had captured during and after the Battle of Moores Creek Bridge, North Carolina's first Revolutionary War battle, in February 1776. The captured leaders, and others who were killed or escaped, had recruited Loyalists in the previous weeks, acting under commissions from Gov. Josiah Martin. The governor had thought that former Regulators and the upper Cape Fear Valley Highland Scots would support his royal authority against the initiatives of revolutionaries. In August 1774 the lower house of the assembly had declared itself a provincial congress and proceeded to conduct business without the governor. This body continued to be controlled by the easterners whose policies and political networks had provoked the Regulator Movement. Like most of the Scottish High-landers who had arrived in America in recent years, the former Regulators appeared to be natural opponents of the revolutionaries, and the governor acted on the expectation that both groups wanted protection from those who were moving the colony in a revolutionary direction. When Martin called on those loyal to the Crown to assemble at Cross Creek in February 1776, far more Scottish Highlanders than former Regulators reached the rendezvous area, about fifteen hundred compared with about two hundred. The backcountry men had farther to go, and most of their companies were stopped by a gauntlet of Patriot attacks as they rode eastward.

Holt told Smyth, while they were prisoners in Philadelphia, that "almost all the Chiefs of the former Regulators" had raised men for the Loyalist effort. Among the Regulator leaders who reached Moores Creek Bridge with their recruits from the Orange-Chatham-Guilford area were James Hunter, John Pyle, John Pyle Jr., Jeremiah Field, and three other "persons named Field." Most of the captured recruiters were imprisoned at Halifax following the battle, but Hunter was kept in Bute County. He took the oath of allegiance to the state in September 1776, but in February 1781, when the British army commanded by Charles Lord Cornwallis marched through the backcountry, Hunter united with the Pyles and other Loyalists in an effort to join Cornwallis's forces at Hillsborough.[6]

While jailed in Philadelphia in 1776, Holt sent apologies to his fellow Orange County JPs on the county's committee of safety, promising not to oppose the provincial congress in the future, and they got the state committee of safety to intervene for his release. Or as Smyth, who remained a Loyalist longer, put it, Holt "contrived to make interest with the Congress to permit him to return again to his family and home." Smyth made no criticism of Holt's course.

Jeremiah Field was imprisoned at Frederick Town, Maryland. The Guilford County Committee of Safety intervened in his behalf at the same time its counterpart in Orange co-opted Holt for the revolutionary cause. Joseph, Robert, John Jr., and William Field, on the other hand, remained active Loyalists.[7] Northern Chatham County resident Eli Branson was also imprisoned in Philadelphia with Holt. Branson had been a Quaker until he became an active Regulator. Unlike Holt and Jeremiah Field, Branson spurned the revolutionaries. He would command a Loyalist provincial company throughout the war. Branson died, as he said in his 1796 will, as "One of his majesty's Subjects . . . now resident in the state of South Carolina."[8]

Moreover, Reuben Searcy and George Sims, framers of the Granville County documents that are regarded as forerunners of Regulator statements, followed different paths during the revolutionary years. There is no indication that either of them participated in the Regulator Movement. Searcy married into the numerous and influential family of Richard Henderson (later a superior court judge) in 1760 and obtained Granville District grants shortly before the land office closed the following year; he had filed for the grants several years prior to his 1759 petition to the county court. Searcy enjoyed local office in the 1760s, serving briefly as sheriff and tax collector and then as clerk of court from 1771 to 1783. In the early 1770s, he and his brothers joined his in-laws and other investors in forming the Transylvania Company. Led by Richard Henderson, the company negotiated with Cherokees for land in present-day Kentucky and Tennessee. Although North Carolina and Virginia refused to acknowledge the purchases, the speculators were rewarded for their settlement efforts with state grants in the area. Searcy also purchased military grants there and moved to his western lands around 1790.[9]

Sims kept a lower but active profile. He was living in northern Orange County when Caswell County was created from it in 1777, and when the state land office opened, he entered a claim for the land on which he lived along Country Line Creek. He was named constable at the first county court and served as deputy sheriff, road juror, and tax assessor for his locale in 1778–1779. However, soon after the British took Charleston and sent recruiters into the backcountry, Sims left home to join them, and his name does not again appear in Caswell County records until September 1782. Sims joined the loyal militia in western South Carolina, served under Patrick Ferguson, and continued in service after the British defeat at Kings Mountain. In February 1781 he and his brother joined the Royal North Carolina Regiment at Hillsborough. Sims became a corporal and completed his service in June 1782 in the Charleston area. He was back in Caswell County three months later. What his neighbors knew of his war service is not known, but he successfully completed the paperwork for the land he had entered in 1778 and 1779, receiving three grants totaling more than one thousand acres, where he died in 1809.[10]

The question of Regulator allegiance at the start of the Revolution involved public opinion in the Piedmont. There is no assumption that all people living in the backcountry were Regulators or sympathized with them; evidence of social tension during the Regulator upheavals suggests the contrary. On the other hand, some broad identification with the Regulator cause may be assumed. It would also appear that after May 1771, outrage over the one-sided bloodshed at Alamance enhanced popular sympathy with issues the Regulators had raised. Coming from one who had opposed the Regulators, Holt's recruiting for the Crown in 1776—alongside "the chiefs of the former regulators"—may have reflected the backcountry's widespread sympathy with the Regulator cause after 1771.

The men who started and shaped the Revolution in North Carolina were the oligarchs whom the Regulators had opposed, who had ignored Regulator petitions in the legislature, who had expelled Husband from the lower house, and who had led the militia into the Piedmont to put down the Regulators. Similarly, the revolutionaries' initial allies in the Piedmont had been their allies as suppressors and targets of the Regulators, with the conspicuous exceptions of Fanning, who left North Carolina for good in 1771, and Frohock, who died in 1772. The connections between local and eastern Regulator targets in the minds of people who had been affected by the Regulator Movement presented a challenge for the revolutionary leaders. John Adams noted that "the back part of North Carolina" resisted the Revolution because of "hatred" that former Regulators held for "their fellow-citizens." Husband himself supported the Revolution, but he shunned the North Carolina revolutionaries. A student of politics and society in North Carolina before the Revolution concluded that "in few other colonies did revolutionaries go to war with so little popular support."[11]

10

Politics at Work
before the Revolution

Courting the Regulators: "The Country is as Much Master Now as Ever"

Even before Moores Creek Bridge, Governor Martin's challengers had begun to court former Regulators in response to the new governor's good relationship with them. In seeking to attract former Regulators, the eastern politicians who shaped the Revolution in North Carolina incorporated some Piedmont concerns into their political agenda at its crucial beginnings. In this way, the approach of the Revolution and the lingering tensions that had exploded during the Regulator years increased the political importance of the backcountry.

The eastern legislators who challenged the new governor's authority were advantaged by the strength, initiative, and political experience they had attained in facing down the Regulators with Tryon. Martin, on the other hand, on his arrival saw an opportunity to advance his career by bringing peace and reconciliation to the Piedmont. Accordingly, he visited Hillsborough and Salisbury soon after reaching North Carolina and met Regulator leaders on their own ground. He won the praise and respect of their rank and file in the Orange-Chatham-Guilford area. In November 1772 James Hunter wrote to William Butler, advising him that it was safe to come home from Fincastle County, Virginia. "Things have taken a mighty turn," Hunter said:

> Our new governor has been up with us and given us every satisfaction we could expect of him and has had our public tax settled and has found our gentry behind in . . . the public tax, £66,443-9 shillings besides the parish and county tax, and I think our officers hate him as bad as we hated Tryon only they don't speak so free. He has turned . . . out every officer that any complaint has been supported against. In short I think he has determined to purge the country of them.

Hunter described two conferences the outlawed Regulator leaders had with Martin: "We petitioned him as soon as he came, and when he received our petition he came up amongst us and sent for all the outlawed men to meet him at Wm. Fields." At Fields's home in south-eastern Guilford County, Martin counseled them on the pardoning process, and they soon followed it with success. "He came to see us the second time," Hunter said, "and advised for fear of ill-designing fellows to go to Hillsboro and enter into recognizance till the assembly met, which eleven of us did." The outcome, according to Hunter, was that "the country is as much master now as ever." Elated, Hunter continued his account of events in the Regulator country in the fall of 1772:

> Our governor has got Fanning to forgive the pulling down of his house and he has published it in print advertisements all over the country. The governor has published a statement of the public accounts at every church and court house in the province for seventeen years back in print, with the sheriffs' names and the sum they have in hand for each year, and a great many of their extortionate actions—a thing we never expected—to the great grief and shame of our gentry. . . . I have so much to tell you that I could not write it in two days. The outlawed all live on their places again and I think as free from want as ever. I came home in ten months after the battle, entered a piece of vacant land adjoining my old place and rented out my old place.[1]

The Regulators and other backcountry men with whom Martin talked unloaded their grievances concerning land. One of the governor's first proposals to the government in London was that the Crown purchase the Granville District so that the land office could be reopened and the ungranted land administered in the routine manner. In November 1771, Martin wrote to the secretary of state for the colonies, the Earl of Hillsborough:

> The proprietary right of the Earl Granville, in the heart of this province, I learn from all hands My Lord, to be a very principal cause of the discontents that have so long prevailed. . . . the superior excellence of the soil in his District . . . invites emigrants from all the northern Colonies, who many of them bring money to take up Lands, but [the heirs of] Lord Granville having empowered no person here to give them titles, they set themselves down where they please, and because they cannot establish freeholds, under these circumstances; they refuse to pay taxes, which has been and still is, a source of perpetual discord and uneasiness.[2]

Courting the Regulators: The Provincial Congress in the Piedmont

With a Regulator of Hunter's status singing the new governor's praises in late 1772, the men who contested Martin for the political high ground in 1775 had work to do in the backcountry. Accordingly, they brought the third "provincial congress," which had developed out of the lower house of the colonial assembly in two previous sessions, to Hillsborough for its August 21–September 10, 1775, session. Thomas Hart and Francis Nash continued to represent Orange County, and Samuel Johnston, author of the Johnston Riot Act, was elected Speaker. Even so, the old order was joined by new men.[3] The Orange-Granville Presbyterian minister Henry Pattillo participated in the congress, though apparently not as a member. In particular, he was requested to counsel former Regulators to be prepared to break their oaths to the Crown. Without using the word "Regulator," the provincial congress instructed Pattillo and a committee of twelve to "confer with such of the Inhabitants . . . who entertain any religious or political Scruples, with respect to associating in the common Cause of America, to remove any ill impressions." Similarly, a committee was to "confer with the Gentlemen who have lately arrived [in the upper Cape Fear Valley] from the highlands in Scotland." The provincial congress made some moves toward military preparation, most notably by planning for two regiments of Continental Line and by reorganizing the militia. They rejected Benjamin Franklin's suggestion for a colonial confederation, however, on the grounds that it would impede reconciliation with the British government.

In these circumstances, some statement of principle seemed appropriate. The third provincial congress imposed an oath on its members and stipulated that delegates to the next provincial congress must take it as well. The oath professed "Allegiance to the King" and acknowledged "the Constitutional executive power of Government." The oath did not use the word "swear" or invoke the deity:

> We do absolutely believe that neither the Parliament of Great Britain, nor any Member or Constituent Branch thereof, have a right to impose Taxes upon these Colonies to regulate the internal police thereof; and that all attempts . . . to establish and exercise such Claims . . . ought to be resisted . . . and that the people of this province, singly and collectively, are bound by the Acts and resolutions of the Continental and Provincial Congresses.[4]

Money had to be found as some actions taken by the third provincial congress involved expenditures. It issued a new paper currency to replace the "proclamation money" of former legislatures. The new money floated on the expectation of collecting all back taxes, as well as a poll tax to begin in 1777 and run for nine years. Old script was supposed to be exchanged for new and then burned. The legislature expected this action to be controversial, particularly in the backcountry, and fortified it with stiff enforcement provisions. A skeptical Wachovia Moravian observed after a year of the "new proclamation" currency:

One is told on good authority that those who were to burn [the old money] gave some of it out again. Many thousands of pounds were not brought in, and circulated at face value among the people who hoped the King would yet regain control, or who doubted whether the State could maintain itself. There is much of this old Proc. still in existence, which will never be redeemed.[5]

If the currency act could be expected to arouse hostility in the Piedmont, it was accompanied by another measure that was sure to be appreciated there. The provincial congress specified that voters for its successor would include landholders in the Granville District who had no title, but who had made improvements on the land they occupied. They would be qualified to vote, "in like manner as Freeholders in the other counties." Although temporary, this measure showed that revolutionaries could reach out to people whose grievances the Regulators had articulated.

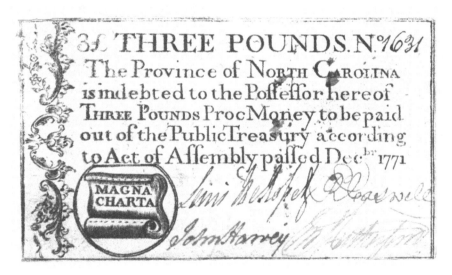

This three-pound note is part of the "Cornell Hoard," proclamation money collected by Samuel Cornell (1730–1781), a transplanted New Yorker who became a wealthy merchant in New Bern. He helped finance the construction of Tryon Palace *and* the Battle of Alamance using proclamation money. Image provided courtesy of an anonymous gift to The Colonial Williamsburg Foundation, Williamsburg, Va.

Orange County's October 1776 Election

The subsequent fourth provincial congress was unable to hammer out a state constitution and called a special election for a fifth provincial congress, which was to serve as a constitutional convention. For the first time, counties would have equal representation: the thirty-six counties would send five members each and nine towns one representative apiece. Free men who headed households and had resided in the state for a minimum of six months could vote for this particular body.

The October 1776 election for the fifth and final provincial congress was especially spirited in Orange County. On October 15, voters elected James Saunders, William Moore, John McCabe, John Atkinson, and John Pine. William Johnston narrowly won the Hillsborough seat. But when these gentlemen presented themselves at the convention in Halifax, they faced a call for a scrutiny of all six seats. The committee on elections upheld the result and the house concurred, but a few days later the house reversed itself and called for a new election.

The committee's report described the voting in Orange, drawing on testimony from "sundry Persons," who presumably had traveled to Halifax from Orange County. The problem was not fraud or violence but "Tumult" caused by overcrowding in the courthouse on the single day set aside for voting. Witnesses said "that the People pressed into the house in such numbers to vote, that the Clerks could not write down their names." Three times, the candidates ordered the polling suspended because of the "tumultuous and disorderly manner." Finally, "an hour and a half before sunset," the candidates and clerks left, "by reason of the Tumult," and did not return again until sunset, when they closed the poll. Witnesses estimated that those who voted were fewer than one-quarter of the "Inhabitants," by which they seemed to mean men who had come to vote.

John Butler was one of the unsuccessful candidates in this election. Colonel and commanding officer of the southern battalion of Orange County militia, Butler discussed the recent election at the next general muster. One supposes it to have been a general topic of conversation among the men gathered. Butler pointedly "recommended . . . that it was incumbent on all of them that were dissatisfied with the former Election, to immediately petition" the fifth provincial congress for a new election. The ensuing petition was presented on the first working

Thomas Burke (1744–1783) was a colonial official and governor. He served as a delegate from Orange County in all but the first of the five provincial congresses. Though a newcomer to the area, he represented Orange County in the House of Commons in 1777 and 1778 and served briefly as governor in 1781–1782. Image provided courtesy of the North Carolina State Archives.

day of the session and resulted in the scrutiny. When the committee upheld the October election, its grounds were that there appeared to be no "violence or bodily injury offered to any person whatever, but that the Tumult and disorderly Behaviour was occasioned by People over anxious to get into the Court-house to vote." The congress accepted the report and validated the election. Five days later, however, it reconsidered the committee's report, rescinded the former order, and scheduled a new election for December 10. The congress appointed a commission of five men, stipulating that any two of them could conduct the election, and that they could use up to three days for voting if necessary. In the new contest, only one candidate elected in October was returned: John McCabe. Others elected on December 10 were John Butler, Thomas Burke, Nathaniel Rochester, and Alexander Mebane Jr.[6] Butler, as sheriff briefly in 1770, had testified against some Regulator activities, but he seems to have avoided the ire of the movement. Regulator leader William Butler was his brother. A Regulator petition had named John Butler and James Watson as those

Nathaniel Rochester (1752–1831), merchant, land developer, and colonial official, represented Orange County in the fourth provincial congress. He had been a merchant in Hillsborough since 1768 and would later serve as clerk of court for Orange County. Image provided courtesy of the North Carolina State Archives.

rare officials who observed the table of fees. Butler was an early proponent of the revolutionary cause. In February 1776 he had commanded the militia unit from the western part of the Hawfields (the area between the Haw and Eno rivers) that went out against Highlanders and former Regulators. Alexander Mebane Jr. was the son of the first sheriff of colonial Orange County. From the 1750s, members of the Mebane family had operated public houses in the Hawfields, important centers for communication and petitioning during the Regulator years. Thomas Burke, by contrast, was a newcomer to Orange County. He had moved to Hillsborough in 1772 from Tidewater Virginia, where his legal career had focused on debt collection for merchants. Nathaniel Rochester had been a merchant in Hillsborough since 1768. Burke and Rochester had been members of the third provincial congress, at which revolutionaries had initiated overtures to former Regulators.

By the time the new Orange and Hillsborough members arrived at Halifax, the constitution had been written. Even so, a set of

"Instructions to the Delegates from Orange" on the subject of a constitution reached the fifth provincial congress. As it is entirely in Burke's handwriting, one associates it with the second set of members. The "Instructions," or parts of it, may have been used in the electoral campaigns, or at least the first campaign; its wording anticipates the opening of the legislature. The Orange document is nearly identical to one from Mecklenburg County. Both stressed popular sovereignty and particularly admonished against an established church. Also, they advocated three separate branches of government, including a bicameral legislature elected by ballot. Both called for the constitution to be voted on in all the counties. Except for this last consideration, the constitution that was put into effect by the fifth provincial congress met the broad goals of its delegates from Orange and Mecklenburg counties.[7]

11

Land Ownership and Local Power

If Any Man Would . . . Take Away His Land
He Would Shoot Him

In the 1760s, stresses related to landholding and, in particular, corruption surrounding the processes of establishing legal ownership of land had been integral to Regulator complaints. Landholding issues remained unresolved in the next decade. As the revolutionary conflict progressed, land became the ultimate issue in which revolutionary leaders could wield power. Land was inseparable from the political framework that ensured or threatened the landholder's legal title.

In 1778 the legislature set up a land entry process by which a person could "enter," or register a claim to purchase, a tract of land from the state. The price of the land was fifty shillings per one hundred acres, and there were standard fees established for the entry taker and the surveyors. A claimant could reserve up to 640 acres for purchase in this way. If any of the surrounding land had not been surveyed, the limit was one thousand acres, and the price per acre doubled beyond 640 acres. This was the long-standing Crown practice, but it had not been used in the Piedmont during the years marked by Regulator activities. The political potential of the state land-granting process was enormous. An oath of allegiance to the state was required for entering land. Like using the new currency, relying upon the authority of the state government to register a claim on a tract of land was an investment of support for that government, but with far greater rewards for the investor if the colonies won their bid for independence. For farmers of the Granville District who already held clear title to their land, the logic of revolution was less compelling.

There was a rush to enter land claims in the Piedmont. Five hundred and thirty-eight entries that eventually resulted in grants were made in Orange County alone in 1778, the year the process was instituted. June, the first month of activity, saw 119 entries there. Likewise, in Guilford County nearly one hundred entries were filed in the month of December 1778. There was similar demand in Chatham County. In 1779, 375 land entries in Orange County continued the trend.[1]

The new land entries raised new questions about land security, however. A person in possession of a piece of land, particularly if he had a deed, could consider himself threatened by the land entry process. A glimpse of such disgruntlement can be seen in the statements that James Dickey attributed to Elijah Lyon in February

Deposition of James Dickey, March 12, 1778, giving evidence that Elijah Lyon had made threatening statements against the new land entry process. From Salisbury District Superior Court Civil Action Papers, 1754–1807. Image provided courtesy of the North Carolina State Archives.

1778, when Dickey gave evidence against Lyon. Spending the night in a Rowan County public house soon after the land law had passed, Dickey overheard Lyon speaking too freely over his drink. Dickey later quoted Lyon as declaring that "our Assembly had no Right to open ye Land Office & that if any man would Molest him or Take away his Land he would shoot him." Dickey reminded Lyon that he did not have the power to disobey the legislature. Lyon further aroused Dickey's concern when he replied that he could recruit a company of men in twenty-four hours. Lyon concluded his dangerous display of opinion by attacking the state currency; he said, "it was Damnd Liberty to take our money when they had no Right & there would be other Laws in ye Land before long." The next morning, a sober and fearful Lyon went upstairs to Dickey's room and asked him to disregard his unguarded speech. Dickey refused and promptly swore a warrant for Lyon's arrest.[2]

If Lyon could convince a jury of prior possession of and improvement to his land, there was legal recourse by which he could protect himself against a land entry, just as there had been under the Crown.

Many land entries were challenged by people who claimed to have a previous right to the land. To defend a pre-existing claim, one filed a caveat against the entry. Some people said they had bought the land from the Granville land office, and others claimed a right by prior possession. The volume of caveats filed against land entries reveals that many of the new entries were contested. Court records indicate also that land entries and caveats were accompanied by charges of trespass, forcible entry, and assault. Such circumstances suggest that people were fighting over land well before they stood in military formation against either each other or outsiders.[3] The state land act provided for settlement of such disputes. Juries selected by the sheriff were to hear both claimants, under the authority of the justices of the county court. In land disputes, sheriffs and JPs still mattered.

The Continuity of County Officials

The sheriff and the justices of the peace who selected him were still powerful men, as they had been during the colonial period. In the Regulator areas, they were the same men as well, with a few marked exceptions. The 1776 state constitution retained the practice of county justices of the peace selecting the sheriff. Justices of the peace continued to be appointed by the governor on the advice of the county's members of the lower house of the assembly (now called the House of Commons). The state constitution forbade multiple office-holding in general but made an exception for JPs and militia officers, who long had held more than one position. Thus local authority continued to facilitate courthouse rings connected with the legislature, as it had before and during the Regulator years. Ultimately, the makeup of the county officers and JPs remained in the hands of the county's representatives in the lower house of the General Assembly.

The new constitution made the General Assembly more powerful than the governor. The assembly annually elected the governor and all other executive officers. The legislature itself, however, was subject to annual elections for members of both the House and the Senate. Only men who owned at least fifty acres could vote for state senators, but all freemen who held land or paid public taxes could vote for members of the House. Race was not yet a criterion. The General Assembly, exposed to voter approval every year, stood between the county officers and the state executive and controlled both.

State of North Carolina Lincoln County
A Return of Men Summoned by order of the Commitioners of Confiscated property to Shew Cause Why Their Estates Shall not be Confiscated agreeable to an Act of assembly
Fredrick Sumey
Peter Peker
Thomas Hoover
Jacob Laots
William Keenor
Barney Snayder
Conrod Heckelman
John Hekelman
Jacob Heckelman
John Bumgarner
Andrew Craisley
John Keenar
Robert Blackburn
Antony Holman
Henry Crase
John Crase
Christain Cras
George Havner
Danial Hungory
[illegible]

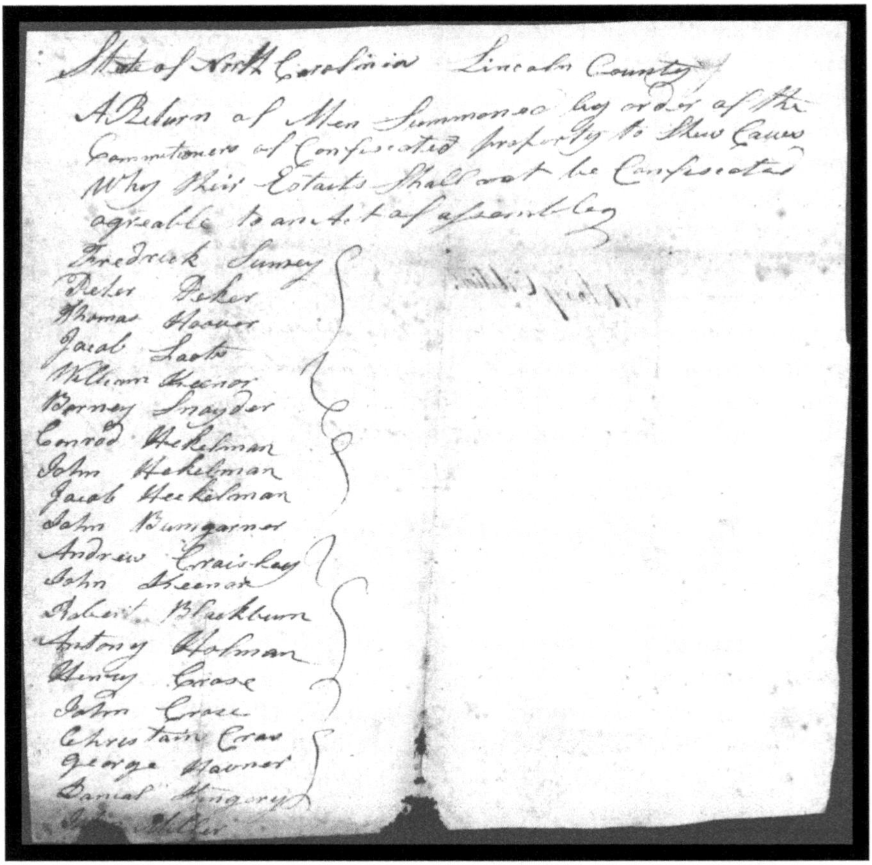

"A tory Citation," shown here, is a list of men summoned by order of the Commissioners of Confiscated Property to show just cause why their estates should not be confiscated according to an act of the General Assembly. From Lincoln County Miscellaneous Papers, Agreements—Coroner's Inquests, 1764–1923, "Confiscation of Property from Tory Sympathizers, 1782." Image provided courtesy of the North Carolina State Archives.

Countywide alliances of speculators and revolutionaries in the Piedmont used their land-granting apparatus to build support for the Revolution and to enlarge their own holdings during and after the war. Land confiscated from absentee Loyalists with large holdings, primarily Edmund Fanning and the McCullohs, was their ample resource. It was supplemented by smaller holdings of local Loyalists and others who resisted overt support of the revolutionaries. Quaker farms in Surry County and land occupied by Dunkards in Tryon/Lincoln and Mecklenburg counties were easy prey for county officers. Even the Wachovia Tract was threatened, in spite of the wartime *modus vivendi* between Moravian spokesmen and the county officials of Guilford, Rowan, and Surry.[4]

In Guilford County, the revolutionary and postwar courthouse ring was headed by legislators Alexander Martin and Ralph Gorrell, and included James Martin, Robert Gorrell, John and Daniel Gillespie, Thomas Henderson, Thomas Searcy, John Hamilton, Charles Bruce, William Dent, and John Paisley. Paisley and John Gillespie had participated in Regulator activities, but most of the others had been JPs and militia officers who were targets or opponents of Regulators.

In Orange County, neither the departure of Edmund Fanning nor the 1767–1777 gap in court minutes obscures the continuity of county personnel with the coming of the American Revolution. The first justices of the peace under state authority included at least five men who had held the office prior to 1767: John Butler, Thomas Hart, James Watson, Alexander Mebane Sr., and Alexander Mebane Jr. How many of the eighteen other first state-authorized JPs for Orange County had served during the ten-year lacuna in the records is unknown, but they included several with surnames from the pre-1766 roster of magistrates. In 1777, Orange County still included present-day Alamance, Durham, and Orange counties; Chatham, Guilford, and Wake had been created in 1770 during the Regulator scare and Caswell in 1777. About half of the post-1776 Orange County officials lived in the Hawfields east of the Haw River, with most of the remainder in Hillsborough.[5]

Paying Taxes to Own Land—Unfolding the Revolution in the Heart of the Regulator Country

By enabling free householders to vote for members of the House of Commons, both the fourth and the fifth provincial congresses addressed a basic concern that lingered after the Regulator years throughout the Granville District, namely a widespread lack of clear title to land. This was a directly political issue, for in the political culture inherited from England, ownership of land was understood to give a man a "stake in the country," or a right to participate in its governance. In this widely accepted belief, which local and state revolutionaries as well as Loyalists shared, neither leasing, renting, nor occupying land could bestow political participation. There is no direct evidence that allowing the householder, as distinct from the

First and last pages of the 1779 Orange County tax list. Note Nathaniel Rochester's signature. From General Assembly Records, Tax Lists, GA 30.1. Image provided courtesy of the North Carolina State Archives.

landowner, to vote for members of the lower house in 1776 carried any understanding that the householder would in fact come to own his land as payment for standing with the revolutionaries. Even so, in Orange County at least, that was the outcome.

Evidence of the process begins to appear in the first state-authorized tax lists. State law specified the taxes on property and polls (men, female heads of household, and people of African ancestry, whether enslaved or free). Even a man without taxable property paid a poll tax on himself. In theory, taxed property included money at interest, debts, stock in trade, and pleasure vehicles, as well as slaves, land, horses, and cattle. Only a few merchants and others who had loaned money paid in the first four categories. As William McCauley, tax assessor in the northern Hawfields, scrawled as he filled in the form: "There is no Stock in trade nor Carrages of pleasure in Said District." For most taxpayers, tax was levied on men, slaves, land, cattle, and horses.

It is the use of the "land" category of taxable property that is politically significant. Although state law set the terms of the tax, local JPs, who were also court-appointed tax assessors for their districts, could decide whether a householder should be listed as a landowner for tax purposes. Most of the names on the Orange County tax lists during the Revolutionary War appear neither in the prewar land records (not surprising in view of their incomplete nature), *nor* in the land entry records, which were carefully kept and survive intact.[6] Obviously, it was in the state's interest to have as many people pay tax on "their" land as possible, motivation for the tax assessor to encourage men who had no legal claim to their land to list it anyway. But who decided who listed land for which there were conflicting claims, either formally lodged as entry and caveat or informally contested by rival claimants who might never reach the courthouse with their claims? Tax districts were small enough for the JP/tax assessor to know all the taxpayers that he listed. The keeper of the district tax list was part of a control network linking county officials with the legislators who selected them and with the voters who selected the legislators. In Orange County, there was little wartime change in the personnel of JPs, other county officials, and representatives in the General Assembly; even that change is accounted for in large part by military or other official demands. The householder, as defined by the tax list, was also a voter. If a man's name was on the tax list, he could vote.

In the Hawfields: "Mr Studwicks Tenants, Almost to a Man"

In the Hawfields area of Orange County in particular, the continuity of land issues between the Regulator and revolutionary years compels examination. How typical such continuity was throughout the Regulator area is an open question that begs further research. In Orange

County, if a man with no title to land was listed for land tax, every year the tax assessor listed land under his name increased his likelihood of eventually owning it. Samuel Strudwick's weakening grasp on much of the Hawfields illustrates this process.

The circumstances of Strudwick's ownership of Piedmont land goes back to the governorship of George Burrington from 1723 to 1734. Burrington fed speculators with "blank patents" in the 1720s and amassed at least 18,400 acres himself, including much of the Hawfields. Burrington obtained some or all of this land from Edward Moseley, a London orphan who became arguably the most influential North Carolina politician of the first half of the eighteenth century and one of the first to take large grants along the Trading Path across the backcountry. Burrington died in 1759, killed at age seventy-seven by a robber while walking in a London park. Much of his estate quickly passed through the hands of his son as gambling debts. Strudwick's father, a London merchant, bought Burrington's land in the Hawfields and New Hanover County in 1761. Apparently, Strudwick also bought other Hawfields land that dated back to the blank patents. Strudwick took possession of the land in 1764 and moved permanently to North Carolina in 1767, building residences in Orange and New Hanover counties. He promptly became a member of Tryon's council, a JP, and a militia officer.[7]

What the dynamics of Burrington's absentee administration of his valuable lands had been is not known. Strudwick, on the other hand, was not an absentee. In the spring of 1768, when the Regulator Movement was gaining momentum, the occupants of Strudwick's land organized. That April, Francis Nash and Thomas Hart urged their business partner Edmund Fanning to advise Governor Tryon to bring in a military force from eastern North Carolina, advice Tryon would refuse for three years. Nash and Hart implored:

> We really think it a matter worthy the Governor's notice, as we are apprehensive a force must be brought from some other part of the Province. . . . In short Sir, the matter is of so new & of so extraordinary a nature to us that we are at the greatest loss what is to be done, but certain we are, that unless some measures can be fallen upon, of suppressing . . . those who have offended that no man will be safe among us in the possession either of his life or property. . . . And as an instance of the Evil & destructive consequence . . . we are creditably informed that Mr Strudwicks Tenants almost to a man have entered into an association among themselves to keep forcible possession of his lands and for that purpose, had a meeting yesterday in the Haw Fields.[8]

During the 1768 militia campaign against the Regulators, Strudwick was a lieutenant general.[9] Following a post-Alamance quiescence, people living on Strudwick's Hawfields land resumed their efforts to cast off his landlordship during the Revolution. They did so by listing and paying taxes on the land they occupied and by obstructing several parties of surveyors that Strudwick sent into the area for the purpose of documenting their trespasses. For Strudwick to be able to use the revolutionary courts to enforce his ownership, he had to make some acknowledgment of the Revolution and not give any indication of resisting it. He was among those who did not rush to take the loyalty oath when a state law made it mandatory for all free men over the age of sixteen. Accordingly, the county court ordered him and several

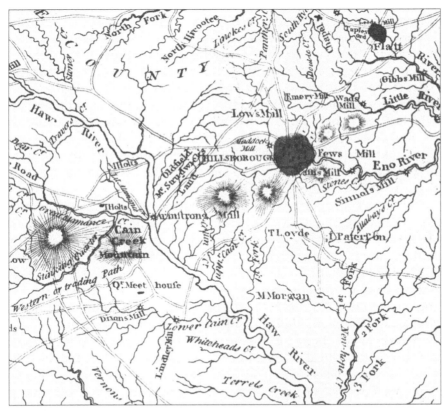

A portion of the 1770 Collet Map shows "Mr. Strudwick's Land" west of Hillsborough. From "A Compleat Map of North-Carolina from an actual Survey. By Captn. Collet, Governor of Fort Johnston. Engraved by I. Bayly." Image provided courtesy of the North Carolina Office of Archives and History.

others to appear in court and take the oath. Apparently, he did so quietly before a neighboring justice of the peace, which was the usual way, for he was named to the district superior court grand jury pool a few months later, his first public function under the new government.

By all appearances, Strudwick came to terms with his allegiance and its risks in a cautious and subdued manner. In the summer of 1777, he spent a month in quiet seclusion in Salem, rooming in the tavern, worshiping with the Moravians, reading an English translation of an account of their Greenland missions, and no doubt, thinking. After the first few days, his Salem hosts assumed that he was there to avoid taking the state oath, and they avoided the subject of politics.[10]

By 1780 Strudwick went on the offensive. With the legal and political assistance of Thomas Burke, he sued people for illegally occupying his lands and obstructing the surveyors. More than once the superior court ordered new surveys of the twenty-four thousand acres for which Strudwick provided legal documentation. In these court-ordered surveys, each side named a surveyor, but still the surveys were stopped. Strudwick described to Burke one incident: "the Chain was cutt by a Fellow of no property" (later identified as William Ray, who had registered a purchase of two hundred acres in Orange County in 1764), while the persons in whose interest he acted had not interfered with the surveyors. "Too much intimidated to join the links and make a second attempt: [the surveyors demand] a Guard for the Security of their persons," Strudwick said.[11]

Strudwick struck back at the next court in October 1780, obtaining an order for the sheriff to protect the survey party with a posse. Sheriff Alexander Mebane Jr. seems to have had a reasonable relationship with Strudwick, having bought 214 acres on Back Creek from him in 1772, paying what appears to have been a fair price. But whatever Sheriff Mebane did with a posse, the survey did not proceed, and in the November 1780 county court, Strudwick tried to protect himself financially. His method played into the hands of his "tenants."

Strudwick petitioned the county court to be taxed on one hundred acres of land instead of twenty-four thousand. He declared that the land was being taxed twice: He listed it on the tax inventory, as did the "Sundrie Persons" occupying the land. Strudwick concluded that he could not sell, rent, lease, cultivate, or use the land in any way and therefore should not be charged taxes on it. The people who had the use of it could pay the taxes. The court recorded no response to

Strudwick but apparently referred the matter to the General Assembly, for Strudwick then petitioned that body with his request. The assembly complied in early February 1781, allowing Strudwick to avoid the tax. It is likely that Strudwick understood the strategy of his challengers. The legislature's resolution noted that "this resolve shall not be considered in any sense to affect the title of these lands." The revolutionaries' political response to Strudwick's financial maneuvering came during the weeks prior to the Battle of Guilford Courthouse, when fighting in the area briefly provided the military momentum of the war. A string of encounters in Orange and Guilford counties thwarted Cornwallis's recruiting efforts before his showdown with Gen. Nathanael Greene on March 15. The damage to British forces at Guilford Courthouse would eventually pay off at Yorktown.[12]

In October 1782, with independence assured, the superior court ordered another survey and repeated the county court's order that the sheriff use "the power of the county" to protect the survey party. Meanwhile, the tenants' campaign to own the land outright by paying tax on it had continued through the war. The issue of ownership had never been separate from the survey obstructions; two of the three men whom Strudwick mentioned as directing the obstruction in 1780 were tax assessors at the time.[13]

Strudwick left an image of himself during those beleaguered days, when he confided his land troubles to Burke in September 1780. Burke was helping him buttress his legal documentation for all his New Hanover and Orange County land, but Strudwick's mind was on the place where he lived on Haw Creek. Someone, he said, had filed a land entry for it: "one Bowles . . . has got a new Patent [or grant] for a small plantation lying in sight of my house." James Bowles had entered eighty acres on the waters of Haw Creek in November 1778 and received a grant in September 1779. On the land for which Bowles now had a deed, Strudwick had planted corn and an orchard. Bowles, Strudwick related, "came and told me he intended in a few days to fetch away the peaches to distill: On my saying I would not consent to it, he answered he could get a Posse to assist him, which I suppose he will: and it is very probable the other man who has got a Patent for my house will raise another (or the same) Posse, and drive us into the woods." In a postscript to this letter, Strudwick apologized for not visiting Burke in person but explained, "at the one time the dread of losing my house, and at another that of loosing my peaches, keeps me almost a Prisoner at home." Samuel Strudwick handsomely survived the loss of much of his land and died in the Hawfields in 1797.[14]

Paying Taxes to Own Land—A Second Look

Strudwick's Hawfields tenants were exceptional among settlers on expansive colonial tracts to which they had no legal claim. Generally, owners of large grants comparable to Strudwick's were absentee landlords, and the state legislature confiscated their holdings in 1779. The disposition of one of Edmund Fanning's tracts in the Hawfields illustrates the ease by which residents who paid taxes during the Revolution could enter land that was not already claimed by revolutionaries, even if it had not been confiscated. In addition, the episode illustrates the continuity of title difficulties stemming from early-eighteenth-century tract grants, as well as farmers' fears of powerful litigators.

Fanning already owned land elsewhere in Orange County when he bought a ten-thousand-acre tract in the Hawfields, north and west of Strudwick's, in 1770. Fanning bought the tract at a court-ordered sale presided over by Sheriff John Butler. The superior court ordering the sale was not the Hillsborough court but its counterpart in Halifax District, where Fanning was not a touchstone for controversy. A debt suit initiated by George Lathbury against the estate of Gov. Sir Richard Everard's grandson had resulted in the court order to the Orange County sheriff to sell the Everard family holdings. Everard had granted the tract to himself while governor in the 1720s. Fanning bought an undivided share of the ten-thousand-acre tract in 1770 for about 600, paying slightly more than 930 proclamation currency.[15] The Everard/Fanning tract stretched eastward from a point west of the Stony Creek confluence with the Haw River to include the upper portions of Back Creek. The Moseley/Burrington/Strudwick land was adjacent, beginning at the lower section of Back Creek and extending southeastward to Motes Creek, where an early-eighteenth-century grant to Lewis Conner began. Together, Fanning's and Strudwick's lands included almost half of present-day Alamance County and stretched into present-day Orange County. Strudwick owned all of today's Melville Township and roughly half of Thompson Township. After 1770, Fanning held title to a wide swath of present-day Faucette, Pleasant Grove, and Haw River townships of Alamance County.

The legislature passed a series of confiscation laws and ordinances during 1776–1783. A 1779 statute named persons whose property was to be seized, and it authorized commissioners of confiscated estates in

All confiscated and directed to be fold for the use of the state.

The conditions of sale are twelve months credit, with six per cent. interest from the day of sale, payable in specie, or current money of said state, or certificates granted the officers and soldiers of the continental line of the state.

The sales to continue from day to day until all is sold. When and where the commissioner will attend in person, who, with the surveyor, will by shewing the plots give every necessary description and possible information.

Archibald Lytle, Commissioner.

Feb. 2, 1786

N. B. The late Assembly resolved, That Final Settlements, Specie Audited, County Commissioners, and Comptrollers Certificates should be received in payment of the said property, to which due respect will be paid.

Terms for purchasing grants from the Commissioners of Confiscated Property, as printed in the February 16, 1786, issue of the *North Carolina Gazette*. Image provided from microfilm, courtesy of the North Carolina State Archives.

each superior court district to inventory the property to facilitate future sales. The other statutes did not specify names but left interpretation to the county courts.[16] When Commissioners of Confiscated Property sold land and movable property at auction, it was a separate process from entering land for a state grant, sparingly used in the Piedmont until after the Revolutionary War. Fifteen men petitioned the legislature in 1789, claiming ownership of the Fanning tract in the Hawfields. They said they had bought the land from Granville. They feared it would be sold as confiscated property, because "a certain George Lathbury [a litigant concerning Fanning's Everard tract] claims the land as his." There is documentation in the Granville land records for only one of the fifteen, but the claimants had made uncontested entries for state grants of the land in 1778, prior to the 1779 law confiscating Fanning's property. They emphasized that they had paid state taxes on the land.[17]

Paying taxes to establish legal possession of a piece of land or to block another's entry worked during the war years, when it was politically expedient. Without a purchase from the state, however, there was no lasting security after the crisis passed. Closing some remaining loopholes, the legislature in 1785 confiscated large grants in the Piedmont dating from the 1720s. The presumption was that occupants of any of this land were renting, leasing, or squatting. The new move against the 1720s grants put that land in the same category as the Fanning and McCulloh tracts already seized; anyone could buy the land outright from the Commissioners of Confiscated Property. Terms for purchasing the grants were printed in the only newspaper in the state, which at the time was published in Hillsborough.

The commissioners' announcement offered more than fifteen thousand acres, including McCulloh lands west of the Haw River on Travis, Gun, Stinking Quarter, Alamance, and Euliss creeks. Persons in occupation of the land could specify to the commissioners where "their" land was, for which they now finally had to pay. The February 1786 announcement read: "Those lands are now occupied and in possession of sundry persons who hold them under . . . titles . . . contrary to law. The property will be sold for the use and benefit of the state in such surveys as is by the present possessor claimed." Purchasers had up to one year to pay, with 6 percent credit. Buyers could pay in specie, North Carolina currency, certificates from the North Carolina Continental Line, or audited certificates from state comptrollers or county commissioners.[18]

The Orange County court altered the sale somewhat at the start to exclude land claimed by John Butler. Still a JP in his home county, Butler usually sat as a presiding justice in the court but recused himself for the February 1786 session. He had petitioned the court to stop the commissioners from selling some of the lands formerly belonging to McCulloh, to which he now claimed title, and his fellow justices William McCauley, John Hawkins, and William Courtney complied, enabling Butler to keep the land.[19]

The Continuities of Local Power

Four years later, Michael Holt II had to petition the legislature to keep more than two thousand acres of McCulloh lands. Holt had bought the land from a speculator who had purchased the tract from one of the Commissioners of Confiscated Property. Most of the sales of McCulloh's Piedmont land went to speculators, not to settlers. In Orange County, only about a dozen individual farm-sized purchases of confiscated McCulloh land had been made by April 1788. Most of the McCulloh land in Orange County was bought by James Williams. By the late 1780s, Williams had mortgaged the lands to a partner and moved to Georgia. At some point, Williams sold more than two thousand acres of his purchases to Holt. In 1789 Williams's partner asked the state legislature to direct the attorney general to foreclose on the mortgages. The legislature's resolution authorized Williams's partner (or, possibly, victim) to sell the lands.

Holt and two others petitioned the legislature in 1790 to rescind its resolution insofar as it applied to lands they had bought from Williams. Williams had begun buying confiscated McCulloh lands in 1784, with twelve farm tracts in the area of Alamance and Stinking Quarter creeks, totaling 2,379 acres. Variations in size and price indicate that these were not fresh tracts of wilderness land but parcels that had been occupied, with some improvements. Apparently the land consisted of scattered active farms of some of Holt's neighbors, to which no one had established title by filing entries during the revolutionary years. Ten of these farms were on Great Alamance Creek, Stinking Quarter Creek, or their tributaries. The two others were on nearby Gun and Varnals creeks. All the tracts were west of the Haw River.

Like the Hawfields on the other side of the river, this largely German area had supported petitions and other expressions of outrage during the Regulator years, and the site of the Battle of Alamance lay within its bounds. It had not produced striking support for the Revolution, however. Cornwallis had felt comfortable enough in the area for his forces to spend a week there after leaving Hillsborough in the winter of 1781, the time of greatest military activity in what Cornwallis called "the Regulator country." Moravians in Wachovia were friends of Germans in the area west of the Haw River, but in 1782 a Moravian writer remarked on their reputations as "Tories." Moreover, a mid-nineteenth-century resident of the Alamance-Stinking Quarter area recorded an oral tradition that prosperous German farmers had been targets of extortion by a militia commander during the Revolution.[20] These factors raise the likelihood that the farms that Holt bought within this particular McCulloh tract had been occupied by people who were out of favor with the county government during the war years.

After the legislature cleared Holt's title in 1790, his German neighbors could rent or purchase their farms from him or his heirs. This process continued well into the nineteenth century and helped Holt accumulate the capital that enabled his grandson, Edwin Michael Holt, to pioneer textile manufacturing in the Piedmont in the 1830s. The fact that residents of the confiscated farms that Holt bought had not filed entries for state grants contrasts with the action of the fifteen Hawfields petitioners who protected their farms from sale as Fanning's confiscated property about the same time that Holt petitioned the legislature to save his purchase of confiscated McCulloh land. One supposes that neither the Hawfields petitioners nor the residents of the farms that Holt bought had paid for their land, given the severe currency shortage and the difficulties of acquiring land titles in the Granville District and in large tracts such as McCulloh's and Burrington/Fanning's. In the area of the lands that Holt purchased, there had been a large-scale community effort in the 1760s to impede the Granville agents from selling farms that residents were in the process of buying from McCulloh. Between 1763 and 1766, about 130 individuals in the largely German settlements west of the Haw River, including the Alamance-Stinking Quarter region, mortgaged tracts of approximately 350 acres each to Henry Eustace McCulloh. Recording the mortgages prevented the tracts from being sold by the Granville land office, as they were on McCulloh land that had been found to be in the Granville tract. Holt's parents had facilitated the paperwork for these mortgages at their store and blacksmith operation.[21] Whether the buyers had paid off their mortgages is not known, for a segment of Orange County land records did not survive the Revolution. Among the continuities apparent in these decades of land transactions is the interface that the Holts provided between German-speaking farmers and the respective colonial and revolutionary officialdoms. Whipped by Regulator-inspired rioters for being a member of the closed loop of county power, Holt came to champion Regulator principles and personnel following their defeat. Opposing the Revolution at its inception, he adapted well and became one of its major financial beneficiaries. Holt understood the continuities of local power and legislative partnership.

12

Religious Divergence and Growing Support for Revolution

The Repudiation of Nonviolence and
the Eclipse of Shubal Stearns

The Regulator Movement from its inception included people who rejected violence on religious grounds, primarily Separate Baptists and Quakers, as well as others who accepted violence as a political tool. Quaker meetings disowned men for infractions such as "making warlike preparation"[1] during the Regulator years and later during the Revolutionary War. Such men were a minority among the Friends, and as with other breaches of conduct, repentance (usually following the respective crises) brought readmission. Moreover, Quakers as a group, like Moravians, Dunkards, and Mennonites, managed to protect themselves from military service during the Revolution by shrewd negotiations involving trade and extra taxes.

For Separate Baptists, the issue of violence came to a head during the excitement that followed the election of Regulators to the lower house in July 1769. Beginning on October 14, representatives of the churches of the Sandy Creek Association met at Sandy Creek Church. This was less than two weeks before the colonial assembly would convene, with new members from Anson, Granville, Halifax, Orange, and Rowan counties bringing Regulator issues to New Bern. Shubal Stearns, who had founded the Sandy Creek Association and led it for more than a decade, presided over the meeting. Stearns had worked closely with Husband from the beginning of the Sandy Creek settlement. He recently had petitioned for the release of Regulator prisoners. He remained, however, unflinchingly opposed to violence. The embodiment of Separate Baptist zeal in the interior of Virginia and the Carolinas, Stearns grounded his repudiation of violence on his understanding of the New Testament. If Regulators who wanted to do more than deliberate and petition were to recruit successfully among Separate Baptists, by then a far larger and more influential body than the Quakers, the old man would have to be dealt with.

Association meetings, like later camp meetings and revivals, lasted for several days and attracted visitors and traders who did not participate in the sessions. Routinely, outdoor preachings and other activities clustered about the church. There is no record of business transacted in the October 1769 session, but according to Morgan Edwards, who visited the Sandy Creek area in 1772, a resolution, or "order," was passed at that time, stating that "If any of our members shall take up arms against the legal authority and abbet them that do he shall be excommunicated." News of this "order" would have traveled fast through the gathered crowds into the surrounding country. Edwards further related that shortly after the order had passed, four Regulator "chiefs" strode angrily into the church, confronted Stearns as he stood in the pulpit, and demanded to know if what they had heard regarding the order were true. Stearns hesitated, then gave what Edwards described as an "evasive" answer, for Stearns and the other delegates "were in bodily fear." Edwards (and presumably his informants in the community) credited Stearns's evasion with forestalling a violent breakup of the association meeting by the Regulator chiefs and their adherents. Stearns's biographer viewed the evasion as a self-inflicted death wound.[2]

Stearns lived until November 1771, but the pacifism of Separate Baptists was cracked in the October 1769 incident. Edwards noted subsequent Regulator attacks on Separate Baptists, including the disarming of members of the Haw River Church after it reaffirmed the association's resolution in November 1769 and specified that "if any of their members should join the Regulators and take up arms against the lawful authority he should be excommunicated." During the Revolutionary War, Patriots jailed two preachers from the Haw River Church for preaching nonresistance.[3]

During Edwards's 1772 visit, he concluded that the trauma connected with the Regulator Movement caused the Separate Baptist exodus from the Sandy Creek settlement and from clusters of churches in present-day Sampson and Montgomery counties. He heard stories about Tryon's foraging and depredations following the Battle of Alamance and knew that Baptists remained vulnerable. Accordingly, Edwards took pains to disassociate them from the Regulator Movement. Even so, his sympathy with the causes of the Regulator disturbances rendered his remarks ambivalent. The only contemporary source to address the issue directly, Edwards's comments are capable of opposing interpretations as to why most Separate Baptists left the area after the Regulator defeat: either the Separate Baptists supported and participated in the Regulator Movement and the Battle of Alamance and suffered as a result of the bloodshed and Tryon's exactions; or the Separate Baptists resisted Regulator efforts to recruit them and suffered at the hands of Regulators. It seems likely that both explanations are true, and that the resulting conflict within the churches and communities added impetus for removal and separation. Stearns's death at age sixty-five, six months after the Battle of

Alamance, can only have added to the communal grief and sense of ending. Edwards's oft-summarized words are as follows:

> The cause of this dispersion was the abuse of power which too much prevailed in the province and caused the inhabitants at last to rise up in arms, and fight for their privileges; but being routed they despaired of seeing better times, and therefore quitted the province. It is said that 1500 families departed since the battle of Almance; and, to my knowledge, great many more are only waiting to dispose of their plantations in order to follow them. This is to me an argument that their grievances were real, and their oppression great notwithstanding all that has been said to the contrary.[4]

Pacifism survived among some Separate Baptists through the political strain of the Regulator and revolutionary years, but it did not triumph, neither among Separate Baptists nor within the southern and Appalachian religious cultures that they shaped. The exodus following Alamance took Separate Baptist families and entire congregations into western Virginia and South Carolina. Quaker movement from the Regulator country into South Carolina and Georgia increased at the same time. Even before the Piedmont disturbances peaked in the Regulator Movement, Quakers and Separate Baptists from the area had initiated settlements in frontier areas of South Carolina and Georgia. These neighborhoods, notably Raeburn's Creek, Deep Creek, and Bush River in South Carolina and Wrightsborough in Georgia, continued to draw Separate Baptists, Quakers, and others who left the Piedmont following the Battle of Alamance. As pacifists, or at least as people who held themselves aloof from the revolutionary conflict, Quakers and Separate Baptists could be confused with each other; British officers at Augusta in 1779 thought a delegation of Wrights-borough Quakers were "Anabaptists" (and one referred to them as "Crackers.")[5] During the Revolutionary War, such communities were suspected of harboring Loyalists and in some cases produced conspicuous ones. David Fanning, for example, who was neither Quaker nor Baptist, ran away from home following the Regulator campaign, apparently in rebellion against his adoptive father, a Johnston County justice of the peace who had commanded militia against the Regulators. By 1773, eighteen-year-old Fanning was living on Raeburn's Creek. Former pacifists were active on both sides during the Revolutionary War. Even at Sandy Creek, Seymour York, who had given land to build Stearns's founding church, recruited and led thirty-four neighbors to join the expected British landing in February 1776.[6]

A shadow of Separate Baptist pacifism was recorded in the South Carolina up-country after the Revolutionary War. The South Carolina Constitution of 1778 required churches to present their principles and a list of members to the legislature. Congregations that had been Separate Baptists dropped the word "Separate" with its pacifist connotation, and there was little mention of aversion to war in their stated principles. An exception was a church on Padgett's Creek in present-day Union County, South Carolina, near two Quaker meetings with which it shared migrational ties to the North Carolina Regulator area. The Padgett's Creek Baptist Church "principles" acknowledged their compromise but still maintained, "We do hold to open our doors to any orderly minister or church of the Separate Order, that doth not tolerate War."[7] Rapid postwar migration from the South Carolina congregations into Georgia and from the North Carolina and western Virginia congregations into Kentucky and Tennessee further hastened Baptists' amnesia of their denominational forebears' rejection of violence, even violence mandated by lawful government, that stretched back from New England to sixteenth-century Anabaptists and Mennonites in Europe.

Preaching Revolution: David Caldwell and "The Character and Doom of the Sluggard"

During the religious excitement that framed the Regulator Movement, generally referred to as the Great Awakening, Baptist churches appear to have been the fastest growing congregations in the Carolina Piedmont. Following the Revolution, Methodist expansion would parallel the Baptist and further etch a distinctive religious style into the general culture entering the nineteenth century. During the Regulator years, the Piedmont's most numerous ethnic group, the Scotch-Irish, was subject to the influence of Presbyterian clergymen, clearly the largest educated group among the backcountry's clergy-poor populace. The handful of Presbyterian ministers active in the Piedmont during the Regulator and revolutionary years discouraged the Regulator Movement but encouraged the Revolution. Their political evolution paralleled the nationalistic and decidedly non-pacifistic tone with which the dominant religious culture of the southern Piedmont and Appalachian regions entered the new nation. Any push-pull relationship between Piedmont Presbyterian clergy and their over-whelmingly revolutionary laity has not been explored, but a precedent of clergy-laity dynamic in the middle colonies during 1740–1760 is suggestive. A careful study of the Great Awakening among Scotch-Irish there concluded that it had been the Presbyterian laity, not the clergy, who had propelled revivalism, particularly in Pennsylvania, on the cusp of Scotch-Irish mass migration to the North Carolina Piedmont.[8]

When Presbyterian ministers disapproved of Regulator activities but later promoted the Revolution, they stood with the secular leaders of the Scotch-Irish settlements, such as the Mebanes and some of the Butlers in the Hawfields and the Alexanders and Polks of Mecklenburg County. In the greater Mecklenburg area, Scotch-Irish leaders maintained control throughout the Regulator upheavals and smoothly continued their alliances with eastern North Carolina challengers of Gov. Josiah Martin after he replaced Tryon. Theirs was a direct and easy progression. They used dissenter grievances that fed the Regulator Movement as negotiating points with Tryon and Fanning. Though useful for bolstering local control during the Regulator crises, such negotiations did not advance religious freedom; that would come later. With revolutionary victory, Mecklenburg leaders in the new state government faced no great obstacles to fulfilling their promises to fellow dissenters with a state constitution forbidding an established church.

In Guilford, Orange, and nearby counties where the Regulator Movement was played out, Presbyterian ministers openly opposed Regulator threats of violence and their refusal to pay taxes but did not condemn the movement's intentions. Henry Pattillo served congregations in the Hawfields, as did David Caldwell in eastern Guilford County. As the Regulator crisis deepened, both struggled to reconcile Regulators with government officials, particularly Tryon. They were joined by George Micklejohn in Hillsborough, whose Anglicanism did not deter Regulators from embracing his efforts to help them obtain redress. They referred to him as "our Rector." As an Anglican, he was more a pillar of authority than were the Presbyterians. Pattillo, Caldwell, and Micklejohn were active as couriers and mediators. They preached plainly against breaking the law, and, from their more nuanced perspectives, they grasped Tryon's sympathies with the Regulator grievances.[9]

So too did Samuel Suther, initially in the Cabarrus area where Tryon helped German-speaking congregations obtain the young teacher's services in 1768. He became pastor of a joint Lutheran and Reformed congregation west of the Haw River in October 1771.

On the important Duty of SUBJECTION to the
CIVIL POWERS.

A

SERMON

Preached before his EXCELLENCY

WILLIAM TRYON, Efquire,
GOVERNOR, and Commander in Chief of the
Province of NORTH-CAROLINA,

AND THE

TROOPS raifed to quell the late

INSURRECTION,

AT

HILLSBOROUGH, in ORANGE County,

On SUNDAY *September* 25, 1768.

By GEO. MICKLEJOHN, S. T. D.

N E W B E R N:

Printed by JAMES DAVIS,

M,DCC,LXVIII.

George Micklejohn (1717–1818) was an Anglican clergyman referred to by Regulators as "our Rector" because he tried to help them obtain redress from their grievances without violence. Like David Caldwell, he had served as a mediator between Tryon and the insurgents. While supportive of the Regulator cause he remained loyal to the Crown, even when the American Revolution broke out. This is the title page of a sermon delivered to Governor Tryon and his troops at Hillsborough, September 25, 1768. Image provided courtesy of the North Carolina State Archives.

A late-nineteenth-century Reformed pastor and historian there was told that Suther had "lived on a farm hard by the [Alamance] battle-ground, and perhaps owned it." Suther identified strongly with Reformed bodies. The Presbyterian and Reformed communions shared a Calvinist theology, which since the late sixteenth century had embraced a duty of revolution in certain circumstances. This political teaching departed from Calvin's instructions and originated among French Calvinists (or Huguenots) following his death. John Knox took the new teaching to southeastern Scotland, and there it underlay the foundational Presbyterian revolution against Mary, Queen of Scots. Likewise, in a number of German states, teachings that fostered a religious duty of revolution undergirded the auto-nomy with which local rulers encouraged Calvinist-style reform of churches in their territories during the late sixteenth and seventeenth centuries. Students of the American Revolution find something like an intellectual fault line between Calvinist and Arminian premises, drawn by the Calvinist inclination toward proactive political behavior.[10]

During the Revolution, Suther bonded some Germans west of the Haw River with the Scotch-Irish leadership of the Revolution that flanked them on the east and west. The fact that Suther's Reformed flock withdrew from a Lutheran-Reformed union arrangement during his ministry suggests a political difference early in the revolutionary crisis. Oral memory, collected about a century later, recalled that during the Revolution, the Reformed congregation, or "Clapp's" church, built a separate meeting house for themselves, no longer sharing the facility used by the "Low's" Lutherans.[11]

Suther's Presbyterian ministerial neighbor in the Hawfields was John DeBow. Freshly graduated from the College of New Jersey (later Princeton University) and licensed by the Synod of New York and Philadelphia, the thirty-year-old DeBow traveled to North Carolina to serve congregations without ministers in 1775, about the time that Pattillo moved from the Hawfields to Bute County. In February 1776, when revolutionary militia massed to face the expected Highlander and Regulator Loyalist uprising, DeBow joined John Butler's Hawfields unit as chaplain and accompanied its expedition to Moores Creek Bridge. Three months later, DeBow became the pastor of Hawfields and Eno Presbyterian churches, and he continued to serve vacant congregations from time to time. He also served as a chaplain throughout the war, a symbol of Scotch-Irish revolutionary solidarity throughout the greater Hawfields area.[12]

Closer to Suther was a more seasoned Presbyterian minister than young DeBow. Whatever else may have been involved in shaping Suther as a revolutionary, his exposure to the mind of Presbyterian David Caldwell was important. Caldwell's congregation on the headwaters of Alamance Creek was near Suther's congregation on a tributary of that creek. Both men were in their fifties in the 1770s. Little is known of the Swiss-born Suther's education, but Moravian innuendo suggests that it was slim, a circumstance that would have enhanced Caldwell's influence on him.[13] Suther's neighbor was a graduate of the College of New Jersey and a physician. Beginning in 1767, "Dr. David Caldwell's Log College" came to be recognized as the most advanced school in North Carolina and one of the finest classical and theological academies in the South.

As a New Light Presbyterian, Caldwell had long been exposed to heady declamations directed toward the individual hearer. Not least was his exposure to the thought of Alexander Craighead, whose daughter Rachel, reputed to be a spirited woman of intellectual accomplishments, became Caldwell's wife in 1766. Craighead died that year, but Rachel lived with Caldwell until his death in 1824 at age one hundred. From his pulpit, Caldwell repeatedly advocated independence during the war years. His fervor was rekindled during the War of 1812, when he was informed that volunteers were lacking in Guilford County, and that a draft might be necessary. Frail with age, Caldwell raised volunteers with a sermon at the courthouse, using the text from Luke 22:36, "He that hath no sword, let him sell his garment, and buy one." His direct appeal to individual responsibility resonates with Craighead's insistence on personal commitment to the two Presbyterian covenants:

> You will say, They are National Covenants, and therefore what can we do? The Nation will not join us, and we are not a Nation? *Answer,* Tho' you are not a Nation, yet certainly you are a Part, tho' never so small; and as such, there is some Duty lieth upon you to renew these Covenants, yea, even as much Duty as on any in your Station; for in the Covenant every individual Person swears for himself in his Station, to endeavour to prosecute the End and Design of the Covenants.[14]

Whether Caldwell had a copy of his father-in-law's 1746 publication that includes this quotation is not known, for in 1781 British forces burned his personal papers and library. A sermon of Caldwell's that Eli Caruthers published in 1842 does lend insight into the cleric's role as advocate for revolution. Caldwell delivered the sermon in 1775, seven years after he and three other Presbyterian ministers, together at Hawfields, had told Regulators in no uncertain terms to recant their Regulator oaths. The oaths bound Regulators, in the ministers' estimation, "to call Officers to a Settlement, in a way the Law has not allowed, and . . . not to pay their Taxes."[15]

Caldwell's purpose in his 1775 sermon was to call his neighbors to arms against parliamentary authority in the colonies. He directed his criticism at what he called parliamentary usurpations, rather than at the authority of the Crown, a convention typical of revolutionaries at the start of the crisis. Even so, the minister did not attempt to disguise what he acknowledged to be revolution. What is most interesting is the argument by which Caldwell did not simply justify revolution but presented it as a duty, springing from the bedrock of Christian responsibility.

The sermon was titled, "The Character and Doom of the Sluggard." Analyzing the sermon, a historian of religion thought that it gave the Protestant ethic a "more powerful and novel application" than did Caldwell's contemporaries, who also preached that "self-denial in the cause of liberty, zealousness for the common good, and a refusal to profit personally by the upheaval of the times were Christian duties." "It was not enough to practice thrift and self-denial in the patriot cause, [Caldwell] declared; the people must gather and exert their psychic energy: they must focus, concentrate, and obey their own self-consciousness and thereby move with swiftness and grace instead of habitual heaviness, clumsiness, and indecision."[16] The minister's unstated premise was that only sloth could hold one back from joining the Revolution.

Caldwell's text was Prov. 12:24, "The hand of the diligent shall bear rule; but the slothful shall be under tribute." He presented the slothful man as a target for the greedy, recalling recent events to the minds of his hearers. There was an element of threat in Caldwell's denunciation of the slothful man: "Let not the friends of the constitution, or the 'Sons of Liberty,' know that such an enemy to the common interests of mankind anywhere exists, lest their patriotic zeal should raise undue resentment and cause it to burst upon his devoted head." After describing the ruin the "sluggard" would bring to himself, his children, and his society by remaining aloof from the revolutionary movement, Caldwell turned to the individual listener in a style reminiscent of Craighead's:

You are perhaps saying, . . . if the sluggard's character be so odious and his punishment so terrible, we will not indulge in sloth ourselves, nor connive at it in others. These are good resolutions, . . . but these distempered times call for more than resolutions. You know that some years ago the British Parliament took a notion to be arbitrary; and proceeded to pass acts that were unknown to the constitution, alarming to the wise and prudent in Great Britain. . . . We sent forth our grievances. . . . Our petitions were rejected. . . . We have therefore come to that trying period in our history in which . . . Americans must either stoop . . . or resist. . . .

The preacher's crescendo drew on the Christian aspiration for the Kingdom of God. It drew as well on the faith in reason and the perfectibility of a well-ordered society that inspired the Founding Fathers. If his listeners refused to actively support the Revolution, whether through laziness, cowardice, or indecision, he said:

We must continue in our present state of bondage and oppression, while that bondage and oppression may be increased until life itself will become a burden; but . . . if we act our part well, as men and as christians, . . . we may, with the help of the Lord, obtain a complete and final deliverance from the power that has oppressed us, or at least secure our rights, and attain a prosperity and happiness which no nation has ever enjoyed, or even dared to hope.[17]

Caldwell's stirring sermon did not mention the Regulator crisis or any of its issues. Nevertheless, the sermon came less than five years since Caldwell himself had desperately shuttled messages between the Regulators and Tryon in a vain effort to prevent the Battle of Alamance. If the Regulator Movement itself did not contribute to Caldwell's becoming a revolutionary and a propagandist for the Revolution, it is yet likely that the manner in which Tryon dealt with the Regulators did.

Appendix 1

An Incomplete Compilation of Names in a Regulator Context

CAVEAT: The following set of names is not a list of "the Regulators." It is a compilation of names on petitions and depositions backing issues advocated by Regulators during 1766–1771; in letters or statements indicating sympathy with Regulator individuals or causes; in indictments or other official actions against individuals as Regulators; or in descriptions by contemporaries. The compilation omits obvious duplicates, except when a name appears twice in the same document; one in each pair is marked with the suggestion, "Jr. or Sr.?" though they may be duplicative. Other actual Jr. and Sr. appellations are transcribed. Most names are from published documents, and spellings are limited by the editors' knowledge of eighteenth-century Piedmont names. In addition to these English, Anglicized, and quasi-Anglicized German names, about fifty names appear in German script.

SOURCES: *Colonial Records of North Carolina; The Correspondence of William Tryon and Other Selected Papers; Records of the Moravians in North Carolina; The Regulators of North Carolina: A Documentary History 1759– 1776*; and unpublished petitions in the General Assembly Session Records, 1767–1789 passim, North Carolina State Archives.

Daniel [blank]	William Alrid Jr.	William Barber
Richard [blank]	William Alrid Sr.	James Barindine
Samuel [blank]	Thomas Anderson	William Barindine Jr.
Isaac __?	Adam Andriss	William Barindine Sr.
[blank] Aaronson	Conrad Andriss	James Barker
John Acuage	Isaac Armstrong	Nicholas Barker
James Adams	Jas. E. Arnet	Samuel Barker
George Admire	Thomas Arrington	Brinceley Barnes
James Aiken	James Arrowood	James Barnes
James Aikin	Nathl. Ashley	Thomas Barnes
William Albright	Walter Ashmore	James Barns
James Aldridge	Alexander Awtry	Benjamin Barritt
Nathan Aldridge	John Bailey	Thomas Barrot
Nicholas Aldridge	Thomas Bailey	Richard Bartleson
Thomas Alexanders	Abner Baker	John Barton
Joseph Allen	Silvesley Baker	John Baxtor
J. W. Allison	Thomas Baley	Thomas Beaty
Edward Almond	Thomas Balice	Jeffrey Beck
Seamor Almond	William Bannistor	Thomas Beel

Thomas Belhany
Abraham Belieu
George Belieu
Isaac Belieu
John Bell
Abraham Bellew
   [Jr. or Sr.?]
John Bennet
William Benton
John Bery
William Betten
James Bignour
Jas. Billingley
James Binnum
Thomas Black
Philip Blasé Jr.
William Blewet
James Bly
Waterman Boatman
John Boe
Patrick Boggen Jr.
Joseph Boggs
William Boilstone
John Bond
William Bond
Charles Booler
[blank] Boothe
[the elder] Borg
[the younger] Borg
William Bosil
James Bound
Abram Bradley
Laurence Bradley
Ayen Brady
William Brakin
Eli Branson
Thomas Branson
James Brantley
Benj. Braswell
George Braswell
Richard Braswell
Edward Bray
Henry Bray
Alexander Brewer

Howell Brewer
Nickless Brewer
John Bricks
Peter Brisley
Robert Broadaway
Howel Brooer [Jr. or
   Sr.?]
Isaac Brooks
James Brooks
John Brooks
John Brooks Jr.
[blank] Brown
Daniel Brown
David Brown
James Brown
Robert Brown
John Brox
John Brus
Samuel Bruton
John Bryan
Jams. Buchanan
John Bullen
William Bulter/Butler
Benjamin Bunt
Henry Burcham
James Burcham
John Burcham
Joseph Burcham
James Burgiss
Darass Burns
William Burns
John Burston
William Burt
Stephen Bush
Thom Bush
Abraham Buskin
Christopher Butler
William Butler
William Buzen
Patrick Calley
William Cane
John Capin
William Caps
John Carpenter

Josseph Carr
John Cartright
John Caterham
Peter Ceingth
John Cerow
Joseph Chafen
Edward Chambers
Randal Cheek
Randolph Cheek
Richard Cheek
Francis Cheney
Christopher Christian
James Christian
Thomas Christian
Jacob Christman
Job Cilleadon
Benjamin Clanton
Charles Clanton
George Clap
John Clap
Tobias Clap
Lodwick Clapp
Elija Clark
Francis Clark
John Clark
Joseph Clark
Nicholas Coble
Jacob Cockerham
John Cockerham
Timothy Code
James Colbon
John Coleman
William Coleman
Jacob Collins
Joshua Collons
Harklis Conkwrite
Stephen Cook
John Cooper
James Copeland
Richard Copeland
William Copeland Jr.
William Copeland Sr.
Nichlos Coplin
Thomas Coplin

Valentine Corlin
John Corry
George Cortner
John Cory
Henry Cotes
Benjamin Covington
John Cowen
David Cox
Harmon Cox
Solomon Cox
Thomas Cox
John Craswill
Joseph Craven
Peter Craven
Thomas Craven
Patrick Crayton
William Creaswill
Solomon Crofts
Abraham Crosson
Gilbard Croswell
John Croswell
Willliam Croswell
Mansfield Crow
Samuel Culberson
Andrew Culbison
John Culpepper
Thomas Culpepper
William Culpepper
William Culpepper Jr.
Ezekel Cure
John Curry
Sam Curtis
Samuel Dark
John Davidson
Enoch Davis
Gabrill Davis
James Davis
John Davis
Jonathan Davis
Matthew Davis
Thomas Davis
Samuel Debury
Robert Delap

John Dennis
James Denson
Shadrack Denson
Samuel Devine
Samuel Deviney
Samuel Dibury
William Digge
Thomas Dinkins
William Dinkins
Calib Dixon
Jacob Dobbins
Thomas Donnor
Somon Dorph?
Francis Dorset
Owen Dowd
Daniel Dowdy
Richard Downs
William Drinkin
Jacob Drox[Troxler]
Jeremiah Duckworth
Benjamin Dumas
David Dumas
Bartol Dun [Jr. or Sr.?]
John Duncun
William Dunkin
Barth. Dunn
Meeager Edwards
James Ellis
James Emberson
Matthew English
John Enyart
John Erwin
George Estess
William Estess
Aaron Evans
Joshua Evans
Andrew Falconbery
Henry Falconbery
Isaac Falconbery Jr.
John Falconbery
Christen Fall
John Fanin
William Fany

Jacob Felker
Aquilla Felp
John Felps
Thomas Feutral
James Few Jr.
William Fielding
Jeremiah Fields
John Fike
Marton Firnier
Thomas Flack
Samuel Flake
John Flemmin
John Flowel
William Forbis
Henry Fortenbury
John Fortenbury
Joseph Foshea
Thomas Fox [Fee?]
Leonard Franklyn
Joseph French
Neal French
John Fruit
Thomas Frull
Jacob Fudge
John Fudge
Joseph Fulk
Thomas Fulla
John Fuller
Joshay Fuller
Thomas Fuller
Thomas Fuller
William Galbreath
Daniell Galespie
John Gapen
Parrish Gardner
Samuel Gaylord
Joseph George
James Gibson
Silvester Gibson
Walter Gibson
William Gibson
Gideon Gilbert Jr.
Gideon Gilbert Sr.

Jonathan Gilbert
Joshua Gilbert
William Gillmore
Peter Givil [Cavel?]
Christian Glase
George Glase
Philip Glase Sr.
Powel Glase
Thomas Glover
George Goble
John Goble
Charles Goldstone
Phillip Goodbraid
Frank Gordon
Jonathan Gowers
Thomas Gowers
James Graham
Thomas Grames
John Grappen
John Graves
Thomas Greaves
William Greaves
Thomas Green
William Green
Andrew Griffin
James Griffin
Jacob Grigg
Solon Gross
Benjamin Grubbs
John Grubbs
Johan H_
Joshua Hadley
Simon Hadley
Jesse Hadly
Isam Haley
Silas Haley
William Haley
William Haley Jr.
Arch. Hamilton
Ninian Hamilton
Thomas Hamilton
Thomas Hamm
Abraham Hammer
J. L. Harbison

James Haridon
Stephen Harlan
Aaron Harland Sr.
Ebron Harlow
Zach. Harman
Thomas Harper
Adam Hartman
Joseph Harris
Jesse Harrison
Jno. Harrison
Joseph Harrison
John Hart
Jno. Philip Hartzo
Philip Hartzo
William Hattocks
James Hearndon
George Heitziel
Jonathan Helms
Tilmon Helms
Argulus Henderson
John Henderson
Nathaniel Henderson
Richard Henderson
William Henderson
George Hendrey
Thomas Hendrey Jr.
Thomas Hendrey Sr.
John Hennen
George Henry
Joseph Henson
William Henson
Delany Herring
William Hickman
John Hickory
James Higgins
John Higgins
William Higgins
Thos. Hill
Nicholas Hillerman
Abraham Hilton
John Hilton
Joseph Hindes
Charles Hines
William Hintrand

Shadrick Hogins
Thadwick Hogins
William Grifen Hogon
Julius Holley
Christopher Holt
John Holt
Peter Holt
Michael Honest
David Hopkins
Wm. Hopkins
Thomas Hopper
John Horback
Jacob Horn
Jn. Hornaday
John Hornbeck Jr.
Nehemiah Howard
Nehemiah Howard [Jr.
  or Sr.?]
Rednap Howell
Joseph Howelt
James Hugh
Edward Hughes
William Hull
Joseph Hunt
James Hunter
Hermon Husbands
Authd Hutchins
Richard Hutson
William Hutson
William Inglish
John Inyard
David Jackson
John Jackson
Stephen Jackson
Jimmey James
John James Jr.
John James Sr.
Robert Jarman
Jno. Jeffery
John Jenkins
David Jernigan
Jacob Johns Jr.
Jacob Johns Sr.
Stephen Johns

John Johnson
Andre Jones
Aquila Jones
Charles Jones
John Jones
John Jones Jr.
Sam Jones
Stephen Jones
Thomas Jones
Thomas Jones [Jr. or Sr.?]
William Jones
Jos. Jonson
Thomas Jordan
Francis Jourden
William Jowers
Peter Julian Jr.
Peter Julian Sr.
Thos. Kanid
Patrick Kelly
Alexander Kenedy
John Kimborough
William Kiniman
Thomas Kinniman
James [Tiery?] Klann
Thomas Lacy
Charles Landron
Rubin Landrum
Archey Lane
Edward Lang
Adam Larence
Cornelius Latham
Samuel Latham
Samuel Law
Daniel Laws
Marverick Layieu
Richard Leak
William Learey
William Leaton
Michael Leel [Leal?]
John Leveritt
William Leveritt
William Levy
Jonathan Lewellyn

James Liles
John Liles
Henry Linterman
Mincher Littler
Yomond Lloyd
Mathew Locke
John Long
Lewis Lord
James Lowe
John Lowe
Robt. Lowery
Lewis Lowry
William Lucas
William Lucas Jr.
John Luin
George Mabry
Thomas Mackness
Joseph Macpherson
John Macvay
Joseph Maddocks
William Maffet
Richard Maner
Robt. Marbey
George Marchbanks
John Marchill
Roger Marfey
William Marly
Larance Marmanee
John Marshall
Jacob Marshill
John Marshills
Jno. Marswaine
Joseph Martin
Thomas Mason Jr.
Ned Mathes
John Mathews
Antho Mathis
Benjamin Maudlin
Benjamin Maudlin [Jr. or Sr.?]
James Maudlin
John Maudlin
John Maudlin [Jr. or Sr.?]

Jonie Maudlin
James McCane
Daniel McCay
Jno. McClewland
Archibald McCoy
John McCoy
James McCrane
John McDaniel
Jacob McDanil
John McDonald
John McGee
John McIlvaill
James McMeot
John McNish
Alexander McPherson
Patrick McSwain
John McVey
Jason Meadow
Jason Meadow Jr.
Thomas Melone
Jeremiah Melton
Jeremiah Melton [Jr. or Sr.?]
Thomas Merns
John Merrie
James Merrow
Charles Miles
John Miles Jr.
John Miles Sr.
Thomas Miles
Jero Miller
John Mims
Thomas Mims
William Mims
William Mitchell
William Moffit
James Moffitt
Thomas Moon
Edward Moore
Thomas Moore
Archelam Moorman
Bennakia Moorman
Thomas Moorman
Goin Morgan

James Morgan
John Morgan
Ruddy Morgan
Solomon Morgan
John Moris
Edward Morris
John Morris [Jr. or Sr.?]
Joseph Morris
William Morris
William Morris Jr.
William Morrow
Adam Moser
Larance Murchisons
John Murphey of
     Orange
John Murphy of Anson
James Murray
Chrisr Nation
George Navil
Thomas Needom
William Needom
Thomas Nelson
William Newberry
John Noe
Denes Norlen
William Norton
Nehemiah Odle
James Oliver
James Oliver [Jr. or Sr.?]
William O'neal
Stephen Owen
Elisha Owins
Wm. Paine
John Par
Joseph Park
Samuel Parks
John Paterson
William Payne
John Penton
Timothy Penton
Thomas Person
Thos. Persons
David Phelps

David Phillips
William Phillips
James Phipps
John Phipps
Joseph Phipps
E. Pickett
Thomas Pickett
Henry Pickral
Amons Pilgrim
John Pleourt
Francis Pooey
Umfreh Pooey
James Porter
John Poston
John Poston Sr.
Nathaniel Powel
John Powitt
Thomas Preslar
John Preslie
Augustine Prestwood
Mathias Prok
John Pryor
Enoch Pugh
Enoch Pugh [Jr. or Sr.?]
James Pugh
Jesse Pugh
John Pugh
Thomas Pugh
John Pyle
Matthew Raiford Jr.
William Raiford
George Raines
John Raines
John Rainey
John Ramsel
James Ramsey
Michael Ramsouer
William Rancy
Thomas Ranetalor
Wm. Raney
Elisha Ratcliff
Samll Ratcliff
Samuel Ratcliff Jr.

Samuel Ray
Abraham Relyon
     [Kelyon?]
Petter Rennolds
John Richard
Sian Richardson
Joseph Richerson
Peter Richerson
Thomas Riddle
Thomas Roberson
Joseph Robins
Luke Robinson
Tirey Robinson
Hyram Rogers
Jacob Rogers
Josiah Rogers
Sion Rogers
Damsey Roles
Drury Rollins
James Round
Wm. Rousbrock
Josseph Routh
John Row
Burlingham Rudd
David Ruine
Mark Rushen
John Ryle
Samuel Saglar
     [Haglar?]
George Adam Salling
Jacob Samuel
Daniel Sanders
James Sanders
Patrick Sanders
William Sanders
Reuben Sanderson
Richard Sands
John Savor
Charles Saxon
[blank] Schwim
Joseph Scott
Job Self
Thomas Sellers

Hendry Senderman
Philip Shaw Jr.
Philip Shaw Sr.
John Shiphard
Conrad Shoemaker
John Shor
Daniel Short
William Short
William Sidden
John Sidewell
Christian Sike
John Simmons
Philip Sitton
Samuel Skin
John Skinner
Barnabee Skipper
George Skipper
Owen Slaughter
Alexander Smith
Benjamin Smith
Charles Smith
Daniel Smith
David Smith
Edward Smith
Francis Smith
Henry Smith
John Smith
John Smith
John Smith [Jr. or Sr.?]
Peter Smith
Richard Smith
Richard Smith [Jr. or Sr.?]
Robert Smith
Thomas Smith
Will Smith
Zechariah Smith
John Snider
John Smith Sondhill
Jacob Soots
Charles Sowel
John Sowel
Samuel Sowel
William Sowel

Lewis Sowell
Henry Sower
William Spencer
William Spere
Enoch Spinks
Jacob Stelie
John Stewart
John Stinkberry
Eron Stinton
Thomas Stockstil
Henry Stokes
Henry Strader
Jn. Stringer
William Stringfellow
Abraham Stroud
John Thos. Suggs
Joseph Sutton
James Sweany
Joseph Sweany
Thos. Swearinger
Barnit Swing [Zwing]
Lodwick Swing [Zwing]
John Swor Jr.
John Swor Sr.
Jonathan Swor Jr.
William Tague
Moses M. Tallant
Thomas Tallant
John Tarrance
Thomas Taylor
Edward Teage
Joshua Teague
Frederick Temple
Jeremiah Terrell
James Teruit
John Thomas
Zekel Thomas
James Thompson
Elisha Thomson
John Thomson
William Thomson
Robert Thorn
Edward Thornsbury

William Thornsbury
Abraham Thornton
David Thornton
Thomas Thorntown
William Thredgill
William Tomson
John Touchberry
Saml. Touchbery
Thomas Tree
William Treneen
George Troat
William Trousdale
Thomas Trull
Timothy Tukins
Jonathan Turner
James Upton
Thomas Ussery
Welcome Ussery
William Ussery
[blank] Van
  Swearingen
Amos Vernon
John Vickery
Johan Jacob Von
  Heilmer
Peter Von Stradoer
Henry Wade
Samuel Waggoner
Isaac Wainscott
Silvanus Waker
John Walker
Robert Walker
William Walker
Charles Walkinford
Jesse Wallas
Thomas Waller
Walter Walsh
William Ward
Wm. Ward Jr.
Jacob Watson
John Watts
Hyram Waver
Beaty Web
Joseph Web

John Webb
Lennard Webb
Richard Webb
Robert Webb
John Wed
William Weeb
Henry Welch
Walter Welch
Wm. Wellborn
Luke Welsh
Jacob Whit
Ulrick Whit
Augustin White
Charles White
Charles White [Jr. or Sr.?]
James White
John White
John White [Jr. or Sr.?]
Joseph White
Uldric White [Jr. or Sr.?]
William Wilborn Jr.
Thomas Wilborne
John Wilcox

William Wiley
James Wilkerson
Alex Wilkins [Jr. or Sr.?]
Alexander Wilkins
John Wilkins
John Wilkins [Jr. or Sr.?]
Robert Wilkins
Robert Wilkins [Jr. or Sr.?]
William Wilkins
James Will
James Willet
James Willet [Jr. or Sr.?]
Eshmael Williams
James Williams
James Williams
John Williams
Nehemiah Williams
Theofilis Williams
Geo. Wilson
George Wilson
James Wilson
John Wilson
Thomas Wilson

Richard Wineham
John Winkler
Daniel Winter
Nathaniel Wood
Reuben Woodward
Robert Woody
Thomas Word
Presley Wren
Philbert Wright
Thomas Wright
Hugh Wyley
Stokey Yeamons
John York
Robinson York
Saml. Young
James Youngblood
John Youngblood
Jno. Youngblood
Peter Youngblood
Peter Youngblood [Jr. or Sr.?]
Thomas Youngblood
James Younger

Appendix 2

Bibliographic Essay:
The Historians and the Regulators

"It proves to my mind, a disputed fact of history whether they [the Regulators] were a noble and chivalrous people or a lawless mob."

"I never looked upon the Regulators or the battle of Alamance as a patriotic measure—Herman Husband was a hypocritical Yankee Quaker, neither 'fish, flesh, food, nor good bed burring.' "

The first statement was made by a young Hillsborough lawyer in 1857, shocked by perusing the cryptic court records that survived the 1770 Regulator intrusion in the courthouse. His correspondent, a former North Carolina governor and current university president, was attempting to collect documents through which the state's history might be researched and reconstructed in the future. The squeamish comment expressed more than class-based distaste for the anger of farmers. It reflected as well an imperative for civic judgment to which elements of history were subject in the new nation. The caustic second comment—by an elite Hillsborough woman early in the twentieth century—adds bitterness born of her society's nineteenth-century experiences with "Yankees" and (abolitionist) "Quakers."[1]

Arguments for and against considering the Regulators as heroes had been published within a generation or so of the Revolution. The earliest ones, written by Hugh Williamson and Joseph Seawell Jones, reflected their sectional and ideological differences.[2] The "for or against" approach framed discussions of the Regulator Movement and Herman Husband among American historians in general and students of North Carolina in particular for the remainder of the nineteenth century.[3] Their basic lines of argument concerned morality and civic expediency: had the Regulators been "good men," or had they been "bad men"? (Considering them proto-revolutionaries was understood to argue that they were "good men.") Were they worthy to be upheld as exemplars of American liberty or merely ruffians whose only connection with the patriotism of the revolutionary era was the time sequence?

A positive contribution was made in the 1840s by Eli Caruthers, who sifted local traditions and, like Jones, interviewed former Regulators. About one-third of Caruthers's biography of David Caldwell devoted unprecedented attention to the Regulator Movement and the Battle of Alamance.[4] Subsequent pro-Regulator treatments relied heavily on Caruthers for specifics, sometimes without acknowledgment. As sectional tensions mounted, and particularly after the Civil War, some pro-Regulator writings degenerated into arguments for celebrating Alamance, rather than some northern event, as the first battle of the Revolution. Attempts to evaluate Husband apart from his followers added only a slight complexity to these efforts.[5] In 1880, John Wheeler Moore published the fullest treatment of North Carolina history to that point. While Moore found merit in the Regulators' grievances, he concluded that Husband was a demagogue who hijacked the movement and ran it aground.[6] In the same year, a marker commemorating the Battle of Alamance was erected following a year of private fund-raising in Alamance County. Subsequent booster emphasis on the "first battle of the Revolution" theme, along with Moore's conclusion that the Regulators did not question the legitimacy of the British government, lowered the appeal of the Regulator Movement among North Carolina scholars for a time.

Developments within the historical profession redirected interest to the eighteenth-century Piedmont, however, and the Regulators have not lacked attention for long since 1893, when Frederick Jackson Turner presented a paper to the American Historical Association titled, "The Significance of the Frontier in American History." For several decades, Turner and his students, most of whom were from the Midwest, South, and West, emphasized the importance of the frontier in shaping American character and institutions. Regarding the Regulators, Turner and his school generally credited democratic tendencies in the Piedmont frontier with challenging the established classes of the eastern seaboard, both before and after the American Revolution.[7] Moreover, in 1894, North Carolinian John Spencer Bassett, using questions about sectionalism and class conflict, researched the Regulator Movement more fully than it had been studied up to that time. Unlike earlier historians, Bassett had available the multivolume *Colonial Records of North Carolina* (eighteenth-century government documents) that William L. Saunders had recently edited and the State had published. Bassett's work had the effect of discrediting a direct connection between the Regulation and the Revolution. He concluded that the Regulator Movement was a widespread revolt by backcountry farmers against corruption and taxes brought on by eastern domination of the colonial government.[8] Bassett raised the stakes in Regulator research by sweeping away some of its distractions, and Turner's impact lifted the topic out of provincial confinement.

In the second half of the twentieth century, new questions and broader sources of information fed a rich stream of Regulator-related historical research. An enduring magnet for graduate students envisioning blockbuster theses, the Regulator Movement has drawn generations of researchers to apply fresh skills and insights to the colonial southern backcountry, a process that promises to remain productive. Explorations of specific aspects of backcountry life and Regulator activity revealed connections and nuances that had lain unknown when the Regulator Movement had been perceived simply as a tax revolt or a sectional conflict. At the same time, the disparities, variations, and contradictions thrown up by these investigations rendered narrative writing about the Regulator Movement far more challenging and probably postponed its accomplishment. The first published book-length monograph on the Regulator Movement, Marjoleine Kars's *Breaking Loose Together* in 2002, drew skillfully on the post-1950 findings to present a three-part Regulator context: economics, religion, and politics.

The most influential of a half century of Regulator studies include the following:

- William Stevens Powell, *The War of the Regulation and the Battle of Alamance, May 16, 1771* (Raleigh: State Department of Archives and History, 1949).

- Hugh T. Lefler, "Orange County and the War of the Regulation," in *Orange County 1752–1952*, Hugh Lefler and Paul Wager, eds. (Chapel Hill: University of North Carolina Press, 1953).

- F. Wilbur Helmbold, "Religious Aspects of the Regulator Movement in North Carolina," (typescript, North Carolina Collection, Wilson Library, University of North Carolina at Chapel Hill, Chapel Hill, 1953).

- Elisha P. Douglass, *Rebels and Democrats; The Struggle for Equal Political Rights and Majority Rule during the American Revolution* (Chapel Hill: University of North Carolina Press, 1955).

- Marvin L. Michael Kay, "The Payment of Local and Provincial Taxes in North Carolina, 1748–1771." *William and Mary Quarterly* 3rd ser., 29 (April 1969): 218–240.

- William Stevens Powell et al., eds., *The Regulators in North Carolina: A Documentary History 1759–1776* (Raleigh: Division of Archives and History, 1971).

- James Penn Whittenburg, "Backwoods Revolutionaries: Social Context and Constitutional Theories of North Carolina Regulators, 1765–1771" (Ph.D. diss., University of Georgia, 1974).

- Marvin L. Michael Kay, "The North Carolina Regulation, 1766–1776: A Class Conflict," in *The American Revolution: Explorations in the History of American Radicalism*, Alfred F. Young, ed. (DeKalb, Ill.: Northern Illinois University Press, 1976), 71–123.

- Roger Ekirch, "The North Carolina Regulators on Liberty and Corruption, 1766–1771," in *Perspectives in American History* 11 (1977–1978): 197–256.

- James Penn Whittenburg, "Planters, Merchants, and Lawyers: Social Change and the Origins of the North Carolina Regulation," *William and Mary Quarterly* 3rd ser., 34 (April 1977): 215–238.

- William Stevens Powell, ed., *The Correspondence of William Tryon and Other Selected Papers*, 2 vols. (Raleigh: Division of Archives and History, Department of Cultural Resources, 1980–1981).

- Roger Ekirch, *Poor Carolina: Politics and Society in Colonial North Carolina, 1729–1776* (Chapel Hill: University of North Carolina Press, 1981).

- Mark Haddon Jones, "Herman Husband: Millenarian, Carolina Regulator, and Whiskey Rebel" (Ph.D. diss., Northern Illinois University, 1983).

- Daniel Frederick Blower, "The Orange County and Mecklenburg County Instructions: The Development of Political Individualism in Backcountry North Carolina, 1740–1776" (Ph.D. diss., University of Michigan, 1984).

- Marjoleine Kars, " 'Breaking Loose Together': Religion and Rebellion in the North Carolina Piedmont, 1730–1790" (Ph.D. diss., Duke University, 1994).

- Andrew C. Denson, "Diversity, Religion, and the North Carolina Regulators," *North Carolina Historical Review* 72 (January 1995): 30–53.

- Lars C. Golumbic, "Who Shall Dictate the Law? Political Wrangling between 'Whig' Lawyers and Backcountry Farmers in Revolutionary Era North Carolina," *North Carolina Historical Review* 73 (January 1996): 56–75.

- Wayne Emmett Lee, "Careful Riot, Virtuous War: The Legitimation of Public Violence in Eighteenth-Century North Carolina" (Ph.D. diss., Duke University, 1999).

- Wayne Emmett Lee, *Crowds and Soldiers in Revolutionary North Carolina: The Culture of Violence in Riot and War* (Gainesville: University Press of Florida, 2001).

- Marjoleine Kars, *Breaking Loose Together: The Regulator Rebellion in Pre-Revolutionary North Carolina* (Chapel Hill: University of North Carolina Press, 2002).

Endnotes

Chapter 1

1. William L. Saunders, ed. *The Colonial Records of North Carolina*, 10 vols. (Raleigh: State of North Carolina, 1886–1890), 4:807 (quotation); Thornton W. Mitchell, "The Granville District and Its Land Records," *North Carolina Historical Review* 70 (April 1993): 103–129; W. N. Watt, *The Granville District* (Taylorsville, N.C.: W. N. Watt, 1992).

2. Saunders, *Colonial Records*, 5: 24 (quotation); William P. Cumming, "Wimble's Maps and the Colonial Cartography of the North Carolina Coast," *North Carolina Historical Review* 46 (Spring 1969): 157–170.

3. A. Roger Ekirch, " 'A New Government of Liberty': Hermon Husband's Vision of Backcountry North Carolina, 1755," *William and Mary Quarterly*, 3rd ser., 34 (October 1977): 639–641 (quotation, 639).

4. Orange County Court of Pleas and Quarter Sessions, Minute Docket, 1752–1754, North Carolina State Archives, Office of Archives and History, Raleigh; William S. Powell, ed., *Dictionary of North Carolina Biography*, 6 vols. (Chapel Hill: University of North Carolina Press, 1979–1996), s.v. "Corbin, Francis."

5. Ekirch, "New Government of Liberty," 639–640. For Carter and John Frohock (below) see Joshua Lee McKaughan, "People of Desperate Fortune: Power and Populations in the North Carolina Backcountry," *Journal of Backcountry Studies* 2 (Spring 2007) http://libjournal.uncg.edu/ojs/index.php/jbc.

6. *Dictionary of North Carolina Biography*, s.v. "Corbin, Francis"; A. Roger Ekirch, *"Poor Carolina": Politics and Society in Colonial North Carolina, 1729–1776* (Chapel Hill: University of North Carolina Press, 1981), 139–142; Wayne E. Lee, *Crowds and Soldiers in Revolutionary North Carolina: The Culture of Violence in Riot and War* (Gainesville: University Press of Florida, 2001), 24–28.

7. Saunders, *Colonial Records*, 4:1086 (quotation). The McCullohs' opportunities for speculation in North Carolina sprang from their ties with the Board of Trade, exemplifying the power that networks of mercantile and landholding families exercised over the British Isles and the colonies by the mid-eighteenth century. Charles G. Sellers Jr., "Private Profits and British Colonial Policy: The Speculations of Henry McCulloh," *William and Mary Quarterly*, 3rd ser., 8 (October 1951): 548; Daniel Frederick Blower, "The Orange County and Mecklenburg County Instructions: The Development of Political Individualism in Backcountry North Carolina, 1740–1776" (Ph.D. diss., University of Michigan, 1984), 228–240; Marjoleine Kars, *Breaking Loose Together: The Regulator Rebellion in Pre-Revolutionary North Carolina* (Chapel Hill: University of North Carolina Press, 2002), 39; *Dictionary of North Carolina Biography*, s.v. "Fanning, Edmund"; Saunders, *Colonial Records*, 8:230; William S. Powell et al., eds., *The Regulators in North Carolina: A Documentary History, 1759–1776* (Raleigh: Division of Archives and History, 1971), 31–32.

8. Saunders, *Colonial Records*, 7:22, quoted in Lee, *Crowds and Soldiers*, 31 (quotation); McCulloh's account of events is in William S. Powell, ed., *The Correspondence of William Tryon and Other Selected Papers*, 2 vols. (Raleigh: Division

of Archives and History, Department of Cultural Resources, 1980–1981), 1:66–82 (quotation, 75); Kevin L. Yeager, "The Power of Ethnicity: The Preservation of Scots-Irish Culture in the Eighteenth-Century American Backcountry" (Ph.D. diss., Louisiana State University, 2000), 186–188; Norris W. Preyer, *Hezekiah Alexander and the Revolution in the Backcountry* (Charlotte: Heritage Printers, 1987), 56–57; Powell, *Regulators*, 17–22; Edward Palmer Thompson, *Customs in Common* (New York: New Press, 1993), 1–15, 517–519.

9. Henry Eustace McCulloh to Edmund Fanning, May 5, 1765, Saunders, *Colonial Records*, 7:32–33. For the English context of the 1723 law, see Edward Palmer Thompson, *Whigs and Hunters: The Origin of the Black Act* (London: Allen Lane, 1975).

10. Gov. Josiah Martin to Lord Hillsborough, September 5, 1772, Colonial Office 5/303, 22, British Records, North Carolina State Archives.

11. Orange County Court of Pleas and Quarter Sessions, Minute Docket, March 1754; Rowan County Court of Pleas and Quarter Sessions, Minute Docket, 1753–1766, North Carolina State Archives. The minutes are abstracted in Ruth Herndon Shields, *Orange County, N.C. Abstracts of the Minutes of the Court of Pleas and Quarter Sessions of Sept. 1752–Aug. 1766* (Greenville, S.C.: Southern Historical Press, 1991), and Jo White Linn, comp., *Abstracts of the Minutes of the Court of Pleas and Quarter Sessions, Rowan County, North Carolina*, 3 vols. (Salisbury, N.C.: Mrs. Stahle Linn Jr., 1979–1982), vol. 1.

12. Orange County Court of Pleas and Quarter Sessions, Minute Docket, 1752–1766 (quotation, August 17, 1765); Powell, *Regulators*, 581–582; John L. Cheney Jr., ed., *North Carolina Government, 1585–1974: A Narrative and Statistical History* (Raleigh: Department of the Secretary of State, 1981), 46; Saunders, *Colonial Records*, 9:372, 470, 471; Walter Clark, ed., *The State Records of North Carolina*, 16 vols. (11–26) (Raleigh: State of North Carolina, 1895–1906), 23:627–629; 25:520–521.

13. For western Orange County, the lack of road orders during the Regulator period may reflect the inflammatory role of this issue. During and after the Revolutionary War, there was a fresh spate of road maintenance. Orange County Court of Pleas and Quarter Sessions, Minute Docket, 1777–1795. The 1777–1788 minutes are abstracted in Alma Cheek Redden, *Orange Co., N.C. Abstracts of the Minutes of the Inferior Court of Pleas & Quarter Sessions, 1777–1788* (Greenville, S.C.: Southern Historical Press, 1991); Marvin Lawrence Michael Kay, "The North Carolina Regulation, 1766–1776: A Class Conflict," in *The American Revolution: Explorations in the History of American Radicalism*, ed. Alfred F. Young (DeKalb, Ill.: Northern Illinois University Press, 1976), 71–123; Marvin Lawrence Michael Kay and William S. Price Jr., " 'To Ride the Wood Mare': Road Building and Militia Service in Colonial North Carolina, 1740–1775," *North Carolina Historical Review* 57 (Autumn 1980): 361–409 (quotation, 377).

14. Hugh T. Lefler, "Orange County and the War of the Regulation," in *Orange County 1752–1952*, eds. Hugh Lefler and Paul Wager (Chapel Hill: University of North Carolina Press, 1953), 26.

15. Robert L. Ganyard, *The Emergence of North Carolina's Revolutionary State Government* (Raleigh: Division of Archives and History, 1978), 5–13.

16. Julian P. Boyd, "The Sheriff in Colonial North Carolina," *North Carolina Historical Review* 5 (April 1928): 151–180 (quotation, 180).

17. Alamance, Caswell, Chatham, Durham, Guilford, Johnston, Lee., Orange, Person, Randolph, Rockingham, and Wake. Ruth Blackwelder, *The Age of Orange: Political and Intellectual Leadership in North Carolina, 1752–1861* (Charlotte: William Loftin, 1961), 2.

18. Powell, *Regulators*, 81 (quotation); James Penn Whittenburg, "Backwoods Revolutionaries: Social Context and Constitutional Theories of the North Carolina Regulators, 1765–1771" (Ph.D. diss., University of Georgia, 1974), 90–91; *Dictionary of North Carolina Biography*, s.v. "Fanning, William."

19. Powell, *Regulators*, 81 (first quotation); Henry Eustace McCulloh to Edmund Fanning, May 9, 1765, Saunders, *Colonial Records*, 7:32.

20. Powell, *Regulators*, 564–565, 567.

Chapter 2

1. François-Xavier Martin, *The History of North Carolina from the Earliest Period*, 2 vols. (New Orleans: A. T. Penniman, 1829), 2:227.

2. Lefler, "Orange County and the Regulation," 29.

3. The Boston *Chronicle* printed the remark on November 7, 1768. Powell, *Regulators*, 195–196.

4. The text of Searcy's petition and the subsequent Nutbush Address were first published in Archibald Henderson, "The Origin of the Regulation in North Carolina," *American Historical Review* 21 (January 1916): 320–332. They were subsequently published in William K. Boyd, ed., *Some Eighteenth Century Tracts concerning North Carolina* (Raleigh: Edwards and Broughton, 1927), 175–192. The North Carolina Office of Archives and History has made them available at http://www.ncpublications.com/colonial/Bookshelf/Tracts/Nutbush%20Address/introduction.htm.

5. Emphasis added. Quoted in Henderson, "Origin of the Regulation," 324. As with lawyers, the level of resentment of local planters by farmers whose views spokesmen such as Searcy and George Sims reflected depended on how they used their position, particularly regarding debt collection in court. James P. Whittenburg, "Planters, Merchants, and Lawyers: Social Change and the Origins of the North Carolina Regulation," *William and Mary Quarterly*, 3rd ser., 34 (April 1977): 215–238. Lars C. Golumbic, "Who Shall Dictate the Law? Political Wrangling between 'Whig' Lawyers and Backcountry Farmers in Revolutionary Era North Carolina," *North Carolina Historical Review* 73 (January 1996): 56–82, examines the lawyer-versus-farmer theme in the 1770s and 1780s.

6. Emphasis added. Archibald Henderson, ed., "Hermon Husband's Continuation of the Impartial Relation," *North Carolina Historical Review* 18 (January 1941): 48-81 (quotation, 80).

7. Saunders, *Colonial Records*, 5:lviii (first quotation); Ekirch, *Poor Carolina*, 141 (second quotation); Saunders, *Colonial Records*, 6:107, 113; *Oxford English Dictionary*, Compact ed., 2 vols. (London: Oxford University Press, 1971), N, 216, "nose-" (17b).

8. "The Nutbush Address," in Boyd, *Eighteenth Century Tracts*, 182–192; *Dictionary of North Carolina Biography*, s.v. "Sims, George."

9. *Dictionary of North Carolina Biography*, s.v. "Benton, Samuel" and "Person, Thomas."

10. Emphasis added. "The Nutbush Address," in Boyd, *Eighteenth Century Tracts*, 186.

11. One example was a 1769 petition from dissenters in Orange and Rowan counties for the legislature to "grant us a Repeal of the [Marriage] Act, prohibiting Dissenting Ministers from marrying according to the Decretals, Rites and Ceremonies, of their Respective Churches: a privilege they were debarred of in no other part of his Majesty's dominions; and as we humbly conceive, a privilege they stand entitled to, by the *Act of Toleration* [1689], and in fine, a privilege granted even to the very Catholics of Ireland." Saunders, *Colonial Records*, 8:82–83.

12. "The Nutbush Address," in Boyd, *Eighteenth Century Tracts*, 185, 187 (quotation).

13. "The Nutbush Address," in Boyd, *Eighteenth Century Tracts*, 187–189.

14. Emphasis added and punctuation adjusted. "The Nutbush Address," in Boyd, *Eighteenth Century Tracts*, 189–190; Sims's illustration typifies actual cases cited in Kars, *Breaking Loose Together*, 72.

15. "The Nutbush Address," in Boyd, *Eighteenth Century Tracts*, 182, 191–192.

16. [Hermon Husband], *A Fan for Fanning, and a Touch-Stone to Tryon*, in Boyd, *Eighteenth Century Tracts*, 347.

17. Emphasis added. "The Nutbush Address," in Boyd, *Eighteenth Century Tracts*, 191-192.

18. Powell, *Regulators*, 27.

Chapter 3

1. Whittenburg, "Backwoods Revolutionaries," 314; *Oxford English Dictionary*, A, 513.

2. William Barlow, *The summe and substance of the conference . . . at Hampton Court, January 14, 1603* (1604; reprint, Gainesville, Fla.: Scholars' Facsimiles and Reprints, 1965), 79 (quotation); Susan Mosteller Rolland, "From the Rhine to the Catawba: A Study of Eighteenth-Century Germanic Migration and Adaptation" (Ph.D. diss., Emory University, 1991).

3. Stephen Jay White, "North Carolina Quakers in the Era of the American Revolution" (master's thesis, University of Tennessee, 1981).

4. Sheridan Gilley and W. J. Sheils, eds., *A History of Religion in Britain: Practice and Belief from Pre-Roman Times to the Present* (Cambridge: Blackwell, 1994); George A. Rawlyk, Mark A. Noll, and David W. Bebbington, eds., *Evangelicalism: Comparative Studies of Popular Protestantism in North America, the British Isles, and Beyond, 1700–1900* (New York: Oxford University Press, 1994).

5. Marilyn Westerkamp, *Triumph of the Laity: Scots-Irish Piety and the Great Awakening, 1625–1760* (New York: Oxford University Press, 1988), 15–42, 186– 189; Eve B. Weeks and Mary B. Warren, eds., *Morgan Edwards Materials towards a History of the Baptists*, 2 vols. (Danielsville, Ga.: Heritage Papers, 1984), 2:91; Mechal Sobel,

The World They Made Together: Black and White Values in Eighteenth-Century Virginia (Princeton: Princeton University Press, 1987), 180–203.

6. [Alexander Craighead], *Renewal of the Covenants, National and Solemn League; A Confession of Sins, and Engagement to Duties; and a Testimony As They Were Carried on at Middle Octarara in Pensylvania, November 11, 1743 Together with an Introductory Preface*, "reprinted" 1746, microfilm of original at Presbyterian Historical Society, Philadelphia, 15; *Dictionary of North Carolina Biography*, s.v. "Craighead, Alexander"; William Henry Foote, *Sketches of North Carolina, Historical and Biographical, Illustrative of the Principles of a Portion of Her Early Settlers* (1846; reprint, Raleigh: Harold J. Dudley, 1965), 163–164, 183–193, 479; Neill Roderick McGeachy, *A History of the Sugaw Creek Presbyterian Church* (Rock Hill, S.C.: Record Print Company, 1954), 14.

7. John B. Boles, *The Great Revival: Beginnings of the Bible Belt* (Lexington: University of Kentucky Press, 1996).

8. James E. Bradley, *Religion, Revolution, and English Radicalism: Nonconformity in Eighteenth-Century Politics and Society* (New York: Cambridge University Press, 1990); Robert Hole, *Pulpits, Politics, and Public Order in England, 1760–1832* (New York: Cambridge University Press, 1989); Geoffrey S. Holmes, *Politics, Religion, and Society in England, 1679–1742* (Roncevert, W. Va.: Hambledon Press, 1986); Margaret Spufford, ed., *The World of Rural Dissenters, 1520–1725* (New York: Cambridge University Press, 1995).

9. Elizabeth Cometti, "Some Early Best Sellers in Piedmont North Carolina," *Journal of Southern History* 16 (August 1950): 327, 335.

10. James Kirk, " 'The Polities of the Best Reformed Kirks': Scottish Achievements and English Aspirations in Church Government after the Reformation," *Scottish Historical Review* 59 (April 1980): 22–54; Ian B. Cowan, *The Scottish Covenanters, 1660–1688* (London: Gollancz, 1976).

11. Edward J. Cowan, "Prophecy and Prophylaxis: A Paradigm for the Scotch-Irish?" in *Ulster and North America: Transatlantic Perspectives on the Scotch-Irish*, eds. H. Tyler Blethen and Curtis W. Wood Jr. (Tuscaloosa: University of Alabama Press, 1997), 15–23; Sean J. Connolly, "Ulster Presbyterians: Religion, Culture, and Politics, 1660–1850," in *Ulster and North America*, 24–40; Gordon Donaldson, *Scotland James V to James VII* (Edinburgh: Oliver and Boyd, 1965), 319–342, 358–384; Westerkamp, *Triumph of Laiety*, 105–135.

12. Craighead, *Renewal of Covenants*, 6.

13. Powell, *Regulators*, 227.

14. Petition to Earl Granville, ca. 1756, Granville District Papers from the Marquis of Bath's Library in Longleat, Wiltshire, English Records (microfilm), North Carolina State Archives; the petition with signatories is published in William D. Bennett, comp., *Orange County Records*, 13 vols. (Raleigh: The compiler, 1987), 7:59–69. Paul Conkin, "The Church Establishment in North Carolina, 1765–1776," *North Carolina Historical Review* 32 (January 1955): 1–30.

15. Adelaide L. Fries, et al., eds., *Records of the Moravians in North Carolina*, 13 vols. (Raleigh: Division of Archives and History, 1922–2006), 1:191–192.

16. Goddard D. Bernheim, *History of the German Settlements and of the Lutheran Church in North and South Carolina* (Philadelphia: Lutheran Book Store, 1872), 196–197; Fries, *Moravian Records*, 1:172, 196–198; Society for the Propagation of the Gospel, Journal 19:88, 207–208, 252 (microfilm), Library of Congress.

Chapter 4

1. "Tour of Rev. Morgan Edwards of Pennsylvania to the American Baptists in North Carolina in 1772–73," copied by Walter Durham, North Carolina Collection, Wilson Library, University of North Carolina at Chapel Hill, 11; Elder John Sparks, *The Roots of Appalachian Christianity: The Life & Legacy of Elder Shubal Stearns* (Lexington: University of Kentucky Press, 2001), 89–91.

2. Eli Washington Caruthers, *A Sketch of the Life and Character of the Reverend David Caldwell, D.D.* (Greensboro, N.C.: Swaim and Sherwood, 1842), 130.

3. *Dictionary of North Carolina Biography*, s.v. "Husband, Herman"; Mark H. Jones, "Herman Husband: Millenarian, Carolina Regulator, and Whiskey Rebel" (Ph.D. diss., Northwestern University, 1983); Sobel, *World They Made Together*, 181, 189, 203; Mechal Sobel, *Trabelin' On: The Slave Journey to an Afro-Baptist Faith* (Princeton: Princeton University Press, 1990); John B. Boles, "Slaves in Biracial Protestant Churches," in *Varieties of Southern Religious Experience*, ed. Samuel S. Hill (Baton Rouge: Louisiana State University Press, 1988), 95–113.

4. Jones, "Herman Husband," 39 (first quotation), 53–57; [Hermon Husband], *Some Remarks on Religion*, in Boyd, *Eighteenth Century Tracts*, 195–246 (second quotation, 240).

5. Ekirch, "New Government of Liberty," 635.

6. Ekirch, "New Government of Liberty," 641, 644; Powell, *Regulators*, 484.

7. Useful abstracts of Orange County Deed Books 1 and 2 are in *Register of Orange County, North Carolina, Deeds 1752–1768 and 1793*, transcribed by Eve B. Weeks (Danielsville, Ga.: Heritage Papers, 1984) and Bennett, *Orange County Records*, vols. 2 and 3. Volumes 1, 5, 6, and 7 of *Orange County Records* contain abstracts of Orange County and some Rowan County material in the Office of Secretary of State, Land Office (Colonial), Granville Proprietary Land Office, Land Entries, Warrants, and Plats of Survey, 1748–1763, North Carolina State Archives. Rowan deed abstracts are in *Rowan County, North Carolina Deed Abstracts*, compiled by Jo White Linn (Salisbury, N.C.: Mrs. Stahle Linn Jr., 1972). These aids are helpful for using land grant records at the North Carolina State Archives from the Office of Secretary of State.

8. Ekirch, "New Government of Liberty," 646.

9. Robert B. Semple, *History of the Rise and Progress of the Baptists in Virginia* (Richmond: John O'Lynch, printer, 1810), 2 (quotation); A. J. Patterson, "In Memoriam. Elder Shubal Stearns. . . ." (Liberty, N.C.: W. H. Eller, 1902), North Carolina Collection; "Rev. Shubal Stearns," in John Wheeler Moore, *Sketches of Pioneer Baptist Preachers in North Carolina*, scrapbook of clippings from *The Biblical Recorder*, North Carolina Collection; Josh Powell, "Shubal Stearns and the Separate Baptist Tradition, " *Founders Journal* 44 (Spring 2001): 16–31; David T. Morgan Jr., "The Great Awakening in North Carolina, 1740–1775: The Baptist Phase," *North Carolina Historical Review* 45 (Summer 1968): 264–283; Sparks, *Roots of Appalachian*

Christianity, 61-62; Orange County Court of Pleas and Quarter Sessions, Minute Docket, March 1759, 352; Grant to Semore York, plat, September 9, 1755, Office of Secretary of State, Land Office (Colonial), Granville Proprietary Land Office, Grants of Deed, 1748–1763, North Carolina State Archives.

10. "Tour of Rev. Morgan Edwards," 7.

11. Weeks, *Register of Orange County Deeds*, 4–50 passim; Bennett, *Orange County Records*, vols. 2, 3; George W. Paschal, "Morgan Edwards' Materials towards a History of the Baptists in the Province of North Carolina," *North Carolina Historical Review* 7 (July 1930): 365–399.

12. Cane Creek Monthly Meeting, December 1755, December 1760, February, April 1761, Friends Historical Collection, Guilford College.

13. Cane Creek Monthly Meeting, May 1761; Western Quarterly Meeting, August 1761, Friends Historical Collection.

14. Emphasis added. Cane Creek Monthly Meeting, April 1776.

15. Algie I. Newlin, *Charity Cook: A Liberated Woman* (Richmond, Ind.: Friends United Press, 1981), 26.

16. Grants to John Wright, Anson County (1755), Pasquotank County (1753, 1759), Office of Secretary of State, Land Office (Colonial), Granville Proprietary Land Office, Land Entries, Warrants, and Plats of Survey, 1748–1763, North Carolina State Archives; grant to John Wright, Orange County (1755), Office of Secretary of State, Land Office (Colonial), Granville Proprietary Land Office, Grants of Deed, 1748–1763, North Carolina State Archives; grant to John Wright, Anson County (1768), Office of Secretary of State, Land Office (Colonial and State), Land Warrants, Plats of Survey, and Related Records, 1663–1959, North Carolina State Archives; John Wright Memorials, 6:124, 10:8, 15; Plats 11:42; Grants 15:86, 17:115, South Carolina State Archives, Columbia; Cane Creek Monthly Meeting, February 1762; Newlin, *Charity Cook*, 29–31.

17. Emphasis added. Western Quarterly Meeting, November 1762, February 1763.

18. Western Quarterly Meeting, May 1763; Cane Creek Monthly Meeting, March 1767.

19. Mary Pugh's family had been at Cane Creek since the 1750s, and she was received into membership in April 1762 in preparation for marriage. Cane Creek Monthly Meeting, April, July 1762; Jones, "Herman Husband," 74–75.

20. Cane Creek Monthly Meeting, November 1763.

21. Jones, "Herman Husband," 87; November 10, 1764, minutes from Western Quarterly Meeting, in Cane Creek Monthly Meeting, November 1764.

22. Emphasis and commas added. Quoted in Jones, "Herman Husband," 88, 89; see also Kars, *Breaking Loose Together*, 114–117.

23. George W. Paschal, *History of North Carolina Baptists*, 2 vols. (Raleigh: General Board, North Carolina Baptist State Convention, 1930, 1955), 1:289; Catherine A. Brekus, *Strangers & Pilgrims: Female Preaching in America, 1740–1845* (Chapel Hill: University of North Carolina Press, 1998), 62.

24. Cane Creek Monthly Meeting, June 1766.

Chapter 5

1. Whittenburg, "Backwoods Revolutionaries," 316; Cane Creek Monthly Meeting, October, December 1765; January, February, September, December 1766; February, March 1767; Guilford County Deed Book 1:242 (microfilm), North Carolina State Archives.

2. The term "Regulator" had come into use in the South Carolina backcountry earlier in the 1760s. There it described informal forces seeking to impose order on marginal people and criminals in the absence of county courts. Powell, *Regulators*, 35; Richard Maxwell Brown, *The South Carolina Regulators* (Cambridge: Harvard University Press, 1963); Rachel N. Klein, *Unification of a Slave State: The Rise of the Planter Class in the South Carolina Backcountry, 1760–1808* (Chapel Hill: University of North Carolina Press, 1992).

3. [Hermon Husband], *An Impartial Relation of the First Rise and Cause of the Recent Differences, in Publick Affairs, in . . . North Carolina* (1770), in Boyd, *Eighteenth Century Tracts*, 245–333.

4. [Husband], *Impartial Relation*, in Boyd, *Eighteenth Century Tracts*, 263.

5. [Husband], *Impartial Relation*, in Boyd, *Eighteenth Century Tracts*, 257n.

6. [Husband], *Impartial Relation*, in Boyd, *Eighteenth Century Tracts*, 304–305.

7. Lefler, "Orange County," 30; Powell, *Regulators*, 117.

8. [Husband], *Impartial Relation*, in Boyd, *Eighteenth Century Tracts*, 261 (first quotation); [Husband], *A Fan for Fanning*, in Boyd, *Eighteenth Century Tracts*, 355 (second quotation).

9. Powell, *Regulators*, 84.

10. Powell, *Regulators*, 115, 119; Saunders, *Colonial Records*, 7:733–737; Cheney, *North Carolina Government*, 47.

11. Clark, *State Records*, 22:569 (quotations); Archibald DeBow Murphey's notes from his interviews with MacPherson are in the Regulator Papers, Southern Historical Collection, Wilson Library, University of North Carolina at Chapel Hill, with portions published in Clark, *State Records*, 22:563–571; *Dictionary of North Carolina Biography*, s.v. "Murphey, Archibald DeBow"; grant to James Hunter, September 1758, Book 93A:215, Office of Secretary of State, Land Office (Colonial and State), Patent Books, 1663–1959, North Carolina State Archives; Henderson, "Herman Husband's Continuation," 54.

12. Powell, *Regulators*, 109, 114–121 (quotation, 120).

13. Benson J. Lossing, *The Pictorial Field-Book of the Revolution*, 2 vols. (New York: Harper and Brothers, 1859), 2:366; Fred Hughes, *Randolph County, North Carolina: Historical Documentation* (Jamestown, N.C.: The Custom House, [1976]).

14. Powell, *Regulators*, 566–567; Murphey notes, Regulator Papers.

Chapter 6

1. E. Thomson Shields, ed., " 'A Modern Poem' by the Mecklenburg Censor: Politics and Satire in Revolutionary North Carolina," *Early American Literature* 29, 3 (1994): 218–225; Foote, *Sketches of North Carolina*, 193–194.

2. James Reed to Secretary of Society for the Propagation of the Gospel, July 20, 1766, Saunders, *Colonial Records*, 7:241 (quotation), 252–253.

3. Saunders, *Colonial Records*, 8:217, 78–83; 10:1015; McGeachy, *Sugaw Creek Presbyterian Church*, 195; Powell, *Regulators*, 128–134.

4. This legislation was passed in December 1770–January 1771. William Tryon to Secretary of State Lord Hillsborough, March 12, 1771, Powell, *Tryon Correspondence*, 628–630; Saunders, *Colonial Records*, 8:486.

5. Mecklenburg County Deed Book 7:268–271, abstracted in Brent Holcomb and Elmer Parker, *Mecklenburg County, North Carolina Deed Abstracts, 1763–1779* (Easley, S.C.: Southern Historical Press, 1979), 205–206 (quotation); Saunders, *Colonial Records*, 5:835, 853–854; Clark, *State Records*, 23:772; *Dictionary of North Carolina Biography*, s.v. "Phifer, Martin"; Tryon to Hillsborough, March 12, 1771, Powell, *Tryon Correspondence*, 628-630; Yeager, "Power of Ethnicity," 235–238.

6. Emphasis and punctuation added. General Assembly Session Records, Session of November–December 1768, Bills, Lower House, November 14–24, 1768.

7. Saunders, *Colonial Records*, 7:929, 939, 942. General Assembly Session Records, Sessions of December 1767–January 1768 and November–December 1768, Lower House.

8. Holcomb and Parker, *Mecklenburg Deed Abstracts*, 205–206.

9. Preyer, *Hezekiah Alexander*, 64; Saunders, *Colonial Records*, 5:835, 853–854; 6:832, 1151; 7:64, 343–344, 378–380, 929–940; 8:633, 747; Powell, *Regulators*, 130–133.

10. Powell, *Regulators*, 129–133, 163–165.

Chapter 7

1. Lefler, "Orange County," 35.

2. Saunders, *Colonial Records*, 8:xxx.

3. Punctuation added. William McPherson, quoted in Powell, *Regulators*, 240–241; Henderson, "Herman Husband's Continuation," 71.

4. [Husband], *Impartial Relation*, in Boyd, *Eighteenth Century Tracts*, 306.

5. Martin, *History of North Carolina*, 2:243–244.

6. Shields, "Modern Poem," 218

7. Jacobus Arminius [d. 1609], a Dutch Calvinist theologian, had opposed the absolute predestination associated with John Calvin. In pre-Civil War England, "Arminian" doctrine had been espoused by champions of royal civil and ecclesiastical authority. That connotation would have been distasteful to Avery, a Presbyterian "of Puritan extraction." *Dictionary of North Carolina Biography*, s.v. "Avery, Waightstill."

8. Powell, *Regulators*, 218.

9. Saunders, *Colonial Records*, 8:32.

10. [Husband], *Impartial Relation*, in Boyd, *Eighteenth Century Tracts*, 306–308.

11. Saunders, *Colonial Records*, 8:225.

12. Lefler, "Orange County," 36; Saunders, *Colonial Records*, 8:803.

13. Husband had a legislative proposal to protect settlers on vacant Granville land: "to Pass a Law, that whoever among us shall enter such Improvements, over the head of any such peaceable first Inhabitant, either by himself or by Virtue of a Purchase, shall be liable to an Action at Common Law, and subject to pay the Owner the Value of his Labour, and Damages of moving to another Place, unless such Person had given six Months Warning." [Husband], *Impartial Relation*, in Boyd, *Eighteenth Century Tracts*, 310. Petition of Inhabitants of Orange County, October 27, 1769, General Assembly Session Records, Session of October–November 1769, Lower House Papers, Petitions rejected or not acted on.

14. Henderson, "Herman Husband's Continuation," 69; Saunders, *Colonial Records*, 8:76, 78; *Dictionary of North Carolina Biography*, s.v. "McCulloh, Henry Eustace." Petition of Inhabitants of Anson County, October 9, 1769, General Assembly Session Records, Session of October–November 1769, Lower House Papers, Committee of Propositions and Grievances.

15. Petition of Inhabitants of Orange County, October 27, 1769; Saunders, *Colonial Records*, 8:111–112.

16. Saunders, *Colonial Records*, 8:111–112; Resolution for Warrant, October 27, 1769, General Assembly Session Records, Session of October–November 1769, Lower House Papers, Committee of Privileges and Elections.

17. Saunders, *Colonial Records*, 8:106–141; General Assembly Session Records, Session of November–December 1768, Lower House Papers.

18. Powell, *Regulators*, 278; Saunders, *Colonial Records*, 8:185; Hillsborough District Superior Court, Minute Docket, March 1770, 11–13, North Carolina State Archives.

19. Hillsborough District Superior Court, Minute Docket, March 1770, 13.

20. Saunders, *Colonial Records*, 8:235; Hillsborough District Superior Court, Minute Docket, March 1770, 13.

21. Emphasis added. Powell, *Regulators*, 268–272 (quotation, 270–271); Saunders, *Colonial Records*, 8:231–234.

22. Emphasis added. Powell, *Regulators*, 245–246.

23. Jeremiah Field was not likely the writer of the comments, as a group of his friends said in 1776 that he could not read. Saunders, *Colonial Records*, 8:236–240.

24. Powell, *Regulators*, 268–272 (quotation, 271–272).

25. Saunders, *Colonial Records*, 8:534.

26. Joseph M. Morehead, "James Hunter, an Address" (Greensboro: Guilford Battle Ground Company, 1897), 18; Saunders, *Colonial Records*, 8:521–522, 545.

27. Emphasis added. Powell, *Regulators*, 266–268 (first quotation); Saunders, *Colonial Records*, 8:542; Paul David Nelson, *William Tryon and the Course of Empire: A Life in British Imperial Service* (Chapel Hill: University of North Carolina Press, 1990), 7.

28. Order of the King in Council, April 22, 1772, CO 5/302, 96–97, British Records, North Carolina State Archives; Martin, *History of North Carolina*, 2:265–270.

29. Powell, *Regulators*, 295–298 (first quotation, 296), 337 (second quotation), 340, 395–396; Jones, "Herman Husband," 175–176; Saunders, *Colonial Records*, 8:262–265.

30. Hunter was aware that Fanning had successfully appealed his penny fine, with the North Carolina Superior Court declaring that he had been "ignorant of or had innocently misinterpreted the law." Henderson, "Herman Husband's Continuation," 55; Powell, *Regulators*, 277–280 (quotation, 280); Whittenburg, "Backwoods Pioneers," 407–410.

Chapter 8

1. William Edwards Fitch, *Some Neglected History of North Carolina*, rev. ed. (New York: The author, 1914), 276.

2. Powell, *Regulators*, 374–375.

3. Punctuation adjusted. Powell, *Regulators*, 373–374; Whittenburg, "Backwoods Pioneers," 312–314.

4. Tryon noted that recruiting was more successful in the southeastern counties than in the northeast, where the certifying treasurer refused to authorize payment to militiamen. General Assembly Session Records, Session of November–December 1768 (oversized), (quotation); Powell, *Regulators*, 496; Fries, *Moravian Records*, 2:735; Saunders, *Colonial Records*, 8:541.

5. Powell, *Regulators*, 304–305.

6. Lefler, "Orange County," 39; Martin, *History of North Carolina*, 2:274; Powell, *Regulators*, 361–362, 461.

7. Tryon to Hillsborough, December 14, 1771, Powell, *Tryon Correspondence*, 2:846; Powell, *Regulators*, xxiii, 487; Saunders, *Colonial Records*, 8:607; Fries, *Moravian Records*, 1:461.

8. Martin, *History of North Carolina*, 2:277–278.

9. Powell, *Regulators*, 427.

10. Tryon had camped there during his 1768 militia maneuvers in Regulator country, and Charles Lord Cornwallis and others would use the site during the Revolutionary War. The campsite was identified near a local landmark known as "Little Buzzard Rock" by local resident James Carleton Lowe, who compared the landforms with terrain details recorded by Claude Joseph Sauthier, Tryon's engineer and geographer. Sauthier prepared several drafts of military charts of the area between Alamance Creek and the site of the Battle of Alamance. On one chart he indicated that the Regulators' camp, which was the site of the battle, was four miles from Tryon's camp, and on another he said five miles. Claude Joseph Sauthier, seven military charts titled, "A Plan of the Camp and Battle of Alamance, the 16th May 1771" and "A Plan of the Camp at Alamance from the 14th to the 19th of May 1771," Map Collection, North Carolina State Archives. Lowe's work is incorporated into a report by the Trading Path Association at http://www.tradingpath.org/content/view/104/28/.

11. Powell, *Regulators*, 426–429; Clark, *State Records*, 19:841–842.

12. William Henry Hoyt, ed., *The Papers of Archibald D. Murphey*, 2 vols. (Raleigh: E. M. Uzzell and Company, 1914); Herbert Snipes Turner, *The Dreamer: Archibald DeBow Murphey* (Verona, Va.: McClure Press, 1971); Eli Washington Caruthers, *Revolutionary Incidents and Sketches of Character Chiefly in the "Old North State"*

(Philadelphia: Hayes and Zell, 1854); Eli Washington Caruthers, *Interesting Revolutionary Incidents and Sketches of Character Chiefly in the "Old North State,"* 2nd ser. (Philadelphia: Hayes and Zell, 1856); Caruthers, *Life of Caldwell.*

13. Caruthers, *Life of Caldwell,* 147–148.

14. An eyewitness in the governor's entourage said the Orange County militia had "200 men exclusive of Officers" at Alamance. The troop return of May 26 reported 165 rank and file, 26 officers, 4 surgeons and mates, 4 clerks, 3 drummers, 3 servants, and 2 wagoners in the Orange detachment. Samuel Cornell to Elias Desbrosses, [June 6, 1771], enclosed in Earl Dunmore to Hillsborough, June 20, 1771, CO 5/154, 1:16–17, English Records [ER 13-10], North Carolina State Archives; Powell, *Regulators,* 461.

15. Powell, *Regulators,* 453–454.

16. Powell, *Regulators,* 453–456.

17. Cornell soon afterwards wrote a letter describing the battle that seems to have been the basis for the *Virginia Gazette* account of June 6. Other newspapers and early histories used the *Virginia Gazette* story, albeit selectively, because Cornell's description defended Tryon's attack. Cornell to Desbrosses, [June 6, 1771].

18. Joseph Seawell Jones, *A Defence of the Revolutionary History of the State of North Carolina from the Aspersions of Mr. Jefferson* (Raleigh: Turner and Hughes, 1834), 61.

19. Powell, *Regulators,* 471.

20. Caruthers, *Life of Caldwell,* 152.

21. Martin, *History of North Carolina,* 2:282; Caruthers, *Life of Caldwell,* 152.

22. Murphey notes, Regulator Papers; see also Caruthers, *Life of Caldwell,* 150–169; Powell, *Regulators,* 569.

23. Murphey notes, Regulator Papers (first quotation); Jones, *Defence of Revolutionary History,* 54 (second quotation); Hugh Williamson, *The History of North Carolina,* 2 vols. (Philadelphia: Thomas Dobson, 1812), 2:148–149 (third quotation); Caruthers, *Life of Caldwell,* 155.

24. Cornell to Desbrosses, [June 6, 1771].

25. Powell, *Regulators,* 380, 495.

26. Tryon added that he "took many of their horses and the little provision and Ammunition they left behind them." Powell, *Tryon Correspondence,* 2:744 (first quotation). John Henry Clewell, *History of Wachovia in North Carolina: The Unitas Fratrum or Moravian Church in North Carolina during a Century and a Half, 1752–1902* (New York: Doubleday, Page and Company, 1902), 110 (second quotation); Fries, *Moravian Records,* 1:456–462.

27. Fitch, *Neglected History,* 224–225 (first quotation); Caruthers, *Life of Caldwell,* 156–157.

28. Nelson, *William Tryon,* 85; Powell, *Tryon Correspondence,* 2:722; Powell, *Regulators,* 570.

29. William Tryon to Hugh Waddell, June 7, 1771, Saunders, *Colonial Records*, 8:717; Proclamations of Governor William Tryon, June 9, 11, 1771, Colonial Governors' Papers, 6, 9, North Carolina State Archives; Tryon to Hillsborough, August 1, 1771, CO 5/314, part 2 (microfilm), Emory University Library, Atlanta, Ga.

30. Saunders, *Colonial Records*, 8:724–725.

Chapter 9

1. Martin, *History of North Carolina*, 2:284 (first quotation); Saunders, *Colonial Records*, 8:xxxix (second quotation); Tryon to Hillsborough, December 14, 1771, Powell, *Tryon Correspondence*, 2:845.

2. Martin to Hillsborough, August 15, 1771, Powell, *Tryon Correspondence*, 2:827; *The Oxford Dictionary of National Biography*, 60 vols. (London: Oxford University Press, 2004), s.v. "Martin, Josiah."

3. Fries, *Moravian Records*, 1:456–458 (first, second, third, fourth, and sixth quotations); Paschal, "Morgan Edwards' Materials," 369 (fifth quotation).

4. Tryon's biographer found that contemporaries noted Tryon's tactfulness, honesty, generosity, and faithfulness to duty but more commonly recorded his vanity. Nelson, *William Tryon*, 6.

5. Emphasis added. John Ferdinand Dalziel Smyth, *A Tour of the United States of America*, 2 vols. (1784; reprint, New York: Arno Press, 1968), 1:226–228.

6. Smyth, *Tour of United States*, 1:228; Carole Watterson Troxler, *Pyle's Defeat: Deception at the Race Path* (Graham, N.C.: Alamance County Historical Association, 2003); Chatham County Court of Pleas and Quarter Sessions, Minute Docket, May 1782, North Carolina State Archives; *Dictionary of North Carolina Biography*, s.v. "Hunter, James."

7. Smyth, *Tour of United States*, 1:228–229, 232; Saunders, *Colonial Records*, 10:486, 560, 601, 803–804, 827–828; Clark, *State Records*, 11:350; 24:263n; General Assembly Session Records, Session of November–December 1785, Senate Bills; General Assembly Session Records, Session of November–December 1787, Committee of Propositions and Grievances.

8. Will of Eli Branson, 1796, Will Book 1:180, Judge of Probate Court, Abbeville County, S.C.

9. Pleasant Henderson statement, Richard Henderson Papers, 2 CC, 44.5–44.6, Lyman C. Draper Collection, State Historical Society of Wisconsin, Madison, photocopy in Draper Manuscripts, North Carolina State Archives; Henderson, "Origin of the Regulation," 322; Durward T. Stokes, "Thomas Hart in North Carolina," *North Carolina Historical Review* 41 (Summer 1964): 329; Susannah Searcy Greer, transcription of Reuben Searcy's list of his children, in Henry B. Brackin Jr., *The Brackin Family in the Southeastern United States* (Nashville, Tenn.: privately published, 1979), 354–355. For the Hendersons, see William Stewart Lester, *The Transylvania Colony* (Spencer, Ind.: S. R. Guard and Company, 1935); Mark F. Miller, "Richard Henderson: The Making of a Land Speculator" (master's thesis, University of North Carolina at Chapel Hill, 1975); *Dictionary of North Carolina Biography*, s.v. "Henderson, Pleasant," "Henderson, Richard," "Henderson, Samuel," and "Henderson, Thomas."

10. Pay abstracts 12, 32 (Daniel Plummer), June–December 1781, Treasury Papers 52:2, microfilm in North Carolina Collection; muster rolls (Nicholas Welch, John Wormley, and Neil McArthur), April, December 1781, June 1782, MG23 D1 Volume 26, Library and Archives Canada, Gatineau, Quebec; John Willis, "Brunswick County, Virginia, Poll List 1748," *William and Mary Quarterly* 26 (July 1917): 59–64; Caswell County Court of Pleas and Quarter Sessions, Minute Docket, 1777–1788, June, September, December 1777, March 1778, June, December 1779, September 1781, September 1783, North Carolina State Archives; Will of George Sims, Caswell County Record of Wills, Book F:22, North Carolina State Archives; grants to George Sims, #299, 320, 578, Caswell County, Office of Secretary of State, Land Office (Colonial and State), Land Warrants, Plats of Survey, and Related Records, 1663–1959, North Carolina State Archives.

11. Ekirch, *"Poor Carolina,"* 211.

Chapter 10

1. Morehead, "James Hunter," 43–45 (Hunter quotation); John Butler to William Butler, June 25, 1775, Regulator Papers.

2. Martin stood to earn additional fees if the Crown purchased the Granville Tract. Josiah Martin to Earl of Hillsborough, November 10, 1771, CO 5/315, 18, British Records, North Carolina State Archives.

3. Other Orange County representatives were Thomas Burke, John Kinchen, John Atkinson, and John Williams. Nathaniel Rochester and William Armstrong represented Hillsborough. John Butler told his brother that "John Kinchin & James Saunders" had been elected from Orange County. John Butler to William Butler, June 25, 1775, Regulator Papers; Saunders, *Colonial Records*, 10:166–167.

4. Saunders, *Colonial Records*, 10:169–174, 191–192.

5. Fries, *Moravian Records*, 3:1038.

6. Richard Bennehan, James Martin, Archibald Murphy, John Hogan, and John Kelly were the commissioners. Robert L. Ganyard concluded that the Orange election was not part of any radical/conservative standoff. Robert L. Ganyard, "Radicals and Conservatives in Revolutionary North Carolina: A Point at Issue, the October Election, 1776," *William and Mary Quarterly*, 3rd ser., 24 (October 1967): 568–587 (quotation, 572); Saunders, *Colonial Records*, 10:932–933, 945, 970; *Dictionary of North Carolina Biography*, s.v. "Mebane, Alexander."

7. Saunders, *Colonial Records*, 10:870f–870h.

Chapter 11

1. Pat Shaw Bailey, *Land Grant Records of North Carolina, Volume I, Orange County 1752–1885* (Graham, N.C.: The compiler, 1990); Pat Shaw Bailey, *Land Grant Records of North Carolina, Volume II, Chatham County 1778–1928* (Graham, N.C.: The compiler, 1991); Pat Shaw Bailey, *Guilford County, North Carolina Land Grants, 1778–1934* (Signal Mountain, Tenn.: Mountain Press, 2001); William D. Bennett, ed., *Guilford County Deed Book One* (Raleigh: The editor, 1990); Bennett, *Orange County Records*, vol. 9.

2. Deposition of James Dickey, March 12, 1778, Salisbury District Superior Court, Civil Action Papers, North Carolina State Archives (quotations). Lyon was a militia captain during the Revolution, and he kept his land in present-day Davie County, though he did not make his ownership official until 1790–1792. Jo White Linn, comp., *Rowan County, North Carolina Tax Lists, 1757–1800* (Salisbury, N.C.: Mrs. Stahle Linn Jr., 1995), 143, 286, 306, 356; Jo White Linn, comp., *Abstracts of the Minutes of the Court of Pleas and Quarter Sessions, Rowan County, North Carolina, 1775–1789*, vol. 3 (Salisbury, N.C.: Mrs. Stahle Linn Jr., 1982) 23, 28; land grant to Elijah Lyon, 1792, Book 80:125, Office of Secretary of State, Land Office (Colonial and State), Patent Books, 1663–1959, North Carolina State Archives.

3. Ganyard, *Emergence of State Government*, 87; Hillsborough District Superior Court, Minute Docket, 1768–1783, passim, North Carolina State Archives; Orange County Court of Pleas and Quarter Sessions, Minute Docket, 1780– 1783, passim.

4. Lists of summoned men, n.d., September 19, 1782, and December 12, 1782, Lincoln County Miscellaneous Papers, 1764–1923, North Carolina State Archives; Treasurer's and Comptroller's Papers, Lands, Estates, Boundaries, and Surveys, 1760–1901, Boxes 2–5, North Carolina State Archives; Fries, *Moravian Records*, 2:897, 1027–1029, 1032, 1044–1048; Saunders, *Colonial Records*, 7:702; 8:273–274; Powell, *Regulators*, 368–373, 540; Fred Hughes, *Guilford County, N.C.—A Map Supplement* (Jamestown, N.C.: The Custom House, 1988), 6-8; Albert Bruce Pruitt, *Abstracts of Land Entrys [sic]: Guilford Co., NC, 1779–1796 and Rockingham Co., NC, 1790–1795* (Raleigh: A. B. Pruitt, ca. 1987), 1–74.

5. Orange County Court of Pleas and Quarter Sessions, Minute Docket, 1765, 1777–1778; Bailey, *Land Grant Records of Orange County*, passim; Cheney, *North Carolina Government*, 201–207; *Dictionary of North Carolina Biography*, s.v. "Burke, Thomas," "Butler, John," and "Rochester, Nathaniel."

6. Orange County district tax lists, March 1770–1783, North Carolina State Archives; Bailey, *Land Grant Records of Orange County*, passim; Orange County Court of Pleas and Quarter Sessions, Minute Docket, 1777–1784; Cheney, *North Carolina Government*, 201–211.

7. *Dictionary of North Carolina Biography*, s.v. "Burrington, George" and "Strudwick, Samuel"; Powell, *Tryon Correspondence*, 2:5.

8. Saunders, *Colonial Records*, 7:711–712.

9. Powell, *Tryon Correspondence*, 1:19; Saunders, *Colonial Records*, 7:831, 833; 22:870–871.

10. Fries, *Moravian Records*, 3:1135, 1159, 1365–1366.

11. Clark, *State Records*, 15:409; Weeks, *Register of Orange County Deeds*, 30.

12. Engagements including Hart's Mill, Pyle's Defeat, Clapp's Mill, Hawkins' Plantation, and Weitzel's Mill are narrated in Troxler and Vincent, *Shuttle & Plow*, 108–137. Maps, commentaries, and extracts of selected documents of the battles are in Jeffrey G. Bright and Stewart E. Dunaway, *Like a Bear with his Stern in a Corner* (Privately published, 2009).

13. Clark, *State Records*, 17:661; Orange County Court of Pleas and Quarter Sessions, Minute Docket, 1779–1781; Hillsborough District Superior Court, Minute Docket, October 1782.

14. Clark, *State Records*, 15:409–410; Bailey, *Land Grant Records of Orange County*, 5; *Dictionary of North Carolina Biography*, s.v. "Strudwick, Samuel."

15. After Fanning went to New York, he turned the land over to agents to lease or sell. Orange County Deed Book 3:441, 462, 492 (microfilm), North Carolina State Archives.

16. Clark, *State Records*, 24:263.

17. They were George Hodge, William Hodge, John McCrory, John Stockard, James Stockard, James Hutcheson, William Means, William Scott, James Anderson, James McAdams, Hugh Crawford, William Galbreath, William Creoge, and two men whose first names were Jacob and John. The land included the tract where the 1752–1754 courthouse stood. General Assembly Session Records, Session of November–December 1789, Petitions; land grant to George Hodge(s), September 1779, Office of Secretary of State, Land Office (Colonial and State), Patent Books, 1663–1959, 40:294; Bailey, *Land Grant Records of Orange County*, 1:21; Clark, *State Records*, 24:263; Orange County Deed Book 3:462 (microfilm), North Carolina State Archives.

18. *North Carolina Gazette*, February 16, 1786; Clark, *State Records*, 17:491.

19. Orange County Court of Pleas and Quarter Sessions, Minute Docket, February 1786.

20. Extracts from Office of Secretary of State of North Carolina, 1788, AO 12/91, 18–39, British Records, North Carolina State Archives; Salem Memorabilia, July 1782, Moravian Archives Southern Province, Winston-Salem; Caruthers, *Life of Caldwell*, 213–215.

21. Orange County Deed Books 1 and 3, passim (microfilm), North Carolina State Archives; Clark, *State Records*, 21:984–985, 998, 1034, 1042; Orange County Court of Pleas and Quarter Sessions, Minute Docket, 1752–1753.

Chapter 12

1. Cane Creek Monthly Meeting, November 1768.

2. "Tour of Rev. Morgan Edwards," 12; Paschal, "Morgan Edwards' Materials," 96; Sparks, *Roots of Appalachian Christianity*, 150–155 (quotation, 151).

3. According to Baptist historian George W. Paschal, this church was near present-day Bynum. Paschal, *History of North Carolina Baptists*, 1:365 (quotation), 366, 391, 471–473; Sparks, *Roots of Appalachian Christianity*, 157; Clark, *State Records*, 11:655; Kars, *Breaking Loose Together*, 213–214, 261.

4. Paschal, *History of North Carolina Baptists*, 1:381–384; Paschal, "Morgan Edwards' Materials," 365–399.

5. Robert Scott Davis Jr., *Quaker Records in Georgia: Wrightsborough, 1772–1793; Friendsborough, 1776–1777* (Augusta, Ga.: Augusta Genealogical Society, 1986), 1–38, 61; Robert Scott Davis Jr., "Lessons from Kettle Creek: Patriotism and Loyalism at Askance on the Southern Frontier," *Journal of Backcountry Studies* 1 (Spring 2006), http://libjournal.uncg.edu/ojs/index.php/jbc/; Jesse Hogan Motes III and Margaret Peckham Motes, comps., *Laurens and Newberry Counties South Carolina: Saluda and Little Rivers Settlements, 1749–1775* (Greenville, S.C.: Southern Historical Press, 1994), 5, 233; Brown, *South Carolina Regulators*, 21.

6. About a dozen of the 136 backcountry South Carolina Loyalists who were captured on Cherokee land following the November 1775 uprising at Ninety Six held land at Raeburn's Creek. Robert W. Gibbes, *Documentary History of the American Revolution . . . in South Carolina*, 3 vols. (New York and Columbia, S.C.: 1853–1857; reprint, Spartanburg, S.C.: The Reprint Company, 1972), 1:246, 249–251; Raeburn's Creek entries (various spellings), 1755–1775, Combined Index to Records Series, 1675–1925, South Carolina State Archives; David Fanning claim, AO 1312/109, 142–143, British Records; Saunders, *Colonial Records*, 10:598.

7. Padgett's Creek Church Book, November 1784, quoted in Leah Townsend, *South Carolina Baptists, 1670–1805* (Florence, S.C.: Florence Printing Company, 1935), 248.

8. Westerkamp, *Truimph of Laiety*, 195–213.

9. Micklejohn's behavior during the Regulator crisis mirrored that of his Calvinist colleagues. Later, although he did not support the Revolution, he remained in North Carolina. *Dictionary of North Carolina Biography*, s.v. "Micklejohn, George."

10. See Chapter 7, note 7 for Arminian. Saunders, *Colonial Records*, 8:740 (quotation); John W. Allen, *A History of Political Thought in the Sixteenth Century* (London: Methuen, 1957); Robert M. Calhoon, *The Loyalists in Revolutionary America, 1760–1781* (New York: Harcourt Brace Jovanovich, 1973).

11. *Dictionary of North Carolina Biography*, s.v. "Caldwell, David," "Pattillo, Henry," and "Suther, Samuel"; Orange County Deed Book 3:375 (microfilm), North Carolina State Archives; Clapp Family in "Genealogical Records of Early German and other Families that Settled in the Area of North Carolina of Alamance, Chatham, Guilford, Randolph, Rowan Co[unties]," compiled by David Isaiah Offman and Paul G. Kinney, n.d. (microfilm), North Carolina Collection; John Conrad O'Briant, "The Establishment of the Lutheran Church in North Carolina's Alamance and Guilford Counties," seminar paper, Elon College, 1974, copy on file at Low's Lutheran Church, Liberty, N.C.

12. *Dictionary of North Carolina Biography*, s.v. "DeBow, John"; Foote, *Sketches of North Carolina*, 226; Saunders, *Colonial Records*, 10:972.

13. Church Book, Brick United Church of Christ, Guilford County, Folders 1B, 1E, Thornton W. Whitsett Papers, Southern Historical Collection; Fries, *Moravian Records*, 2:800.

14. Caruthers, *Life of Caldwell*, 266 (Caldwell quotation); [Craighead], *Renewal of the Covenants*, vi (Craighead quotation); *Dictionary of North Carolina Biography*, s.v. "Caldwell, David" and "Craighead, Alexander."

15. Powell, *Regulators*, 164.

16. Robert M. Calhoon, *Religion and the American Revolution in North Carolina* (Raleigh: Division of Archives and History, 1976), 9.

17. Caruthers, *Life of Caldwell*, 273–284. The sermon also appears in Calhoon, *Religion and American Revolution*, 7–16.

Bibliographic Essay

1. William Henry Bailey to David L. Swain, March 24, 1857, Orange County Records, 1769–1771, Southern Historical Collection (first quotation); (second quotation). Cameron's line from "Tom Boleyn," a centuries-old insulting song, depicted Husband as worthless.

2. Hugh Williamson, *The History of North Carolina*, 2 vols. (Philadelphia: Thomas Dobson, 1812) reflected eastern commercial, planter, and urban interests and identified the Regulator Movement with agrarian, antifederal, and Jeffersonian causes he distrusted. Twenty years later, Williamson's challenger claimed to vindicate Regulators as "real Fire worshippers," more revolutionary than their eastern contemporaries, the Sons of Liberty: Joseph Seawell Jones, *A Defence of the Revolutionary History of the State of North Carolina from the Aspersions of Mr. Jefferson* (Raleigh: Turner and Hughes, 1834). Despite Jones's reputation for hoaxes in other undertakings, his work encouraged others to champion Regulators as proto-revolutionaries. A more balanced treatment appeared between Williamson's and Jones's publications: François-Xavier Martin, *The History of North Carolina from the Earliest Period* (New Orleans: A. T. Penniman, 1829).

3. Alan D. Watson, "The Origin of the Regulation in North Carolina," *The Mississippi Quarterly* 47 (Fall 1994): 582–600, examines perceptions of the Regulators in the context of national historiography from 1812 through the 1980s.

4. Eli Washington Caruthers, *A Sketch of the Life and Character of the Reverend David Caldwell . . . including . . . Some Account of the Regulation* (Greensboro: Swaim and Sherwood, 1842); Eli Washington Caruthers, *Revolutionary Incidents and Sketches of Character Chiefly in the "Old North State"* (Philadelphia: Hayes and Zell, 1854).

5. William Henry Foote, *Sketches of North Carolina, Historical and Biographical, Illustrative of the Principles of a Portion of Her Early Settlers* (New York: Robert Garter, 1846; reprint, Raleigh: Harold J. Dudley, 1965); Calvin H. Wiley, *Alamance, Or the Great and Final Experiment* (New York: Harper and Brothers, 1847); John Hill Wheeler, *Historical Sketches of North Carolina, from 1584 to 1851* (Philadelphia: Lippincott, Grambo and Company, 1851); Francis L. Hawks, "Battle of Alamance and the War of Regulation," in *Revolutionary History of North Carolina*, ed. William D. Cooke (Raleigh: William D. Cooke and George P. Putnam and Company, 1853); David L. Swain, "The War of the Regulation," *North Carolina University Magazine* 9 (October 1859; February, April 1860), 10 (August 1860); John Fiske, *The American Revolution*, 2 vols. (Boston and New York: Houghton and Company, 1891), 1; Cyrus Lee Hunter, *Sketches of Western North Carolina, Historical and Biographical* (Raleigh: Raleigh New Steam Job Print, 1877); William Edwards Fitch, *Some Neglected History of North Carolina*, rev. ed. (New York: The author, 1914).

6. John Wheeler Moore, *History of North Carolina from the Earliest Discoveries to the Present Time* (Raleigh: Alfred Williams and Company, 1880).

7. Frederick Jackson Turner, *The Significance of the Frontier in American History* (Madison, Wisc.: State Historical Society of Wisconsin, 1894).

8. John Spencer Bassett, "The Regulators of North Carolina (1765–1771)," in *Annual Report of the American Historical Association for the Year 1894* (Washington, D.C.: Government Printing Office, 1895), 141–212.

Bibliography

Primary Sources

Government and Official Records

Abbeville County, Will Book 1. Judge of Probate Court, Abbeville County, S.C.

Auditors Office Records, British Records Collection (microfilm). North Carolina State Archives.

Caswell County Court of Pleas and Quarter Sessions, Minute Docket, 1777–1788. North Carolina State Archives.

Caswell County Record of Wills, Book F, 1808–1814. North Carolina State Archives.

Chatham County Court of Pleas and Quarter Sessions, Minute Docket, 1781–1785. North Carolina State Archives.

Colonial Court Records, Miscellaneous Papers, 1677–1775, CCR 192. North Carolina State Archives.

Colonial Governors' Papers, William Tryon. North Carolina State Archives.

Colonial Office Records, British Records Collection (microfilm). North Carolina State Archives.

Colonial Office Records, English Records Collection (photocopies). North Carolina State Archives.

Colonial Office Records (microfilm), Emory University Library. Atlanta, Ga.

Combined Index to Records Series, 1675–1925. South Carolina State Archives.

General Asembly Records, Tax Lists. North Carolina State Archives.

General Assembly Session Records. Sessions of December 1767–January 1768, November–December 1768, October–November 1769, November–December 1785, November–December 1787, November–December 1789. North Carolina State Archives.

Governors' Letter Books, William Tryon. North Carolina State Archives.

Granville District Papers from the Marquis of Bath's Library in Longleat, Wiltshire, English Records (microfilm). North Carolina State Archives.

Guilford County Deed Book 1, 1771–1778 (microfilm). North Carolina State Archives.

Hillsborough District Superior Court, Minute Docket, 1768–1783. North Carolina State Archives.

Lincoln County Miscellaneous Papers, 1764–1923. North Carolina State Archives.

Military Collection, War of the Regulation (1768–1779), Box 1. North Carolina State Archives.

Muster Rolls, 1781–1782, MG23 D1 Volume 26. Library and Archives Canada, Gatineau, Quebec.

Office of Secretary of State. Land Office (Colonial). Granville Proprietary Land Office. Grants of Deed, 1748–1763. North Carolina State Archives.

Office of Secretary of State. Land Office (Colonial). Granville Proprietary Land Office. Land Entries, Warrants, and Plats of Survey, 1748–1763. North Carolina State Archives.

Office of Secretary of State. Land Office (Colonial and State). Land Warrants, Plats of Survey, and Related Records, 1663–1959. North Carolina State Archives.

Office of Secretary of State. Land Office (Colonial and State). Patent Books, 1663–1959. North Carolina State Archives.

Orange County Court of Pleas and Quarter Sessions, Minute Docket, 1752–1766, 1777–1795. North Carolina State Archives.

Orange County Deed Books 1, 2, and 3, 1755–1785, *passim* (microfilm). North Carolina State Archives.

Orange County District Tax Lists, 1770–1783. North Carolina State Archives.

Rowan County Court of Pleas and Quarter Sessions, Minute Docket, 1753–1766. North Carolina State Archives.

Salisbury District Superior Court, Civil Action Papers, 1778. North Carolina State Archives.

Treasurer's and Comptroller's Papers. Lands, Estates, Boundaries, and Surveys, 1760–1901. North Carolina State Archives.

Treasury Papers (microfilm). North Carolina Collection, Wilson Library, University of North Carolina at Chapel Hill.

John Wright Memorials, 6:124, 10:8, 15; Plats 11:42; Grants 15:86, 17:115. South Carolina State Archives, Columbia.

Manuscript Collections

Friends Historical Collection, Guilford College

Cane Creek Monthly Meeting, 1755–1768, 1776.

Western Quarterly Meeting, 1761–1763.

Southern Historical Collection, Wilson Library, University of North Carolina at Chapel Hill.

Archibald Henderson Papers.

Orange County Records, 1769–1771.

Regulator Papers.

Thornton W. Whitsett Papers.

Library of Congress, Washington, D.C.

Society for the Propagation of the Gospel, Journals (microfilm).

Moravian Archives Southern Province, Winston-Salem

Salem Memorabilia, July 1782.

North Carolina Collection, Wilson Library, University of North Carolina at Chapel Hill

Moore, John Wheeler. *Sketches of Pioneer Baptist Preachers in North Carolina*. Scrapbook of clippings from *The Biblical Recorder*.

"Tour of Rev. Morgan Edwards of Pennsylvania to the American Baptists in North Carolina in 1772–73," copied by Walter Durham.

North Carolina State Archives, Office of Archives and History, Raleigh, N.C.

Draper Manuscripts.

State Historical Society of Wisconsin, Madison, Wisc.

Richard Henderson Papers, Lyman C. Draper Collection.

Maps

Claude Joseph Sauthier, seven military charts titled either "A Plan of the Camp and Battle of Alamance, the 16th May 1771" or "A Plan of the Camp at Alamance from the 14th to the 19th of May 1771." Map Collection, North Carolina State Archives.

Newspapers

North Carolina Gazette, February 16, 1786.

Published

Bailey, Pat Shaw. *Guilford County, North Carolina Land Grants, 1778–1934*. Signal Mountain, Tenn.: Mountain Press, 2001.

_____. *Land Grant Records of North Carolina*. Volume I, *Orange County 1752–1885*. Graham, N.C.: The compiler, 1990.

_____. *Land Grant Records of North Carolina*. Volume II, *Chatham County 1778–1928*. Graham, N.C.: The compiler, 1991.

Barlow, William. *The summe and substance of the conference . . . at Hampton Court, January 14, 1603*. 1604; reprint, Gainesville, Fla.: Scholars' Facsimiles and Reprints, 1965.

Bennett, William D., comp. *Orange County Records*. 13 vols. Raleigh: The compiler, 1987.

_____, ed. *Guilford County Deed Book One*. Raleigh: The editor, 1990.

Boyd, William K., ed. *Some Eighteenth Century Tracts concerning North Carolina*. Raleigh: Edwards and Broughton, 1927.

Cheney, John L., Jr., ed. *North Carolina Government, 1585–1974: A Narrative and Statistical History*. Raleigh: Department of the Secretary of State, 1981.

Clark, Walter, ed. *The State Records of North Carolina*. 16 vols. (11–26) Raleigh: State of North Carolina, 1895–1906.

[Craighead, Alexander]. *Renewal of the Covenants, National and Solemn League; A Confession of Sins, and Engagement to Duties; and a Testimony As They Were Carried on at Middle Octarara in Pensylvania, November 11, 1743 Together with an Introductory Preface*. "reprinted" 1746, microfilm of original at Presbyterian Historical Society, Philadelphia.

Davis, Robert Scott, Jr. *Quaker Records in Georgia: Wrightsborough, 1772–1793; Friendsborough, 1776–1777*. Augusta, Ga.: Augusta Genealogical Society, 1986.

Fries, Adelaide L., et al., eds. *Records of the Moravians in North Carolina*. 13 vols. Raleigh: Division of Archives and History, 1922–2006.

Gibbes, Robert W. *Documentary History of the American Revolution . . . in South Carolina*. 3 vols. New York and Columbia, S.C.: 1853–1857; reprint, Spartanburg, S.C.: The Reprint Company, 1972.

Henderson, Archibald, ed. "Hermon Husband's Continuation of the Impartial Relation." *North Carolina Historical Review* 18 (January 1941): 48–81.

Holcomb, Brent, and Elmer Parker. *Mecklenburg County, North Carolina Deed Abstracts, 1763–1779.* Easley, S.C.: Southern Historical Press, 1979.

Hoyt, William Henry, ed. *The Papers of Archibald D. Murphey.* 2 vols. Raleigh: E. M. Uzzell and Company, 1914.

Linn, Jo White, comp. *Abstracts of the Minutes of the Court of Pleas and Quarter Sessions, Rowan County, North Carolina.* 3 vols. Salisbury, N.C.: Mrs. Stahle Linn Jr., 1979–1982.

_____. *Rowan County, North Carolina Deed Abstracts.* Salisbury, N.C.: Mrs. Stahle Linn Jr., 1972.

_____. *Rowan County, North Carolina Tax Lists, 1757–1800.* Salisbury, N.C.: Mrs. Stahle Linn Jr., 1995.

Motes, Jesse Hogan, III, and Margaret Peckham Motes, comps. *Laurens and Newberry Counties, South Carolina: Saluda and Little Rivers Settlements, 1749–1775.* Greenville, S.C.: Southern Historical Press, 1994.

Paschal, George W. "Morgan Edwards' Materials towards a History of the Baptists in the Province of North Carolina." *North Carolina Historical Review* 7 (July 1930): 365–399.

Powell, William S., ed. *The Correspondence of William Tryon and Other Selected Papers.* 2 vols. Raleigh: Division of Archives and History, Department of Cultural Resources, 1980–1981.

Powell, William S., et al., eds. *The Regulators in North Carolina: A Documentary History, 1759–1776.* Raleigh: Division of Archives and History, 1971.

Pruitt, Albert Bruce. *Abstracts of Land Entrys [sic]: Guilford Co., NC, 1779–1796 and Rockingham Co., NC, 1790–1795.* Raleigh: A. B. Pruitt, ca. 1987.

Redden, Alma Cheek. *Orange Co., N.C. Abstracts of the Minutes of the Inferior Court of Pleas & Quarter Sessions, 1777–1788.* Greenville, S.C.: Southern Historical Press, 1991.

Saunders, William L., ed. *The Colonial Records of North Carolina.* 10 vols. Raleigh: State of North Carolina, 1886–1890.

Shields, Ruth Herndon. *Orange County, N.C. Abstracts of the Minutes of the Court of Pleas and Quarter Sessions of Sept. 1752–Aug. 1766.* Greenville, S.C.: Southern Historical Press, 1991.

Smyth, John Ferdinand Dalziel. *A Tour of the United States of America.* 2 vols. 1784; reprint, New York: Arno Press, 1968.

Weeks, Eve B., trans. *Register of Orange County, North Carolina, Deeds 1752–1768 and 1793.* Danielsville, Ga.: Heritage Papers, 1984.

Weeks, Eve B., and Mary B. Warren, eds. *Morgan Edwards Materials towards a History of the Baptists.* 2 vols. Danielsville, Ga.: Heritage Papers, 1984.

Willis, John. "Brunswick County, Virginia, Poll List 1748." *William and Mary Quarterly* 26 (July 1917): 59–64.

Secondary Sources

Published

Allen, John W. *A History of Political Thought in the Sixteenth Century.* London: Methuen, 1957.

Bassett, John Spencer. "The Regulators of North Carolina (1765–1771)." In *Annual Report of the American Historical Association for the Year 1894.* Washington, D.C.: Government Printing Office, 1895.

Bernheim, Goddard D. *History of the German Settlements and of the Lutheran Church in North and South Carolina.* Philadelphia: Lutheran Book Store, 1872.

Blackwelder, Ruth. *The Age of Orange: Political and Intellectual Leadership in North Carolina, 1752–1861.* Charlotte: William Loftin, 1961.

Boles, John B. *The Great Revival: Beginnings of the Bible Belt.* Lexington: University of Kentucky Press, 1996.

———. "Slaves in Biracial Protestant Churches." In *Varieties of Southern Religious Experience,* edited by Samuel S. Hill. Baton Rouge: Louisiana State University Press, 1988.

Boyd, Julian P. "The Sheriff in Colonial North Carolina." *North Carolina Historical Review* 5 (April 1928): 151–180.

Brackin, Henry B., Jr. *The Brackin Family in the Southeastern United States.* Nashville, Tenn.: privately published, 1979.

Bradley, James E. *Religion, Revolution, and English Radicalism: Nonconformity in Eighteenth-Century Politics and Society*. New York: Cambridge University Press, 1990.

Brekus, Catherine A. *Strangers & Pilgrims: Female Preaching in America, 1740–1845*. Chapel Hill: University of North Carolina Press, 1998.

Bright, Jeffrey G., and Stewart E. Dunaway. *Like a Bear with his Stern in a Corner*. Privately published, 2009.

Brown, Richard Maxwell. *The South Carolina Regulators*. Cambridge: Harvard University Press, 1963.

Calhoon, Robert M. *The Loyalists in Revolutionary America, 1760–1781*. New York: Harcourt Brace Jovanovich, 1973.

_____. *Religion and the American Revolution in North Carolina*. Raleigh: Division of Archives and History, 1976.

Caruthers, Eli Washington. *Interesting Revolutionary Incidents and Sketches of Character Chiefly in the "Old North State."* 2nd ser. Philadelphia: Hayes and Zell, 1856.

_____. *Revolutionary Incidents and Sketches of Character Chiefly in the "Old North State."* Philadelphia: Hayes and Zell, 1854.

_____. *A Sketch of the Life and Character of the Reverend David Caldwell, D.D.* Greensboro, N.C.: Swaim and Sherwood, 1842.

Clewell, John Henry. *History of Wachovia in North Carolina: The Unitas Fratrum or Moravian Church in North Carolina during a Century and a Half, 1752–1902*. New York: Doubleday, Page and Company, 1902.

Cometti, Elizabeth. "Some Early Best Sellers in Piedmont North Carolina." *Journal of Southern History* 16 (August 1950): 324–337.

Conkin, Paul. "The Church Establishment in North Carolina, 1765–1776." *North Carolina Historical Review* 32 (January 1955): 1–30.

Connolly, Sean J. "Ulster Presbyterians: Religion, Culture, and Politics, 1660–1850." In *Ulster and North America: Transatlantic Perspectives on the Scotch-Irish*, edited by H. Tyler Blethen and Curtis W. Wood Jr. Tuscaloosa: University of Alabama Press, 1997.

Cowan, Edward J. "Prophecy and Prophylaxis: A Paradigm for the Scotch-Irish?" In *Ulster and North America: Transatlantic Perspectives on the Scotch-Irish*, edited by H. Tyler Blethen and Curtis W. Wood Jr. Tuscaloosa: University of Alabama Press, 1997.

Cowan, Ian B. *The Scottish Covenanters, 1660–1688*. London: Gollancz, 1976.

Cumming, William P. "Wimble's Maps and the Colonial Cartography of the North Carolina Coast." *North Carolina Historical Review* 46 (Spring 1969): 157–170.

Davis, Robert Scott, Jr. "Lessons from Kettle Creek: Patriotism and Loyalism at Askance on the Southern Frontier." *Journal of Backcountry Studies* 1 (Spring 2006) http://library.uncg.edu/ejournals/backcountry/

Donaldson, Gordon. *Scotland James V to James VII.* Edinburgh: Oliver and Boyd, 1965.

Ekirch, A. Roger. " 'A New Government of Liberty': Hermon Husband's Vision of Backcountry North Carolina, 1755." *William and Mary Quarterly*, 3rd ser., 34 (October 1977): 632–645.

_____. *"Poor Carolina": Politics and Society in Colonial North Carolina, 1729–1776.* Chapel Hill: University of North Carolina Press, 1981.

Fiske, John. *The American Revolution.* 2 vols. Boston and New York: Houghton and Company, 1891.

Fitch, William Edwards. *Some Neglected History of North Carolina; Being an Account of the Revolution of the Regulators and of the Battle of Alamance, the First Battle of the American Revolution.* Rev. ed. New York: The author, 1914.

Foote, William Henry. *Sketches of North Carolina, Historical and Biographical, Illustrative of the Principles of a Portion of Her Early Settlers.* New York: Robert Garter, 1846; reprint, Raleigh: Harold J. Dudley, 1965.

Ganyard, Robert L. *The Emergence of North Carolina's Revolutionary State Government.* Raleigh: Division of Archives and History, 1978.

_____. "Radicals and Conservatives in Revolutionary North Carolina: A Point at Issue, The October Election, 1776." *William and Mary Quarterly*, 3rd ser., 24 (October 1967): 568–587.

Gilley, Sheridan, and W. J. Sheils, eds. *A History of Religion in Britain: Practice and Belief from Pre-Roman Times to the Present.* Cambridge: Blackwell, 1994.

Golumbic, Lars C. "Who Shall Dictate the Law? Political Wrangling between 'Whig' Lawyers and Backcountry Farmers in Revolutionary Era North Carolina." *North Carolina Historical Review* 73 (January 1996): 56–82.

Hawks, Francis L. "Battle of Alamance and the War of Regulation." In *Revolutionary History of North Carolina*, edited by William D. Cooke.

Raleigh: William D. Cooke and George P. Putnam and Company, 1853.

Henderson, Archibald. "The Origin of the Regulation in North Carolina." *American Historical Review* 21 (January 1916): 320–332.

Hole, Robert. *Pulpits, Politics, and Public Order in England, 1760–1832.* New York: Cambridge University Press, 1989.

Holmes, Geoffrey S. *Politics, Religion, and Society in England, 1679–1742.* Roncevert, W.Va.: Hambledon Press, 1986.

Hughes, Fred. *Guilford County, N.C.—A Map Supplement.* Jamestown, N.C.: The Custom House, 1988.

_____. *Randolph County, North Carolina: Historical Documentation.* Jamestown, N.C.: The Custom House, [1976].

Hunter, Cyrus Lee. *Sketches of Western North Carolina, Historical and Biographical.* Raleigh: Raleigh New Steam Job Print, 1877.

Jones, Joseph Seawell. *A Defence of the Revolutionary History of the State of North Carolina from the Aspersions of Mr. Jefferson.* Raleigh: Turner and Hughes, 1834.

Kars, Marjoleine. *Breaking Loose Together: The Regulator Rebellion in Pre-Revolutionary North Carolina.* Chapel Hill: University of North Carolina Press, 2002.

Kay, Marvin Lawrence Michael. "The North Carolina Regulation, 1766–1776: A Class Conflict." In *The American Revolution: Explorations in the History of American Radicalism,* edited by Alfred F. Young. DeKalb, Ill.: Northern Illinois University Press, 1976.

Kay, Marvin Lawrence Michael, and William S. Price Jr. " 'To Ride the Wood Mare': Road Building and Militia Service in Colonial North Carolina, 1740–1775." *North Carolina Historical Review* 57 (Autumn 1980): 361–409.

Kirk, James. " 'The Polities of the Best Reformed Kirks': Scottish Achievements and English Aspirations in Church Government after the Reformation." *Scottish Historical Review* 59 (April 1980): 22–54.

Klein, Rachel N. *Unification of a Slave State: The Rise of the Planter Class in the South Carolina Backcountry, 1760–1808.* Chapel Hill: University of North Carolina Press, 1992.

Lee, Wayne E. *Crowds and Soldiers in Revolutionary North Carolina: The Culture of Violence in Riot and War.* Gainesville: University Press of Florida, 2001.

Lefler, Hugh T. "Orange County and the War of the Regulation." In *Orange County 1752–1952*, edited by Hugh Lefler and Paul Wager. Chapel Hill: University of North Carolina Press, 1953.

Lester, William Stewart. *The Transylvania Colony*. Spencer, Ind.: S. R. Guard and Company, 1935.

Lossing, Benson J. *The Pictorial Field-Book of the Revolution*. 2 vols. New York: Harper and Brothers, 1859.

McGeachy, Neill Roderick. *A History of the Sugaw Creek Presbyterian Church*. Rock Hill, S.C.: Record Print Company, 1954.

McKaughan, Joshua Lee. "People of Desperate Fortune: Power and Populations in the North Carolina Backcountry." *Journal of Backcountry Studies* 2 (Spring 2007) http://libjournal.uncg.edu/ojs/index.php/jbc

Martin, François-Xavier. *The History of North Carolina from the Earliest Period*. 2 vols. New Orleans: A. T. Penniman, 1829.

Mitchell, Thornton W. "The Granville District and Its Land Records." *North Carolina Historical Review* 70 (April 1993): 103–129.

Moore, John Wheeler. *History of North Carolina from the Earliest Discoveries to the Present Time*. Raleigh: Alfred Williams and Company, 1880.

Morehead, Joseph M. "James Hunter, an Address." Greensboro: Guilford Battle Ground Company, 1897.

Morgan, David T., Jr. "The Great Awakening in North Carolina, 1740–1775: The Baptist Phase." *North Carolina Historical Review* 45 (Summer 1968): 264–283.

Nelson, Paul David. *William Tryon and the Course of Empire: A Life in British Imperial Service*. Chapel Hill: University of North Carolina Press, 1990.

Newlin, Algie I. *Charity Cook: A Liberated Woman*. Richmond, Ind.: Friends United Press, 1981.

The Oxford Dictionary of National Biography. 60 vols. London: Oxford University Press, 2004.

Oxford English Dictionary. Compact ed. 2 vols. London: Oxford University Press, 1971.

Paschal, George W. *History of North Carolina Baptists*. 2 vols. Raleigh: General Board, North Carolina Baptist State Convention, 1930, 1955.

Patterson, A. J. "In Memoriam. Elder Shubal Stearns. . . ." Liberty, N.C.: W. H. Eller, 1902. North Carolina Collection.

Powell, Josh. "Shubal Stearns and the Separate Baptist Tradition." *Founders Journal* 44 (Spring 2001): 16–31.

Powell, William S., ed. *Dictionary of North Carolina Biography.* 6 vols. Chapel Hill: University of North Carolina Press, 1979–1996.

Preyer, Norris W. *Hezekiah Alexander and the Revolution in the Backcountry.* Charlotte: Heritage Printers, 1987.

Rawlyk, George A., Mark A. Noll, and David W. Bebbington, eds. *Evangelicalism: Comparative Studies of Popular Protestantism in North America, the British Isles, and Beyond, 1700–1900.* New York: Oxford University Press, 1994.

Sellers, Charles G., Jr. "Private Profits and British Colonial Policy: The Speculations of Henry McCulloh." *William and Mary Quarterly,* 3rd ser., 8 (October 1951): 535–551.

Semple, Robert B. *History of the Rise and Progress of the Baptists in Virginia.* Richmond: John O'Lynch, printer, 1810.

Shields, E. Thomson, ed. " 'A Modern Poem' by the Mecklenburg Censor: Politics and Satire in Revolutionary North Carolina." *Early American Literature* 29, 3 (1994): 218–225.

Sobel, Mechal. *Trabelin On: The Slave Journey to an Afro-Baptist Faith.* Princeton: Princeton University Press, 1990.

_____. *The World They Made Together: Black and White Values in Eighteenth-Century Virginia.* Princeton: Princeton University Press, 1987.

Sparks, Elder John. *The Roots of Appalachian Christianity: The Life & Legacy of Elder Shubal Stearns.* Lexington: University of Kentucky Press, 2001.

Spufford, Margaret, ed. *The World of Rural Dissenters, 1520–1725.* New York: Cambridge University Press, 1995.

Stokes, Durward T. "Thomas Hart in North Carolina." *North Carolina Historical Review* 41 (Summer 1964): 324–337.

Swain, David L. "The War of the Regulation." *North Carolina University Magazine* 9 (October 1859; February, April 1860), 10 (August 1860).

Thompson, Edward Palmer. *Customs in Common.* New York: New Press, 1993.

_____. *Whigs and Hunters: The Origin of the Black Act.* London: Allen Lane, 1975.

Townsend, Leah. *South Carolina Baptists, 1670–1805*. Florence, S.C.: Florence Printing Company, 1935.

Troxler, Carole Watterson. *Pyle's Defeat: Deception at the Race Path*. Graham, N.C.: Alamance County Historical Association, 2003.

Troxler, Carole Watterson, and William Murray Vincent. *Shuttle & Plow: A History of Alamance County, North Carolina*. Graham, N.C.: Alamance County Historical Association, 1999.

Turner, Frederick Jackson. *The Significance of the Frontier in American History*. Madison, Wisc.: State Historical Society of Wisconsin, 1894.

Turner, Herbert Snipes. *The Dreamer: Archibald DeBow Murphey*. Verona, Va.: McClure Press, 1971.

Watson, Alan D. "The Origin of the Regulation in North Carolina." *The Mississippi Quarterly* 47 (Fall 1994): 582–600.

Watt, W. N. *The Granville District*. Taylorsville, N.C.: W. N. Watt, 1992.

Westerkamp, Marilyn. *Triumph of the Laity: Scots-Irish Piety and the Great Awakening, 1625–1760*. New York: Oxford University Press, 1988.

Wheeler, John Hill. *Historical Sketches of North Carolina, from 1584 to 1851*. Philadelphia: Lippincott, Grambo and Company, 1851.

Whittenburg, James P. "Planters, Merchants, and Lawyers: Social Change and the Origins of the North Carolina Regulation." *William and Mary Quarterly*, 3rd ser., 34, (April 1977): 215–238.

Wiley, Calvin H. *Alamance, Or the Great and Final Experiment*. New York: Harper and Brothers, 1847.

Williamson, Hugh. *The History of North Carolina*. 2 vols. Philadelphia: Thomas Dobson, 1812.

Unpublished

Blower, Daniel Frederick. "The Orange County and Mecklenburg County Instructions: The Development of Political Individualism in Backcountry North Carolina, 1740–1776." Ph.D. diss., University of Michigan, 1984.

Jones, Mark H. "Herman Husband: Millenarian, Carolina Regulator, and Whiskey Rebel." Ph.D. diss., Northwestern University, 1983.

Miller, Mark F. "Richard Henderson: The Making of a Land Speculator." Master's thesis, University of North Carolina at Chapel Hill, 1975.

O'Briant, John Conrad. "The Establishment of the Lutheran Church in North Carolina's Alamance and Guilford Counties." Seminar paper, Elon College, 1974. Copy on file at Low's Lutheran Church, Liberty, N.C.

Offman, David Isaiah, and Paul G. Kinney, comps. "Genealogical Records of Early German and other Families that Settled in the Area of North Carolina of Alamance, Chatham, Guilford, Randolph, Rowan Co[unties]." n.d. (microfilm), North Carolina Collection.

Rolland, Susan Mosteller. "From the Rhine to the Catawba: A Study of Eighteenth-Century Germanic Migration and Adaptation." Ph.D. diss., Emory University, 1991.

White, Stephen Jay. "North Carolina Quakers in the Era of the American Revolution." Master's thesis, University of Tennessee, 1981.

Whittenburg, James Penn. "Backwoods Revolutionaries: Social Context and Constitutional Theories of the North Carolina Regulators, 1765–1771." Ph.D. diss., University of Georgia, 1974.

Wylie, James Aitken. *The History of Protestantism with Five Hundred and Fifty Illustrations by the Best Artist*. London: Cassell, 1899.

Yeager, Kevin L. "The Power of Ethnicity: The Preservation of Scots-Irish Culture in the Eighteenth-Century American Backcountry." Ph.D. diss., Louisiana State University, 2000.

Web Sites

http://libjournal.uncg.edu/ojs/index.php/jbc

http://www.nchistoricsites.org/alamance/alamanc.htm

http://www.ncpublications.com/colonial/Bookshelf/Tracts/Nutbush%20Address/introduction.htm

http://www.tradingpath.org/content/view/104/28/

Index

A

Abbotts Creek, 47, 48

Absentee landowners, 2, 136, 140, 144

Activism, political, 34

Acts passed by the Assembly, 38, 69, 70

Adams, John, 124

Adjutants, 108–109

Advertisements, 59, 84

African Americans, 138. *See also* Blacks; Slavery/slaves

Agent(s), land: abuses of, 47; confrontations between settlers and, 8, 33; deputy, 5; detained at Enfield, 23; hired to transact business, 81; Husband served as, 41, 44; for McCulloh, 6, 7, 10, 119; sold backcountry tracts, 2; worked with speculators, 12. *See also* Granville land agents

Alamance, Battle of: aftermath of, 62, 84, 103, 151; financing of, 128; mentioned, 92, 93, 95; outrage over, 124; participation in, 41, 99; prevention of, 158; Regulators defeated at, 32, 73

Alamance Battleground, 110, 117, 147

Alamance Battleground Research Project: artifacts from, pictured, 112

Alamance Campaign: map of, pictured, 100

Alamance County, 47, 103

Alamance County (present-day), 7, 56, 80, 137, 144

Alamance Creek, 47, 121, 146, 147, 156

Albemarle counties, 13

Albemarle Sound, 20

Alexander, Abraham, 9, 72

Alexander, Benjamin, 10

Alexander, Billy, 9

Alexander, Hezekiah, 76

Alexander, Jimmy, 9

Alexander, John McNitt, 76

Alexander, Joseph, 68

Alexander, Moses, 10, 71, 99

Alexander-Polk alliance, 67, 69, 71

Alexanders, 8, 67, 71, 76, 153

Allegheny Mountains, 43

Allegiance, 122, 124, 127, 142

Alsatians, 31

American Revolution: aftermath of, 141, 148, 152; alliances before and during, 124, 155; first battle of, 122; mentioned, 13; militia movements during, 131; supporters of, 151, 152, 156, 158; targets during, 147–148, 150, 151

Ammunition, 101, 111, 112–113, 118

Anabaptist(s), 68, 151, 152

Anabaptist-Mennonites, 61

Anglican(s): Church of Ireland was, 36; Husband was reared as, 42, 57; Micklejohn was, 73, 154; missionary, 68; proposed bill concerning, 71; resented paying taxes, 45. *See also* Church of England

Anglican Church, 38–39. *See also* Church of England

Anglican minister(s), 15, 38, 68, 73, 153, 154

Anglican privilege, 34, 38, 40

Anson County: churches, 41; establishment of, 44; land records in, 52; location of, 5, 67; men mustered from, 99; new courthouse at, 12; population of, 3; representatives from, 71, 149, 78; petitions relating to, 39, 82, 81

Archdale, John, 31

Arminians, 155

Artifacts, 110, 112

Artillery, 111

Artisans, 43

Ashe, John Baptista, 107

Assembly, colonial: authorized governor to raise taxes, 45; cited Crown-Granville boundary line, 3; elected governor and executive officers, 135; geographic imbalance in, 12; investigated Orange County election, 83; lower house of, 122 135; members of, 73, 84, 149; passed laws regulating fees, 63; passed vestry acts, 38, 69; petitioners appeared to, 80; provincial congress developed out of, 122, 126; regulated county officials, 10; Regulators were elected to, 78; representation of, 14, 84; revised militia act, 97. *See also* House of Commons; Legislature; Lower house

Associate justice(s), 75, 86

Association meetings, 41, 149

Atkinson, John, 129

Attorney general, 21, 23, 77

Avery, Waightstill, 76

B

Back Creek, 142, 144

Backcountry: British marched through, 122, 123; creation of new counties in, 92; currency was scarce in, 11; disorder in, 21; grants included large areas of, 1–2, 140; grievances, 38, 40, 79, 126; Hillsborough was capital to, 20; Husband had vision of New Jerusalem in, 43; land abuses and cronyism plagued, 29; officers denounced public meetings, 62; people were viewed as Regulators, 124; political significance of, 13, 33, 59, 125, 126; Regulators won assembly seats in, 72; religion in, 32, 33, 44; Stearns and his followers moved to, 41; superior court was scheduled for, 84; suspicion and fear of, 22; taverns, 24; Tryon wanted further intelligence from, 77; voted based on resentment, 78

Baltimore County, Md., 43

Baptist(s): congregations, 48; considered dissenters, 29–30; John Bunyan was, 35; Sandy Creek Association was composed of, 29; term "association" originated among, 41; Tryon's forces targeted, 115; were fastest growing denomination in Piedmont during Great Awakening, 152; were religious heirs of activist congregations, 34. *See also* Separate Baptist(s)

Barbados, 43

Bath, N.C., 2

Battle of Alamance. *See* Alamance, Battle of

Battle of Guilford Courthouse. *See* Guilford Courthouse, Battle of

Battle of Moores Creek Bridge. *See* Moores Creek Bridge, Battle of

Battleground, Alamance. *See* Alamance Battleground

Bayly, I., 141

Beaufort County, 97

Bell: pictured, 110

Bennehan, Richard, 35

Benton, Samuel, 24, 25, 71, 78

Berry, Richard, 70

Bethabara, 118, 119

Bishop of London, 40

Bishops, 30, 34, 36

"Black act," 9

Blacks, 25, 32, 42. *See also* African Americans; Slavery/slaves

Blacksmith operation, 148

Bladen County, 43

Board of Trade, 5, 10

Bodley, Joshua, 6, 7

Boston, 77

Boundary lines, 2–3, 8, 52, 95

Bounty, 97

Bowles, James, 143

Branson, Eli, 123

Branson, Thomas, 59

Bray, Henry, 78

Bray, Sarah, 78

Bribery, 7

British, 40, 123, 143

British Isles, 9, 29–30, 34, 36, 38

British North America, 29–30

Brown, William, 117

Bruce, Charles, 137

Brunswick County, Va., 23

Bunyan, John, 35

Burke, Thomas, 130, 131, 142, 143

Burlington, N.C. (present-day), 83

Burrington, George, 140, 144

Burrington/Fanning tract, 148

Bush River, S.C., 151

Bute County, 24, 96, 122, 155

Butler, John: claimed title to McCulloh land, 146; commanded militia unit, 155; elected to represent Orange County, 130; followed fee table, 130–131; lost election, 129; presided over court-ordered sale of land, 144; served as justice of the peace, 137

Butler, William: awaited trial, 73; commanded militia, 131; complained to court about Hooper, 78; James Hunter wrote to, 125; outlawed, 96; Regulators assembled under, 85; served as Orange County sheriff, 130; testified against Regulators, 130; Tryon hoped to execute, 115; was arrested, 65; was early proponent of revolutionary cause, 131; was found guilty and fined, 75; was Regulator leader, 130

Butlers (family), 153

C

Cabarrus County, 153
Cabarrus County (present-day), 2, 7, 33, 44, 67
Caldwell, David: advocated revolution, 156; pictured, 108; quotations from sermon by, 157; served congregations in Guilford County, 153; served as mediator between Tryon and insurgents, 73, 107, 108, 154, 158; supported Tryon, 72; told Regulators to recant oaths, 156–157; tried to reconcile Regulators with government officials, 153
Calvin, John, 30, 35, 61
Calvinism, 30, 71, 155
Camp meetings, 149
Cane Creek, 51, 57, 74, 83, 115
Cane Creek disruption, 55, 56–57
Cane Creek Monthly Meeting of Friends, 50, 51, 52, 54, 59
Cape Fear, 20
Cape Fear division, 97
Cape Fear Valley, upper, 122, 127
Capitol, 19
Carter, James, 5, 45
Carteret, John, 2. See also Granville, Earl
Carteret family, 2

Carteret County, 97, 99
Caruthers, Eli W., 89, 103, 108, 156
Casualties, battle, 111, 113
Caswell, Richard, 83
Caswell County, 123–124, 137
Catawba River, 70
Cattle, 11, 25, 139
Cavalry, 119
Cecil County, Md., 42, 43
Cell, Jonathan, 59
"Century of Revolution," 31
"Character and Doom of the Sluggard, The" (sermon), 157
Charles II, 34
Charles Town, S.C., 20, 22, 99
Charleston, S.C. (present-day), 123, 124
Charlotte, N.C., 69, 71
Charlotte, N.C. (present-day), 8
Chatham County, 92, 96, 123, 133, 137
Chatham County (present-day), 16, 56, 64, 80
Cherokees, 123
Chicanery, 8, 21, 25
Childs, Thomas, 5
Childsboro, 5
Chowan County, 13
Church(es), 32, 34, 132, 149
Church of England: administration of, 29, 36; developing religious culture different from, 34; Husband supported, 45; proponents of, resented Quaker political influence, 31; restoration of, 1, 34; vestrymen must conform to, 39. See also Anglican Church
Church governance, 30, 36, 56
Church of Ireland, 36
Church of Scotland, 29, 69
Churton, William, 39, 47, 64
Civil war, 31, 96
"Clapp's" church (Reformed), 155
Clark, Samuel, 104
Class tension(s): 15; continued in Scotland, 36; frustration over, 19; between lawyers and backcountry, 23; occurred during England's "Century of Revolution," 31; between ruling class and activists, 34; by tax-setting legislature, 20; were

common occurrences in eighteenth century, 21
Clergy, 39, 45, 152
Clerk(s) of court, 11, 24, 63, 123, 131
Cleveland County (present-day), 67
Cold Water Creek, 2, 3
College of New Jersey (Princeton), 155
Collet map (1770): portion of, pictured, 141
Collusion, 12, 25, 71, 86
Colonial officers, 78
Colonial officials, 31, 75, 130, 131, 148. *See also* Officials
Commerce, 24, 34
Commissioners of Confiscated Property, 136, 145, 146, 147
Committee of safety, 122, 123
Committee on privileges and elections, 83
Common law, 80, 92
Commons House of Assembly. *See* House of Commons
Communication, 24, 131
Concord (present-day), 72
Confiscation, 2, 136, 144, 145
Congregationalist(s), 29–30, 34, 35, 41
Connecticut, 48
Conner, Lewis, 144
Constable(s), 11, 123
Constitution (1776), 132, 135, 153
Constitution (S.C.), 152
Constitutional convention, 129
Continental Line certificates, 127, 146
Cooke, John, 88
Cooper, _____, 96
Copeland, James, 117
Corbin, Francis, 5, 6–7, 44, 45
Corbinton, 5
Corn, 25, 116, 143
Cornell, Samuel, 107, 109, 111, 113, 128
"Cornell Hoard": a three-pound note from, pictured, 128
Cornwallis, Charles Lord, 11, 122, 143, 147
Coroners, 11
Corruption: frustration over, 19; among Granville's employees, 5, 7, 45; among lawyers and county officials, 5, 61, 64, 81, 94; in local law

enforcement, 21; stresses related to, 133
Council, governor's: approved raising of militia, 95; influenced by Regulator letter, 96; lived in Tidewater area, 12–13; members of, 73, 103, 107, 140; upper house served as, 10
Council of safety, 122–123
Country Line Creek, 123
County court, 92: as authority regarding common law, 21; common practice in, 61; to halt proceedings, 27; jurors for, 11; land matters in, 50, 145; malpractices of officers of, 24; regulated county officials, 10; respect for institution of, 28; Strudwick in, 141–142
County Donegal, Ireland, 33
County officials, 25, 63, 80, 137, 139. *See also* Officials
Couriers, 153
Court of oyer and terminer, 95
Courthouse ring(s): connected local authority with legislature, 15, 135; embodied tax gouging and fee abuse, 20; features of, 12; in Granville District, 13; in Guilford County, 137; leadership of, 69; in Mecklenburg County, 67; power of, 73, 86; prevented use of grand jury presentments, 62; Regulators and, 70, 97
Courthouses, 12
Courtney, William, 146
Covenants/covenanters, 35, 36, 37, 68, 156
Cox, Hermon, 117
Cox family, 59
"Crackers," 151
Craighead, Alexander, 33, 36–37, 68, 156
Craighead, Rachel, 156
Craven, Peter, 75
Craven County, 97
Creswell, James, 72
Crops, 22, 115
Cross Creek, 2, 20, 74, 93, 122
Crown: allegiance to, 122, 127, 154; authority of, 33; criticism of, 157;

encouraged settlement of back-country, 40; land, 2, 5, 10; practice of purchasing land, 126, 133; protection under, 134; restoration of, 1; use of distraint by, 80

Crown-Granville boundary, 2, 7

Culture, religious, 151, 152

Currency: counterfeit, 96; land as security for, 80; new, 127, 133; payment in, 146; shortage of, 11, 148; state, 134. *See also* Proclamation money

Currituck County, 13

D

Davidson County (present-day), 7

Davie County (present-day), 7

DeBow, John, 155, 156

Debt, 22, 81, 96, 131

Deed(s), 73, 133, 143

Deep Creek, S.C., 151

Deep River, 41, 46, 47, 49, 111, 115

Deep River Meeting, 55, 59

Delaware, 57

Dent, William, 137

Deputy officials, 5, 45, 77, 123. *See also* Officials

Desertion, 99

Devinney, Samuel, 85

Dickey, James, 11, 133–134

Discontent, 36, 64, 126

Disfranchisement, 13

Disorder, 21, 111, 129

Disownment, 51, 52, 149

Dissenters: discrimination against, 38, 71; enumerated, 68; followed Calvinistic doctrine, 30; grievances of, 45, 153; humiliation of, 40; Presbyterians in British Isles and British America were considered, 29–30; Quakers were, 56; resented Anglican privilege, 31, 34; restrictions on, 35; were encouraged to settle middle colonies, 31, 38–39; were nonconformists, 29

Distraint, 11, 62, 80

District superior court, 10, 11–12, 117, 142. *See also* Hillsborough court; Salisbury District Superior Court

Dobbs, Arthur: appointed Orange County sheriff, 11; did not suppress riots in Granville District, 23; land belonging to, 8, 20; manipulation of, 21; pictured, 22; was authorized to raise taxes, 45

Dobbs County, 97

Dobbs Parish, 40

"Dr. David Caldwell's Log College," 156

Dry Creek, 83

Dunkard(s), 31, 71, 136, 149

Duplin County, 8

Durham County (present-day), 56, 137

Dutch Reformed, 30

E

Earl Granville. *See* Granville, Earl

Earl of Hillsborough. *See* Hillsborough, Earl of

East, 12, 13, 15, 92, 122, 125

Edenton, 7, 12, 44

Edgecombe County, 7, 21, 96

Education, 45, 64, 108, 156

Edwards, Isaac, 65, 66

Edwards, Morgan, 149, 150, 151

Ekirch, Roger, 44

Election(s): for fifth provincial congress, 129; improprieties in, were alleged, 80; for members of legislature, 13, 135; militia raised to protect, 95; in Orange County, 83, 130; Regulators were successful in, 78; sheriffs conducted, 13; strategies for winning, 61

Emmerson, James, 117

Enfield, N.C., 7, 23

Enfield Riot, 8, 10, 21, 29

England, 30, 31, 35, 36, 38

English, 21, 24, 36

Eno Presbyterian Church, 155

Eno River, 5, 65, 97, 99, 131

Eno River Meeting, 55, 59

Entries, land. *See* Land entries

Episcopalians. *See* Church of England

Euliss Creek, 146

Everard, Richard, 144

Everard family, 144

Everard/Fanning tract, 144

Excommunication, 149–150
Executions, 113, 117
Extortion, 85; Fanning was tried/fined for, 28, 94; Frohock had reputation for, 18; targets of, 64, 147–148
Eyewitnesses, 104, 108, 109

F

Fan for Fanning and a Touch-Stone to Tryon, A (pamphlet), 64
Fanning, David, 151
Fanning, Edmund: accompanied Tryon to New York, 95, 118, 124; allied with Mecklenburg leadership, 69; arrested Butler and Husband, 65; charges against, 73, 75, 76, 93, 113; and Hillsborough riot, 63, 85, 87, 88; interests of, 67, 140; land of, 136, 144, 145, 148; offices and occupations held by, 15, 16, 78, 92; pictured, 16; quotation by, 63; ridiculed in satire and song, 17, 41–42, 89; served as spokesman for local officials, 62; symbolized Regulator grievances, 15, 19, 71
Fanning, William, 15
Farmers: feared powerful litigators, 144; Husband and, 41, 44; interfaced with officials, 148; landowning, 43, 133; in Mecklenburg County, 67; voted resentments, 78; were Enfield rioters, 23; were targets of extortion, 147–148
Farms: Husband and, 44, 48; in McCulloh tract, 147, 148; Quaker, 136; rented or purchased by Germans, 148; surveying crew returned to, 2; targeted by Tryon, 115
Faucette Township (present-day), 144
Favoritism, 7, 45
Fayetteville (present-day), 20
Fee(s): agreements concerning, 62, 80, 91; complaints against excessive, 6, 21, 81, 82, 85, 90; illegal collection of, 12, 15, 18, 23, 25, 86; paid unlawfully to officials, 20, 45, 66, 78, 133; regulation of, 5, 28, 63, 130–131
Ferguson, Patrick, 124
Few, James, 113

Field, _____, 122
Field, Jeremiah, 87, 122, 123
Field, John, Jr., 123
Field, Joseph, 123
Field, Robert, 123
Field, William, 123, 125
Fifth provincial congress. *See* Provincial congress
Fincastle County, Va., 125
Fort Johnston, 111, 141
Fourth provincial congress. *See* Provincial congress
Franklin, Benjamin, 33, 81, 127
Frederick Town, Md., 123
French, 30, 96, 155
French Calvinists/Huguenots. *See* Huguenots
French and Indian War, 3, 39, 70
Friends, 56, 57, 59. *See also* Quakers; Society of Friends
Frohock, John: death of, 124; had reputation for extortion, 18; indictment of, 77; local power of, 10; lost his seat in Rowan County, 78; ridiculed in song, 17; violence against, 9; was incumbent and target of Regulators, 71, 90; worked with Mecklenburg County network of families, 67; wrote Tryon, 91
Frohock-McCulloh interest, 69
Furniture, 22, 25

G

Gaston County (present-day), 67
General Assembly, 135, 142–143
General Court, 74
Geneva, Switzerland, 30
George II, 39
Georgia, 33, 151, 152
German(s): Baptists, 31; bonded with Scotch-Irish, 70, 155; churches, 155; guarded against being called dissenters, 40; influence with, 70; land dealings of, 148; minister and teacher for, 71, 153; petitions signed by, 63, 147; Reformed, 30, 71; residents, 3; shared common ground with Methodists, 31
Gillespie, Daniel, 137

H

Halifax County, 78, 149
Halifax District, 144
Hamilton, John, 137
Hamilton, Mathew, 75
Hamilton, Ninian, 75
Hamilton, Ninian Bell, 65, 75
Hampshire County, W.Va. (present-day), 48
Harris, Tyree, 11, 88
Hart, Thomas: and Fanning, 15, 16–18, 140; offices held by or nominated for, 11, 15, 126–127, 137; was assaulted during Hillsborough court, 88
Harvey, John, 83
Haw Creek, 143
Haw River: area between Eno River and, 131; confluence of, with Stony Creek, 144; Holt's plantation located near, 121; Husband bought land along, 47; joint Lutheran and Reformed congregation was located west of, 153; land west of, was offered for sale, 146, 147; militia crossed, 101, 103, 111; Orange County officials lived east of, 137; original Orange County courthouse located near, 5; surveyors stopped at, 2; Tryon feared Regulators would reach, 99; Van Hook lived near, 83
Haw River Church, 150
Haw River Township (present-day), 144
Hawfields: Orange County officials in, 137, 139; ownership of, 140, 141, 145; preaching in, 153, 155, 157; public houses operated in, 131; tenants/occupants of, 140, 144
Hawfields Presbyterian Church, 155
Hawkins, John, 146
Henderson, Richard: family of, 123; and Hillsborough court, 75, 86, 87, 88; petition presented to, 86; silhouette in relief of, pictured, 75; travel companion of, 76
Henderson, Thomas, 137
Highlanders/Highland Scots, 122, 127, 131, 155. See also Scottish
Hillsborough, Earl of, 63, 70, 126

Hillsborough: Cornwallis's forces at, 122; court held at, 74, 75, 77, 117; hangings were conducted at, 93, 115, 118; horse seized at, 63; incorporation of, 15; land west of, 141; located on backcountry trading route, 20; mentioned, 131; militia camped near, 97; new courthouse at, 12; newspaper published in, 146; Orange County officials lived in, 137; preaching in, 73, 153, 154; Regulators and, 65, 125; representatives of, 92, 129; riots in, 84, 90; Royal North Carolina Regiment at, 124; travel to, 121; was named for first secretary of state, 5
Hillsborough court: events during, 68, 73–75, 76–77, 91, 94; Fanning and his allies triumphed at, 84; Holt was attacked at, 119; Moore was judge at, 93; new law included riot at, 92; Tryon and, 67, 69, 72, 95
Hoare, William, 22
Holt, Edwin Michael, 148
Holt, Michael, II: attitude of, toward Regulators and Revolution, 120, 148; bought McCulloh land, 147, 148; condemned governor's actions, 119–120; recruited for Crown, 124; and Smyth, 121, 122, 123; suit against, 85; was attacked by rioters, 88, 148; was captured at Moores Creek Bridge, 122; wounded were treated at home of, 119
Hooper, William, 76, 77
Horse(s), 25, 63, 73, 139
House of Commons, 10, 21, 130, 135, 137. See also Assembly, colonial; Legislature; Lower house
House of Commons (London), 10
Howard, Martin, 75
Howell, Rednap: presented petition to Tryon, 64, 65, 66; Regulators assembled under, 85; Tryon hoped to execute, 115; writings of, 17, 66, 89, 95
Huguenots, 30, 155
Humiliation, 21, 23, 40

Hunter, James: in Bute County, 122; did not receive pardon, 75; and Fanning case, 85, 93; led delegation disputing excessive fees, 90; presented petition to Tryon, 64, 65, 66; Rednap Howell wrote letter to, 95; Regulators assembled under, 85; and Richard Henderson, 86, 87; served as messenger/spokesman for Regulators, 64; signed petition to Earl Granville, 64; Tryon had hoped to execute, 115; was tried at Hillsborough, 77; withdrew from Caldwell's congregation, 73; wounded were treated at home of, 119; writings of, 85, 93, 94, 125–126

Husband(s), Herman (Harman/Hermon): animosity of, toward Fanning, 94, 97; brief biographical sketch of, 42; deeds and grants for, 46, 49; disownment and appeal of, 55, 56; involvement of, in Rachel Wright affair, 52, 54-57; leadership of, 58, 77, 103; left area before fighting began, 108; moved to Piedmont, 44; prepared and introduced petitions, 79, 81, 83; quoted, 3, 24, 27, 28, 45, 47, 60-61, 75; and Regulators, 41–42, 73–74, 85, 119; representation and expulsion from lower house, 79, 83, 93, 95, 124; and Sandy Creek settlement, 29, 48, 50, 59; saw anger over poll tax as turning point, 60; served as land agent and speculator, 41, 50; Stearns worked closely with, 149; supported Revolution, 124; was arrested, tried, acquitted, and released, 65, 73–77 passim, 93, 95, 115; was disruptive exponent of individualism, 57; writings of, 42–43, 59, 77, 78

I

Immigrants, 3
Impartial Relation, An . . . (pamphlet), 94
Improvements to land, 7, 8, 81, 134, 147
Indians, 3, 44, 70
Indictments, 77, 78

Individualism, 56, 57
Inner Light, 56–57
"Instructions from the Subscribers Inhabitants of Orange County to their Representatives in Assembly," 79
"Instructions to the Delegates from Orange," 131–132
Insurrection, 104, 120
Investment(s), land, 47–48, 50
Iredell County (present-day), 7
Ireland, 30, 31, 36, 37, 38, 39
Irish Protestants, 3

J

Jackson, Isaac, 75
Jacobites, 106
James I of England (James VI of Scotland), 30
James VI of Scotland. *See* James I of England
Jersey (province), 39
Johnston, Gabriel, 2, 7
Johnston, Robert, 35
Johnston, Samuel, 92, 127
Johnston, William, 129
Johnston County, 52, 97, 151
Johnston Riot Act: authorized imprisonment, prosecution, and execution, 92, 113, 117; petitioners attacked use of, 97; Tryon acted under provisions of, 95, 107; was authored by Samuel Johnston, 127; was under consideration, 93
Jones, Robert, 23
Jones, Robert, Jr., 21
Judge(s): feared more violence at Hillsborough court, 95; letter written to, 93; lived in Tidewater area, 12–13; men who served as, named, 75, 86, 103, 123
Juries/jurors, 11, 86–87, 134, 135
Justices of the peace: appointment of, 10–11, 21, 135; could hold multiple offices, 67, 135; dealings with, 23, 122; determined landowners/voters, 13, 139; legal challenges to, 85; loyalty oaths taken before, 142; men

who served as, named, 24, 79, 90, 119, 137, 140, 146, 151; owned land and slaves, 12; petitions to, 21; powers of, 9, 10, 11, 61, 81, 92, 106, 135; were targets of Regulators, 88, 137

K

Kentucky, 33, 152
Kentucky (present-day), 123
King Charles I, 34
King Charles II, 1
King George II, 2
Kings Mountain, 124
Kinston (present-day), 20
Knox, John, 155

L

Land: abuses, 29; access to, 10; cheap, 3; company, 44; Crown, 10; developers, 131; difficulty in obtaining, 3; engrossment, 67; Granville, 10; grievances over, 80, 126, 135; investments, 50; negotiations with Indians over, 123; ownership, 21, 34, 43, 61, 70, 133, 137; and politics, 133, 139; populating the, 10; price of, 3, 5, 8, 9, 47, 133, 144; problems determining ownership of, 1, 133, 139; sales, 50; seizure of, for payment of fees, 25; surveyors, 68; taxes, 5, 139, 140; titles, 7, 137; was confiscated, 136
Land agents. See Agents, land
Land entries, 47, 133, 135, 145, 147
Land speculators. See Speculators
Lathbury, George, 144, 145
Lawsuits, 80, 85, 96
Lawyer(s): corruption by, 25, 81; land speculators connected with, 10, 80; men who served as, named, 21, 90, 103; in Orange County and Virginia, 15; quotation about, 23; resentment against, 22, 78; were physically assaulted at Hillsborough, 87
Lea, John, 76–77
Lefler, Hugh, 20
Legislators, 13, 132, 139

Legislature: cleared titles, 143, 148; dominated by east, 10, 62; encouraged settlement of back-country, 40; established districts, 12; grand jury presentments made before, 61; granted permission for clergy, 39; meeting sites of, 19–20, 92; passed confiscation laws and ordinances, 144–145, 146; petitions to, 27, 45, 97, 124, 145, 147; provided capitol in Tidewater, 19; set up land entry process, 133, 134; supervised local officials, 63; Tryon dissolved, 84; was subject to annual elections, 135. See also Assembly, colonial; House of Commons; Lower house
Libel, 27, 93
Lincoln County, 136
Lincoln County (present-day), 67
Little River (Orange County), 35
Livestock, 22, 115
Lloyd, Thomas, 11, 62, 64, 65, 88
Local officials, 62, 67–68. See also Officials
London, 28, 118, 126
Lord Granville. See Granville, Earl
Lords Proprietors, 1, 31, 34
Lore, 104, 110, 118
Lossing, Benson, 118
Low, Samuel, 104
"Low's" Lutherans, 155
Lower house: bypassed by petitioners, 63; controlled and distributed powers in counties, 10, 11, 12, 135; declared itself provincial congress, 122, 126; Dobbs wrangled with, 22; election of members to, 13, 29, 137–138, 149; expelled Herman Husband, 93, 124; men who served in, named, 21, 24, 92; Phifer lacked allies in, 71; represented dominant class, 10, 13–15, 83; speakers of, lived in Tidewater, 12–13; was alarmed by threats of disorder, 23. See also Assembly, colonial; House of Commons; Legislature
Loyalist(s) (Tories): faced revolutionary militia, 155; former Regulator leaders were, 122; had land

in S.C., 124; officers, 12, 85, 135, 137, 140; punishment practices of, 9; raising of, by Tryon, 63, 67, 68, 72, 92, 95; Regulators fought, 103, 118, 119, 141; reorganization of, 127; stayed in Regulator area after battle, 115; was not present at Hillsborough court, 84

Mills, 22, 44, 115

Minister(s): chaplain as, 155; Friends, 51; German, 72; Presbyterian, 33, 103, 107, 108, 127; taxes to support Anglican, 15, 38, 68. *See also* Preachers

Moffat, William, 75

Monarchy, 30, 34, 35–36

Montgomery County (present-day), 7, 150

Monthly meetings, 51

Moore, James, 111

Moore, Maurice, 73, 75, 85, 93, 94, 107

Moore, William, 129

Moores Creek Bridge, Battle of, 122, 155

Moravian(s): and Germans, 147; had agreement with county officials, 40, 136–137; protected themselves from military service, 149; quotation by, concerning proclamation currency, 127–128; recorded news about Battle of Alamance, 112, 118; speculated about minister, 156; tradition, 31; worship, 142

Moseley, Edward, 140, 144

Motes Creek, 144

Murphey, Archibald DeBow, 17, 103, 109, 113

Murray, James, 38

Muster(s), 97, 98, 99

N

Nash, Abner, 85

Nash, Francis, 15, 88, 89, 111, 127, 140

Nation, Christopher, 75

National Covenant (1638), 35, 36

Negroes. *See* Blacks

Neuse division, 97

Neuse River, 92

New Bern: court of oyer and terminer in, 95; district court met at, 12; general muster held at, 96; governor's residence in, 19; Husband jailed in, 93; lower house in, 149; Regulators planned to march on, 92, 93; supported as seat of government, 20

New England, 41, 48

New Garden Meeting, 57

"New Government of Liberty," 48

New Hanover County, 97, 140, 143

New Jersey, 64

New Jerusalem, 43, 44

New Lights (Presbyterian), 41, 42, 57, 68, 156

New Side Presbyterian Church, 42

New York, 15, 39, 95, 118, 128

Newspapers, 113, 146

North Carolina Gazette, 93, 94, 145

North Carolina Yearly Meeting, 55

Northampton County, 68, 96

Nutbush Address, 24, 25, 27, 29, 78–79

Nutbush Creek, 23, 48

O

O'Neal, John, 75

Oath(s): of allegiance, 115, 122, 133, 141–142; imposed on members of third provincial congress, 127; mentioned, 63; of naturalization, 85; Regulator, threatened nonpayment of taxes, 72; Regulators were to recant their, 127, 156–157

Officeholding, 15, 25, 28, 67, 135

Officials: abuse by, 5, 15; complaints about corrupt, 81, 82, 94; conviction of fiscal irregularity by, 86; county, 10, 11; government, 13; local, 15; observed table of fees, 130–131; tried to intimidate Husband, 85. *See also* Colonial officials; County officials; Deputy officials; Local officials

Oligarchs/oligarchy, 9, 124

Onslow County, 92

Orange County: churches, 41; committee of safety, 123; confiscations in, 146, 147; contained land from Crown and Granville, 5; Corbin and Childs influential in, 5; Cornwallis's recruiting efforts in, 143; court, 59, 85–86, 146; division of, into new counties, 92, 103, 137; election, 83, 129; establishment of, 44; grants in, 46, 133; Husband and, 44, 45, 47, 93; justices of the peace in, 122; land speculation in, 52; landowners in, 139–140, 143, 144; location and size of, 3, 13, 15, 67; loss of records from, 137, 148; militia in and from, 63, 72, 97, 99, 115; ministers in, 72, 127, 153; new members from, 95, 149; open letter written from, 94; petitions from, 29, 39, 63, 79, 81, 83–84, 86, 97; public meeting in, 6; representation in, 13, 71, 78, 79, 126–127; residents of, 15, 16, 64, 74, 113, 123, 140; Separate Baptists in, 32; sheriffs, 11, 76, 131; tax list, 138, 139–140

Orange County (present-day), 56, 144
Ordinaries. *See* Taverns
Overseers, road, 12
"Oxford," 24
Oyer and terminer, court of. *See* Court of oyer and terminer

P

Pacifism: existed on both sides during Revolutionary War, 151; of Separate Baptists, 115, 150, 151; was avowed by Quakers, 52, 61
Padgett's Creek, S.C., 152
Padgett's Creek Baptist Church, 152
Paisley, John, 137
Pamlico Sound, 20
Pardon(s), 115, 117
Parliament, 24, 25, 36, 84, 157
Pasquotank County, 13
Patriot(s), 122, 150
Pattillo, Henry, 72, 127, 153, 155
Payne, William, 75
Pelham, Peter, 2
Pennsylvania: Craighead and, 33, 37; English dissenters founded, 39; farmers and tradesmen from, 44; Granville District settled by people from, 39; Husband and 44, 47, 48;

immigrants from, 3; political disturbance in, 33; Quakers from, settled Piedmont, 31; revivalism grew in, 153

Perquimans County, 13, 83
Person, Thomas, 24, 27, 79
Petersburg, Va., 20, 22
Petition(s): from Anson County, 82; complaining about corrupt land agents, 6; concerning jury selection, 86; to George II and Earl Granville, 39; ignored or tabled, 83, 124; to legislature, 45, 63, 79; for new election, 129; from Orange and Rowan counties, 80, 83–84, 104; quotations from, 39; for redress of grievances by Regulators, 91; for release of Regulator prisoners, 149; to stop selling McCulloh land, 146; by Strudwick, 142–143; to superior court justices, 88; to Tryon, 27, 98, 105, 106; to Tryon and his council, 63, 66

Phifer, Martin, 69, 70, 71, 72, 99
Philadelphia, 54, 121, 122, 123
Piedmont: backcountry was located in, 1; confiscation in, 14; county organization in, 38; district court in, 12; grievances, 23, 24, 128; growth of, 12, 20; Husband moved to, 44; McCulloh land in, 7, 147; militia commanders in, 97; peace in, 125; *Pilgrim's Progress* was popular in, 35; religious climate of, 31, 33, 56, 151, 152; Scotch-Irish migrated to, 36; surveyors reached, 2; textile manufacturing business in, 148; was inclined toward insurrection, 73, 91

Pike, Abigail, 57
Pilgrim's Progress, The, 35
Pine, John, 129
Pittsylvania County, Va., 41
"Plan of the Camp at Alamance from the 14th to the 19th of May 1771, A": pictured, 102
Planter(s), 22, 43, 78, 92
Pleasant Grove Township (present-day), 144
Poems, 16

Politician(s), 75, 125
Polk, Thomas, 70, 71, 72
Polks, 67, 71, 153
Poll tax, 13, 20, 60, 61, 138–139
Polling, 129
Poor, 38, 45, 64, 68
"Pop Goes the Weazel" (tune), 16
Population, 1, 2, 5, 21, 31
Power, 12, 59, 86, 151
Preachers, 32, 35, 57. *See also* Ministers
Presbyterian(s): college, 69; and dissenter tradition, 29–30, 33, 34; in Ireland, 36; men who were, named, 103, 108, 127, 155; ministers, 107, 127, 152, 153, 156–157; open letter to, 72; petitioners, 39; poured into backcountry, 32; religious activities of, 38, 153; revolution occurred against Mary, Queen of Scots, 155; in Scotland, 29; Tryon was obligated to, 69, 72; urged to take Solemn League and Covenant, 37
Presbyterian Church, 36, 39
Presbyterianism, 35, 36, 42
Presbyteries, 29, 30, 35
Prisoner(s): charge of, 101; exchange, 107; hanging of, 113; men held, named, 113, 121, 123; petition for release of Regulator, 149; were tried at special court in Hillsborough, 117
Privy Council, 5, 20, 38–39, 92–93
Proclamation(s), 63, 96
Proclamation money, 20, 78, 127, 128, 144. *See also* Currency
Property, 11, 138, 139
Protestant(s), 1, 3, 29–30, 34
Protestant Reformation, 30
Protestantism, 33
Provincial company, 123
Provincial congress: fourth, 129, 131, 137; fifth, 129, 132, 137; representation in, 130, 131; third, 122–123, 126, 127
Pryor, John, 79, 83
Public house(s), 131, 134
Pugh, James, 113, 117
Pugh, Mary, 54
Pughs, 59
"Pulling-through," 42

Pyle, John, 74, 83
Pyle, John, Jr., 122
Pyles, 122

Q

Quaker(s): Cane Creek, 50; farms were confiscated, 136; had women preachers, 57; Husband and, 50, 57, 74, 103; lost political importance, 31; meetings, 152; men who were, named, 42, 57, 109, 123; moved to S.C. and Ga., 151; quotation by, 16–18; rejected violence on religious grounds, 149; Sandy Creek Association and, 29, 61; and Separate Baptists, 149, 151; settlement of, 44, 48, 56; sympathized with Regulators, 16; Tryon's forces targeted, 115; were considered dissenters, 29–30, 31, 34, 56. *See also* Friends; Society of Friends
Queen's College, 69
Queen's Museum, 69
Quitrents, 80

R

Race, 135
"Rachel Wright's affair," 51–52, 54, 59
Raeburn's Creek, S.C., 151
Randolph County, 117
Randolph County (present-day), 41, 47, 56, 64, 80
"Ranters," 56
Rape, 51, 57, 113
Ray, William, 142
"Reading the Riot Act," 106
Rebellion, 65, 91, 106
Reedy Creek, 8
Reformed Church, 31, 40, 153, 155
Register of deeds, 5, 11
Regulator(s): allegiance of, 121, 124, 127, 155; area, 56, 152; battle between militia and, 91, 92, 99, 103, 141; camp, 90; challenged colonial officials, 11, 70, 75, 8; charges against, 73, 85; decimation and defeat of, 50, 92, 118, 119; elected to assembly, 72, 78, 149; fled battlefield, 112–113, 118;

former, 122, 131; grievances of, 16, 64, 65, 68, 77, 86, 126, 133; at Hillsborough court, 65, 90, 119; and lawyers, 23, 85; Martin and, 122, 125; men identified as or supportive of, 52, 74, 79, 93, 120, 123, 148, 158; perception of activities of, 15, 24, 88, 94, 104, 111; sympathy with, 17, 63, 153; Tryon and, 105, 106–107, 115

Regulator Advertisements, 59, 60–61, 63, 66

Regulator Movement: account of, 27; affected people's psyche, 124; articulated shared grievances, 67, 122; correlation of land ownership with, 12, 140; dissenter-infused culture produced, 31, 33; fed by "Rachel Wright affair," 51–52; Hillsborough court riots marked spread of, 84; Husband and, 41, 59; origins of, 10, 21, 24, 29, 120; participation in, 61, 123, 149; religious excitement framed, 152; represented challenge for revolutionaries, 124, 158; Separate Baptists and, 32, 150; sparked by Sandy Creek Association, 41; Tryon and, 66, 95

Religion, 1, 3, 31, 80

Representation, 13, 14, 62, 78, 79, 129

Restoration of the monarchy, 24–25

Revivals/revivalism, 56, 149, 153

Revolution (philosophy), 152, 155

Revolution of 1688–1689, 25, 36

Revolutionaries, 131, 136, 143

Revolutionary War. *See* American Revolution

Richland Creek, 47, 115

Riot(s), 7, 21, 84, 90, 91, 92

Riot Act (1715), 106

Rioters/rioting, 8–9, 63

Road overseers. *See* Overseers, road

Roads, 3, 119, 123

Rochester, Nathaniel, 130, 131, 138

Rocky Cliff Trail (present-day), 101

Rocky River, 69, 70, 99, 115

Rocky River Presbyterian Church, 33

Rowan County: agents in, 5, 10; churches, 41; contained land from Crown and Granville, 5; dealings with county officials in, 18, 61, 136–137; division of, into new counties, 92; establishment of, 3, 44; Husband and, 45, 47; location and size of, 3, 67; men mustered from, 99; militia in and from, 72; new members from, 149; petitions from, 39, 81, 83-84; public house in, 134; representation in, 71, 78; residents camped near Salisbury, 90; tried to receive exemption from vestry act, 68–69

Rowan County (present-day), 7

Royal governor, 11, 22

Royal North Carolina Regiment, 124

Rutherford County (present-day), 67

S

Salem, 20, 121, 142

Salisbury: gathering of militia at, 97; located on backcountry trading route, 20, 101; new courthouse at, 12; news about skirmish given by men from, 118; Regulators in, 91, 125; Rowan County men camped near, 90; Tryon at, 72, 99; unscrupulous trustee of, 5

Salisbury District, 12

Salisbury District Superior Court, 10, 67, 77, 90

Salisbury general court, 61

Salisbury Road, 119

Sampson County (present-day), 150

Sandy Creek: arrests made near, 65; farms and mills along, were targets, 115; land along, 46, 47, 49, 64; location of, 41

Sandy Creek area/settlement: Husband in, 50, 54, 93; residents recruited to join British, 151; Separate Baptists in, 32, 48, 50, 150

Sandy Creek Association: activity of, 59, 61, 62; formation of, 29, 50, 149; Husband and, 41, 50, 59, 60–61; leaders and representatives of, 59, 149; praised east for opposing Stamp Act, 84; sparked Regulator Movement, 29, 41; used as political label, 41

Sandy Creek Baptist Church, 32, 48, 49, 149
Satire, 16, 67, 89
Saunders, James, 129
Sauthier, Claude Joseph, 102
Scotch-Irish: communal worship practices, 32; comprised large ethnic group, 67, 152; and Germans, 70, 155; petitioners, 39; preachers, 33, 37; Presbyterians and, 152, 153; residents of backcountry were, 3, 40; from Rocky River, 99; support of, 68, 70; viewed Covenanters as folk heroes, 36. *See also* Scottish
Scotland: dissenters in, 30, 31; national church of, 36; new Calvinism in, 155; non-Anglican Protestants in, 35; Presbyterianism in, 29; revivalist tradition in, 33
Scott, Joseph, 104
Scottish: communal worship practices, 32; Covenanters, 36, 37; forces fought army of King Charles I, 36; McCulloh was, 7. *See also* Highlanders/Highland Scots; Scotch-Irish
Scripture, 43, 149, 156, 157
Searcy, Reuben: did not actually participate in Regulator Movement, 123; petitions of, 21, 24, 29; quoted, 22–23
Searcy, Thomas, 137
Seceders/secessions, 36, 68
Secretary of state, 126
Selwyn, George Augustus, 8
Senator(s), 90, 92
"Separate," 152
Separate Baptist(s): had women preachers, 57; Husband and, 41, 50; moved into and out of Sandy Creek area, 29, 32–33, 41, 48, 50; and Quakers, 149, 151; rejected violence on religious grounds, 149; shaped Appalachian religious culture, 151; some, supported Regulator Movement while others resisted it, 150; were advocates of Sandy Creek Association, 61; were both pacifist and nonpacifist, 115, 151. *See also* Baptist(s)

Sermon(s), 38, 154, 156, 158
"Sermon, A" (publication), 38
"Sermon to Asses, A" (pamphlet), 38
Shenandoah Valley, 48
Sheriff: appointment of, 11; authority of, 71; collected poll taxes, 20; conducted elections, 13, 80; embezzled money, 63; men who served as, named, 24, 76, 123, 130, 131; ordered to protect surveyors, 142, 143; selected juries/jurors, 61, 135; support of, 11, 95
Signatures, 82
Sims, George: did not actually participate in Regulator Movement, 123; joined loyal militia in S.C., 124; Nutbush Address was written by, 23, 29, 78–79; quoted, 24, 25–27, 28
Sinking fund, 83
Sitgreaves, Thomas, 93
Sitterell, John, 88
Slavery/slaves, 12, 44, 45, 139. *See also* African Americans; Blacks
Smyth, John Ferdinand Dalziel, 120, 121, 122, 123
Society of Friends, 31, 42, 51. *See also* Friends; Quakers
Society for the Propagation of the Gospel, 38, 40, 68
Solemn League and Covenant (1643), 35, 36, 37, 68
Some Remarks on Religion . . . (pamphlet), 42, 43, 54, 56–57
Song(s), 17, 41, 64, 65–66. *See also* Tunes
Sons of Liberty, 84
South Carolina: boundary with, 8; Constitution, 152; included in charter, 1; land records in, 52; migration to, 33, 123, 151; Sims joined loyal militia in, 124; trade in, 20
Spaniards, 96
Speaker(s), 83, 127
Speculation, land, 12, 80
Speculators: absentee, 2; disturbances caused by, 7, 10; land obtained through, 5; landowners worked for, 67; McCulloh land and, 147; men who served as, named, 44, 48, 50, 52, 57–58, 75; were allied with

revolutionaries, 136; were granted land, 1, 123; were threatened by settlers, 8

Spencer, Samuel, 71

Spirituality, 42, 54, 56

Stamp Act, 68, 84

Stanly County (present-day), 7

Stearns, Shubal: congregations following, migrated westward, 33, 48; founded and led Sandy Creek Association, 41, 149; may have written "Regulator Advertisement," 64; Separate Baptists and, 32, 41; supported women preachers, 57; was chain carrier, 49

Stevenson, George, 8

Stewart, James, 117

Stinking Quarter Creek, 64, 146, 147

Stony Creek, 144

Strudwick, Samuel, 140, 141, 142, 143, 144

Stuart, Jehu, 50, 51, 54, 57

Sugar Creek, 8, 10

Sugar Creek Presbyterian Church, 33

"Sugar Creek War," 8, 10, 29, 67

Suits. *See* Lawsuits

Superior court, 123, 142, 143, 144–145

Surrender, 104, 106, 107, 115

Surry County, 92, 96, 112, 136–137

Surveyor(s): appointed by governor, 2; cheating by, 44; church elders cooperated with, 68; for Granville, 24, 39; included Granville District on maps, 3; named, 5; obstruction of, 141, 142; received standard fees, 133; worked with speculators, 12

Surveys, 2, 47, 48, 52

Suther, Samuel, 72, 153, 155, 156

"Sweet Betsey from Pike" (tune), 89

Swepsonville (present-day), 103

Swiss, 31, 70

Syke, Malachy, 75

Synods, 30, 35, 155

T

Tar division, 97

Tavern(s), 22, 24, 142

Tax/taxes: all who paid, could vote for House, 135; assessor(s)/collector(s),

123, 139, 140; back, 11, 127; districts, 139; effect of vestry act on collection of, 48; excise, 38; list, 138; lowering, 142; mentioned in quotation, 63; militia raised to assist sheriff in levying, 95; movable property was seized for payment of, 62; negotiations involving paying extra, 149; nonpayment of, 61, 72; occupants of Hawfields paid, 141, 143, 146; to pay for Tryon Palace, 19, 20; petition complaining about, 80, 82, 146; poll, 60, 61, 127, 138; to support Anglican ministers, 39, 45, 68

Tazewell, Henry, 15

Tennessee, 33, 152

Tennessee (present-day), 123

Third provincial congress. *See* Provincial congress

Thompson, Lawrence, 11

Thompson, Robert, 107, 109

Thompson Township (present-day), 144

Tidewater, 12–13, 39, 131

Tisdale, William, 19

Titles, 13, 144, 147, 148

Tool(s), 22, 112

Tories. *See* Loyalists

Townsend Acts, 84

Trade/trader(s), 3, 20, 43, 44, 54, 149

Trading Path, 20, 64, 101, 118, 140

Transylvania Company, 123

Travis Creek, 146

Treason, 91

Trent River, 92

Trespass, 135, 141, 142

"True Friends to Government," 97, 98

Tryon, William: actions of, concerning insurrection at Hillsborough court, 75, 76, 86; actions of, during and after battle, 92, 99, 111, 112, 113, 114, 115, 119, 120, 150; appointments made by, 15, 75, 77, 140; communication of, with Piedmont men and Regulators, 32, 65, 66, 106–107; consulted his council, 93, 95; and enforcement of official fee table, 28, 66; executions/hangings by, 107, 109, 113, 117–118; Fanning and, 16, 63, 120; feelings of, toward various people,

68, 73, 91, 120, 153; and legislature, 84, 125; and local politics, 11, 69, 80; mediation occurred between insurgents and, 154, 158; replacement for, 153; toured Piedmont, 67; tried to avoid bloodshed, 104, 140
Tryon County, 3, 68–69, 71, 99, 136
Tryon Palace, 19, 92, 128
Tunes, 16, 17, 89
Tyrrell County, 13

U

Ulster Scots. *See* Scotch-Irish
Union County (present-day), 67
Union County, S.C. (present-day), 152
Upper house, 10

V

Van Hook, Laurance, 83
Vance County (present-day), 23
Varnals Creek, 147
Vernon, Isaac, 59
Vestries, 39, 68
Vestry act(s): complaints about, 45; exemption from, 68–69; kept investors from buying land in N.C., 47; not enforced, 48; objection to new, 38, 39; passed by assembly, 68
Vestry tax, 71
Violence: accepted as political tool, 149; against court, 95; directed at lawyers, 86; at Hillsborough, 84; mentioned in quote, 63; Regulators tried to avoid impending, 106; rejected by Separate Baptists and Quakers, 149; rituals of, 21; used to garner support, 9
Virginia: border of, 2; churches, 41; Great Awakening spread from New England into, 32; land speculators had ties to, 10; map of, 3; preaching in, 37; Quakers and, 31, 44; Separate Baptists in, 33, 151
Virginia Gazette (Williamsburg), 107, 115
Volunteers, 156
Vote(s)/voters/voting: disfranchisement of, 13; included landholders with no title, 128; procedures for, 13;

qualifications for, 13, 129, 135, 137; for Regulators, 79; for sheriff, 11

W

Wachovia, 40, 136, 127–128, 147
Waddell, Hugh, 97, 99, 115
Wake County, 92, 96, 97, 137
Wake County (present-day), 7
Wales, 30, 31, 38
Walker, John, 107
War of 1812, 156
Wateree Monthly Meeting, 52
Wateree River, 52
Watson, James, 130–131, 137
Weapons, 112
West Virginia (present-day), 48
Western Quarterly Meeting, 51, 54, 55, 56
Westminster Confession of Faith, 36
Whitefield, George, 32, 33, 41, 42
Whitsell (Weitzel), Adam, 85
Whitsell (Weitzel), Henry, 85
Wilcox, John, 74
Williams, James, 147
Williams, John, 104
Williamsburg, Va., 15
Williamson, Hugh, 111
Wilmington, N.C., 12, 77, 111
Wilson, James, 104
Women, 20, 50, 51, 57
Worship: alongside blacks, 42; of Covenanters, pictured, 37; disowned members could attend, 51; among dissenters, 35; freedom of, 39; participatory, 32; practices, 32, 34, 142; Quaker, 42; value of, 31
Wright, Charity, 51–57 passim
Wright, Gideon, 112
Wright, John, 52, 53, 57–58
Wright, Rachel, 51–58 passim
Wright family, 52
Wrightsborough, Ga., 151

Y

Yadkin River, 8, 18, 45, 90, 99
York, Seymour (Semore), 48, 49, 151
Yorktown, 143